IT'S SUICIDE BUT IT'S FUN

IT'S SUICIDE BUT IT'S FUN

The Story of Number 102 (Ceylon) Squadron
1917–1956

Chris Goss

CRÉCY BOOKS

Published by Crécy Books Ltd, 1995
ISBN 0 947554 59 9

Typeset in Baskerville by
Ace Filmsetting Ltd, Frome, Somerset
Printed and bound in Great Britain by
Bookcraft (Bath) Ltd
Midsomer Norton, Avon BA3 2BK

Contents

Group Captain Gus Walker and Brenda Walker

Foreword by Lady Brenda Walker

It is more than 50 years since my late husband, Gus Walker, commanded the base at Pocklington. We had been married for four months and this was his first posting after losing his right arm two months previously. We considered the members of the squadrons based at Pocklington as 'our boys'. They were young, warm hearted, fun and very brave and won their way into the hearts of those Yorkshire folk.

Time passed and in 1947, a dinner/dance Reunion was held at the Café Royale. A commemorative booklet 'a proud and glorious War record of 102 (Ceylon) Squadron' had been compiled and the foreword written by Group Captain G A Walker! For this foreword, I cannot do better than quote what my husband wrote then about the Squadron's members:

> 'To all those who have been associated with this great Squadron, the number 102 cannot fail to conjure up moving memories – of gallantry, of sacrifice, of untiring devotion to duty in the air, on the ground and of a wonderful comradeship and esprit de corps between all ranks, both air and ground.'

How very apt are his words still today. Our Squadron reunions continue to be very well supported and they are most happy and interesting weekends, full of reminiscences, good humour and comradeship and when it comes to the 'march past', the marcher's straight backs, slick marching and proud bearing are proof that their pride in 102 Squadron has not diminished over the years; in fact, the glint in their eyes gives lie to the passage of time. Truly they live up to the motto *Tentate et perficite* – 'Straight and true'. I therefore feel sure that the stories contained in this book will be of great interest to all, both young and old.

Norfolk, 1995

Acknowledgements

The two people who must get the credit for starting me off on my quest for knowledge on 102 Squadron must be mentioned first – Win and Jerry Jerrum. I am only sorry that I could not finish the book before Win's untimely passing away in 1994. To Jerry, I hope you approve.

Many people helped me with this book, so many in fact that I am sure that I will forget one or two! If so, please accept my apologies – it was not intentional! So many in fact contributed toward the end result that I am having to leave some names out but I would still like to record my thanks to the following:

102 (Ceylon) Squadron
Sqn Ldr Alfred Abels DFC, Stan Adams, Edward Alderton JP, Alan Arthurson DFC, Peter Bailey DFC, Batch Batchelder DFM, John Bergman (Canada), Eddie Berry, Ted Boorman, Brian Booth, John Bosworth, Harold Brabin (Australia), Ed Brain (Canada), George Butcher, Larry Carr, Monty Clarke, Ed Cooke (USA), Arnie Coope, Basil Cotton, Mr D Cunningham, David Dale (Canada), Carl Dales (Canada), Norman Davies, Dickie Dykes, Leo Etherington, (the late) Stan Fautley, Sqn Ldr John Fell, Bill Graham DFC, John Grist, Graham Hall, Walter Hedges, John Holmes, Sqn Ldr Vic Hunter, John Hurst, Austin Huycke (Canada), Sqn Ldr Bill Jacobs, Eric Kelly DFC (New Zealand), Dick Kinsey, John Kirkby, Sqn Ldr Ken Lang, Sqn Ldr Wally Lashbrook MBE, DFC, DFM, AE, Monty Lamont (New Zeland), Air Cdre J C MacDonald CBE, DFC*, AFC, Dough McLeod (Australia), Noel McPhail DFC, DFM (Australia), Air Cdre Stanley Marchbank DFC, Don McKim (Canada), Hugh Moore, Doug Mourton, Wg Cdr Ted Millson DSO, DFC, Alec Nicholas, Norman Noble, Bill Ollerton, Air Vice Marshall V C Otter CBE, CENG, FRAES, FBIM, Noel Pearce, Jack Powell, Sandy Powell, Brian Purser, Dai Pugh, Robbie Robinson, Jack Sherwin, Frederick Smith, Ken Speer, Alec Taylor, Reid Thomson (USA), Mr P S Thompson, Mr J A Tippins (Lanzarotte), Don Veale, Jim Verran DFC, Tom Vernon, John Watkins (Canada), Jim Weaver (Canada), David Weir, Jock Williamson, Tom Wingham DFC, John Withington, Philip Winter, Sqn Ldr Ken Wright, John Wroughton.

I would like to particularly thank the following for their specific help:
Winfried Bock (Germany) for his help with German nightfighter claims, Graham Day of the Air Historical Branch for his help with the loss lists,

Mark Postlethwaite for the proof reading, John Smith for the cover and Lady Brenda Walker for the foreword.
I would also like to thank the following who in some small way helped with this book:

Mrs M E Barnett, Ger & Christel Boogmans (Holland), Chaz Bowyer, Guenter Brandner (Germany), Dick Breedijk (Holland), Bill Chorley, Mr Fisher, Georg Greiner (Germany), Hans de Haan (Holland), Bill Chorley, Mrs A Hawkes, Hans Ulrich Kettling (Germany), Peter Menges (Germany), Mr L F Painter, Bernd Rauchbach (Germany), David Stanley, Andy Thomas, 'Duke' Warren (Canada).

Finally, I must make mention of the help from my family – daughters Katie for helping with the printing and Megan and Alexandra for not bothering me! Last but not least thanks again to my long-suffering wife Sally – without you and your understanding, this book would not have been written!

Introduction

'And when you come to 102
And think that you will get right through
There's many a fool who thought like you
It's suicide but it's fun.'
(Anonymous 102 Squadron member, 1941)

Back in 1986, my wife changed her job within local government and started working in a new department. The office staff consisted of two – herself and a man who was somewhat older than her. After a week or so, she came home and told me about the new job and also about her colleague. She was sure that he was ex-Royal Air Force as he said things that she knew were Air Force sayings. However, what puzzled her was that he also used the occasional German word. Knowing my interest of all things wartime, she said she though that he was in the Royal Air Force during the last War and assumed that at some stage he had become a prisoner of war.

A few weeks later I had the privilege of meeting her colleague whose name was Jerry and I asked him if it was true that he was ex-Royal Air Force. Yes he was – he was an ex-Halton Apprentice, had flown as a flight engineer during the War, had stayed on in the Royal Air Force after the War and had retired as a Flight Lieutenant in 1974. The seed had been planted – I asked him with what Squadron he had flown and how many operations he had taken part in; '102 Squadron' was the answer and that he had flown 22½. Why the half I asked and was told that he had been shot down over Germany. I asked one final question – when was this last wartime trip? 'October 1943' was the answer.

Armed with this information, I visited the Public Records Office in London and looked at the Operations Record Book for Number 102 Squadron. There were a series of books relating to 102 Squadron – the Squadron must have had an active War, I thought. After a short search, I did find Jerry's details – shot down over the German city of Kassel on the night of 22–23 October 1943. Noting what was written in the Operations Record Book for this night, I took this back to Jerry who was surprised at what I had found and that I was interested in his wartime career. I then promised to find out more on this night and over the following year, succeeded in tracing his pilot living in New Zealand, his navigator living in Kent and his wireless operator living in Cornwall. Furthermore, I traced the German nightfighter pilot who had probably shot him down and contacted the *Burgermeister* of the village in Germany where Jerry's bomber crashed. This was not all. On the same night, 102 Squadron had lost another bomber and from this crew, I traced the three survivors of its crew of seven – the navigator, bomb aimer and wireless operator. Again I was lucky in tracing the German nightfighter pilot who shot this bomber down and in 1991 I was instrumental in arranging for the wireless operator visiting the crash site of his bomber in Germany where his seat cushion, found the day after his crash nearly 48 years ago, was returned to him.

The seed was now germinating. Who were 102 Squadron and what did they do? What was their claim to fame? This was easier to find out – they had flown operationally from virtually the first to the last day of the Second World War. However, the Squadron had also flown operationally during the First World War, between the Wars and for a short period after the War. A few more facts were sobering   third heaviest losses in Bomber Command, highest losses for the bomber group in which it had flown during the War and the highest percentage losses for any Armstrong Whitworth Whitley bomber squadron, the Whitley being the aircraft the Squadron was equipped with when war was declared. I now wanted to know more about this Squadron – what did it do during the years of its existence, what happened to give it such a macabre claim to fame and what happened to some of those men who flew with this squadron? This then is the story of Number 102 (Ceylon) Squadron through the words of many who fought and suffered with it. Its apt motto in latin was 'Tenate et perficite' – 'Attempt and achieve'; as you will read, many attempted and achieved but at a terrible cost.

Abbreviations

AC	Aircraftsman
Ac	Aircraft
AG	Air gunner
Air Cdre	Air Commodore
B	Bomb aimer
Bf	Bayerische Flugzeugwerke (Messerschmitt)
Clag	Thick cloud or fog
CO	Commanding Officer
Cpl	Corporal
Ditch	To force land in the sea
DFC	Distinguished Flying Cross
DFM	Distinguished Flying Medal
DSO	Distinguished Service Order
Dulag Luft	Luftwaffe interrogation centre at Oberursel near Frankfurt
E	Evaded capture
E or Eng	Flight engineer see also FE
FE	Flight engineer
Fg Off	Flying Officer
Fishpond	Apparatus that detected German nightfighter radar
Flak	German term for anti-aircraft adopted by bomber crews
Flt Cdr	Flight Commander
Flt Lt	Flight Lieutenant
FS/Flt Sgt	Flight Sergeant
Feldwebel or *Fw*	Flight Sergeant
FW	Focke Wulf
Gardening	Mine laying
'Gee'	Radar bombing aid
Geschwader	German term for 3 *Gruppen*
Gp Capt	Group Captain
Gruppe/Gruppen	German term for 3 *Staffeln*
Gr Kdr	*Gruppen Kommandeur*
H2S	Airborne ground scanning radar; a bombing aid
I	Injured
Ju	Junkers
Kampfgeschwader	Bomber *geschwader*
LAC	Leading Aircraftsman
Leutnant (Lt)	German equivalent rank of Plt Off

M	Missing
Major (Maj)	German equivalent rank to Sqn Ldr
MC	Military Cross
Me	Messerschmitt
Met	Meteorological
N or Nav	Navigator
Nachtjagdgeschwader (NJG)	Nightfighter *Geschwader*
Nickel	Propaganda leaflet
O	Observer
Oberfeldwebel/ Ofw	German term for Warrant Officer
Oberleutnant (Oblt)	German equivalent rank to Fg Off
Oboe	Blind bombing device fitted to aircraft but controlled by ground stations in England
Ops	Operations
P	Pilot
Plt Off	Pilot Officer
POW	Prisoner of war
Revs	Revolutions
RG	Rear gunner
Sgt	Sergeant
Sqn Ldr	Squadron Leader
Sqn Cdr	Squadron Commander – see also CO
Staffel	German term for a unit of 12 aircraft
St Kap	*Staffel Kapitän*
Tinsel	Small microphone near to a bomber's engine which could be tuned by the wireless operator to jam German nightfighter frequencies
Unteroffizier/ Uffz	German term for Sergeant
W	Wounded
WAAF	Womens' Auxiliary Air Force
Wild Boar (*Wilde Sau*)	German term for freelance night patrol
Window	Small strips of tin foil dropped to help jam German radar
Wg Cdr	Wing Commander
WO	Warrant Officer
WOp	Wireless operator
X Country	Cross country
2P	Second pilot
+	Killed

CHAPTER ONE

Birth of a Squadron — 1917–1919

Number 102 Squadron was formed on the 17th of August 1917 at Hingham in Norfolk under the leadership of Major H Wylie. The Squadron immediately commenced training on its Royal Aircraft Establishment FE2b bombers and on the 24th of September, after being deemed competent to commit to battle, moved to the French airfield of Saint Andre-aux-Bois. Four days later they moved nearer the front line to the airfield at Le Hameau and shortly after commenced flying operational missions. The Squadron was to remain operational on the Western Front until the Armistice which would occur in just over 14 months; some of the Squadron would not live to see that Armistice.

The two-seat FE2b had been designed in 1914 as a fighter reconnaissance aircraft but by 1916 was found to be considerably inferior to the new breed of German fighters and production was stopped towards the end of that year in favour of a new breed of British fighter. Despite this and the fact that its maximum speed of 90 m.p.h. and low service ceiling making it totally unsuitable for daylight operations, the FE2b found a new lease of life as a night bomber. With a maximum bomb load of 230 pounds, the slightly modified FE2b night bomber first appeared over the Western Front in about April 1917. Six months later, 102 Squadron commenced its offensive against the German Army flying its FE2bs.

Exact details of 102 Squadron's operations are sketchy to say the least and one must rely heavily on a narrative written between the Wars for the Air Ministry. Nevertheless, it would appear that the Squadron's first operational mission was flown on the night of the 30th of September–1st of October 1917 when the ammunition dump at Dechy was successfully attacked. With the arrival of Winter, the Squadron had soon settled into a routine of attacking aerodromes and railway stations, primarily Gontrode and Scheldewindeke aerodromes and the railway stations of Courtrai, Menin, Roulers and Douai. By the end of December 1917, the Squadron had flown 32 separate raids and dropped a total of 55,100 pounds of bombs. Very difficult weather conditions must have been experienced on many occasions and most of the attacks, as a result, had to be carried out at low level – a brave act in such a flimsy and, by today's standard's primitive, aircraft. The following gives some idea of what one crew had to go through:

Lieutenant H Hammond MC

'Lt H Hammond MC and Lt H Howard MC, his observer, reported obtaining a direct hit on a hangar at Saint Denis Westrem aerodrome on the 7th of November 1917. This was confirmed by a repatriee who stated that at this aerodrome about this date two sheds were hit and completely destroyed as well as four others being hit. Lt Hammond on this occasion bombed from 500 feet.

'However, Lt Hammond was severely wounded in the arm by machine gun fire on the 26th of November 1917 over Douai after bombing the railway station again from 500 feet. On the return journey he fainted but his machine was brought back and landed a short distance west of the lines by his observer, Lt H Howard MC.'

A rare known photograph of a 102 Sqn FE 2b (via Thomas)

1918 started steadily with a total of 24 raids during the first two months of the year. However, the work load per month tripled during the month of March 1917 whilst the weight of bombs dropped increased nearly ninefold. This was due to the German offensive along the Somme and the only report from this period is as follows:

Lieutenant J Day MC

'During a flight on the 26th of March 1918, my observer, Lt F O Rooks, and myself saw troops on the road between Mametz Wood and Bazantin-Le-Grand and bombed them and fired on them from a height of 300 feet until all our ammunition was expended. The troops retaliated with machine gun and rifle fire. Number of troops estimated to be about two battalions.'

However, almost coinciding with the disbandment of the Royal Flying Corps and creation of the Royal Air Force on the first of April 1918, 102 Squadron moved from being a night bomber squadron to a night reconnaissance and bombing squadron, although it still managed to maintain its tonnage of bombs dropped. An example of the Squadron's new role is best illustrated as follows:

Lieutenant A J E Broomfield DFC

'2320 hours. Beugny. Dropped one flare on Bapaume–Cambrai Road. No movement observed.

'2325 hours. Flew to Beaumetz. No movement observed. Flew on to Boursies and dropped two flares on Bapaume–Cambrai road. Saw about four lorries moving west on main road. From Boursies flew to Fontaine and dropped three flares along the main road. Saw three transports moving west. No other movement.

'2335 hours. We then flew south-west to Hermies and saw two trains moving west. We dropped two flares from 800 feet and then dived on trains which were brightly lit up by our flares. One train was probably loaded with carts and artillery as we could see the wheels. The other was a goods train with approximately 50 trucks. We dropped four bombs on the first train, obtained one okay on train and one on the line directly in front of the engine. We then dived on the next train and bombed it from 500 feet with four 25 pound bombs; knocked one truck off rail next to engine and one in the centre of the train. Fired 100 rounds into engine of second train and 100 into first train. We then flew along the railway and saw three more trains at Velu near the junction of the two railways, one going south, two west. Fired 100 rounds into train. Trains going west were moving at a good speed, the flash from the engine could be seen plainly. Dropped one flare. Flew along railway and saw four trains moving west at Fremicourt. They appeared to be quite close to each other, at 1,500 feet. Fired 200 rounds into them. We then flew to 'F' lighthouse and from there home.'

The Squadron continued to provide a sterling service to the British Army though not without loss. These had been relatively light following October 1917 when the Squadron suffered its heaviest losses of at least 6 aircraft lost or damaged. However, on the 21st of July 1918, the Squadron was destined to lose another aircraft but this time the crew were more fortunate:

Lieutenant J A Hoogterp

'On the night of the 21st–22nd of July 1918, after having bombed Gremicourt, we, Lt E C Harris and myself, were hit in the radiator and had to land near Theipval on the enemy side of the lines. We were both thrown out of our machine but were unhurt. We immediately tried to make for our lines but ran into a swamp near Thiepval Wood. Going north we tried to cross a railway embankment but ran into some Germans so retraced our steps and hid in a shell hole amongst some tall grass as it was nearing dawn and stayed there till the following night. We could pick up the position of our lines by the flashes from machine guns. At 2200 hours, we made up our minds to have another dash for it. We moved along very carefully and managed to cross several German trenches. We were observed by a German outpost and fired on so we had to take cover for a time. Moving on again we were just coming to another line of trenches and were surprised to hear "Halt! Who goes there?". We both dashed forward with our hands up shouting "Don't shoot we are English!". We were then taken down to Company Headquarters under escort and finally came back to the Squadron.'

Soon the German offensive turned into a retreat offering the crews of 102 Squadron numerous targets of opportunity during its night reconnaissance flights. For instance when the enemy retreat started north of the Somme during August, heavy German traffic and favourable weather gave the Squadron opportunities such as had never been met before for attacking enemy troops and transport at extremely low level. This is best illustrated by this account of one such flight on an unspecified night during August 1918:

Lieutenant A J E Broomfield DFC

'Route Surcamps to Adinfer Wood. By compass and land marks to Boursies, then Beaumetz, then junction of Canal du Nord and finally north west to Arras. At 0305 hours we picked up the Bapaume to Cambrai road at Boursies. At 0310 hours at a sunken road just west of the Canal du Nord we observed a column of 20 two-pair transport (horse). We dived on these and dropped two 112 pound bombs and one 25 pound bomb from 300 feet. The bombs burst in the midst of this transport and knocked out six or eight teams. Some of the rear teams took refuge in the sunken road where there were two lorries. We were at 200 feet and dived down right on the sunken road and with the altimeter registering zero, secured a direct hit among the teams and lorries with one 25 pound bomb. Waggons and dead horses could be seen scattered over the road as well as several men. 250 rounds of ammunition were fired into the wreckage. Four teams escaped – two along the road to Bapaume and two towards Cambrai.'

Targets continued to be plentiful, including many trains, but with the arrival of Autumn came misty weather, especially on the fine nights. Although the weight of bombs dropped did not diminish, the successes of the earlier days of the German retreat were not repeated. When the Armistice did come on the 11th of November 1918, the Squadron had flown a total of 295 raids and dropped approximately 823,872 pounds of bombs* for the loss of eight personnel killed and eight prisoners of war – a very impressive account considering the Squadron did not start its war until October 1917. The Squadron's first claim to fame is that it held the

---

* Although this total weight of bombs seems a lot, one should compare it to what was being carried by the bombers of the Second World War. For example, this equates to approximately 65 sorties by Handley Page Halifaxes and approximately 120 sorties by Armstrong Whitworth Whitleys – Author.

record among two-seater night flying squadrons for the weight of bombs dropped in one night when on the night of 23rd–24th of March 1918 a total of 633 × 25 pound bombs were dropped (this was probably a record for any two-seater day bombing squadron as well). However, the Squadron will be better remembered for its role during the German offensive in March 1918. During the month following the German initial attack, the British Army hierarchy was becoming increasingly anxious about the possibility of further massed offensives by the Germans in the Third Army area. The bombers of the Royal Air Force were especially detailed to reconnoitre roads at low altitude and to report back any signs of activity or movement on roads behind the German front line. This was a particularly hazardous task and to 102 Squadron fell the honour of being the first squadron to carry out such night reconnaissance flights, a task in which the pilots and observers of the Squadron soon became expert and was considered by those on the ground as being of paramount importance to their defensive tactics.

However, with the cessation of hostilities came a virtual halt to all flying. The Squadron's surplus and unserviceable aircraft were broken up at their airfield at Serney and the wreckage burned – an ignominious end for an aircraft that although was obsolete by 1916 was still flying operationally at the end of the War; not many other aircraft from that era could claim the same. The Squadron then returned to England in March 1919 where it was based at Lympne near Folkestone in Kent. However, its future was not bright as in little more than three months it was disbanded, its remaining aircraft disposed of and its aircrew and ground crew dispersed. The first chapter in 102 Squadron's history had ended.

Those men who left Lympne during the Spring and Summer of 1919 would not have believed that, in just over twenty years time, Britain would again be at war with Germany and Number 102 Squadron would be back in the front line playing a very active part. 102 Squadron had flown operationally on the very last night of the First World War and was destined to fly operationally on the second night of the Second World War. History would be repeating itself for 102 Squadron.

CHAPTER TWO

Rebirth and Repetition —
1936–1940

102 Squadron rose again on the 1st of October 1935 when it was reformed from 'B' Flight of 7 Squadron. 7 Squadron was equipped with a mixture of Vickers Virginia Mark VII and Handley Page Heyford Mark II heavy bombers, the Heyford being one of the last of the British biplane bombers and both types of aircraft only being a generation removed from their First World War predecessors.

Based at the small Hampshire airfield of Worthy Down, just north of the historic city of Winchester, the Squadron, under the leadership of Squadron Leader C W Attwood, a First World War veteran, soon got to grips with the ungainly Heyford.* In May 1936, the Squadron participated in the Worthy Down Empire Air Day display and in June, featured in the Portsmouth Aero Club 'At Home' meeting. However, the highlight of the year was the Squadron's participation in the prestigious Royal Air Force Hendon Air Display on the 27th of June 1936 when it took part in the 'skittle bombing' event and 'set-piece' finale.

However, things began to change for 102 Squadron when in July 1936, it changed its Heyford Mark IIs for Mark IIIs, with conversion being complete in time to participate in a major nocturnal bombing exercise at the end of the month. The following month, the Squadron departed Worthy Down for the new (and still incomplete) airfield of Finningley near Doncaster and by the end of September 1936, was declared fully operational and recommenced its training. The Squadron had so far had an incident free second life; this was soon to change and was a sign of things to come:

Sergeant Vic Otter

'On the 19th of November 1936, a detachment of seven Heyfords flew to Aldergrove in Northern Ireland for an armament training camp. There we carried out air gunnery and bombing practice on Lough Neagh and the camp was declared highly successful. We were due to return to Finningley on the 11th of December (Abdication time) but this was cancelled due to bad weather conditions. Having obtained confirmation from the Duty Pilot

---

* It is thought that the Squadron flew Virginias for a very short time but this has not been substantiated – Author.

at 0900 hours that the cloud base over the Pennines was 8,000 feet, we set off in formation at 1045 hours on Saturday the 12th of December (it was very unusual for RAF flying to take place over the weekend in those days!).

'My crew were Sgt Church (second pilot), LAC Clements (fitter) and AC Bodenham (wireless operator). I was flying in the centre of the port side of the formation and all was going well in reasonable weather conditions until we reached Morecambe where we ran into what seemed to be a bank of thick sea fog. We entered the 'clag' in fairly close formation at 3,000 feet led by our Squadron Commander, Sqn Ldr Attwood. Thereafter, we were unable to see anything of the rest of the formation. I recall telling my crew that we would continue at our current speed and altitude on a course of 090 degrees. Our ETA (estimated time of arrival) at Finningley was 1345 hours (which pleased Sgt Church who was hoping to catch a train from Doncaster that afternoon to meet his girlfriend in London).

'However, after a short time, flying conditions became even worse. Visibility was virtually nil but on one occasion I was able to get a brief glimpse of the inner port wing where I noticed a considerable build up of ice (and we had no way of removing ice on the Heyford). I immediately put on more power in an endeavour to get above the icing conditions and recall achieving an indicated altitude of 4,000 feet. Our wireless communications depended on a trailing wire aerial which reeled out from the belly of the bomber and when I asked Bodenham to check on weather conditions at Finningley, he told me that he could get nothing on his wireless set and it subsequently transpired that the ground station at Finningley was out of action for servicing. This was probably irrelevant as the aerial must have been iced up.

The exposed cockpit of the Heyford (Hall)

The cramped interior of the Heyford's cockpit (Hall)

'My recollection is that we obtained and maintained an indicated altitude of 4,000 feet but some time later, Sgt Church shouted that we were getting very low. The next I knew was that I was engulfed in blazing wreckage with the windscreen frame round my neck, my scarf burning fiercely and my goggles, which were fur lined, blistering the skin around my eyes. The scene was horrifying. There was snow everywhere and dense freezing fog. I crawled around the burning wreckage seeking and shouting for my crew but without success. It was not possible to establish where I was but eventually I found a narrow track in the snow which led to a shed in which there were poultry. I reasoned that if there were poultry, someone had to come and feed them.

'I lay in the shed until I heard voices in the distance which were those of the Hebden Bridge residents who had heard the crash. They told me that my screams had enabled them to locate me. They led me over very rough ground to the local post office where a dear Mrs Johnson, on seeing my face, turned all children's faces to the wall, laid me on a divan, covered my face with a cloth, applied a cold compress to my damaged right ankle and gave me a stiff brandy. She also despatched my dictated 'crash' telegram to Finningley. My rescuers had in the meantime gone off to look for other possible survivors. They found Sgt Church some distance from the wreckage badly injured but regrettably, he died in the ambulance taking us to Halifax Royal Infirmary. They found no trace of the other two crew members.

'It was during my stay in hospital that I learned that most of the rest of

Sgt Biddulph and his crew (Hall)

the Squadron's aircraft had come to grief. One crew baled out over Oldham, two force-landed at Disley, Cheshire, one landed at Gainsborough and one near York. The seventh flown by Sgt Biddulph landed in a field in Lincolnshire and having checked with a local farmer as to where he was, took off again for Finningley, narrowly missing overhead electricity cables en route.'*

This was to be the first and last serious setback for the Squadron prior to the outbreak of war. The events that followed in the months and years after the 12th of December 1936 disaster were very minor in comparison. In June 1937, the Squadron's 'B' Flight went to form 77 Squadron and the month after, the Squadron moved to Honington in Suffolk. With the clouds of war starting to gather with the rise of Adolf Hitler and his military machine, training not only continued but also intensified. Following another Squadron move to the airfield of Driffield in the east of Yorkshire in July 1938, the Squadron began to relinquish its Heyfords for a newer bomber:

Aircraftsman Bill Jacobs

'In November 1938, I joined 102 Squadron at Driffield and was posted for duty as a wireless operator with 'B' Flight. At this time, the Squadron was in the process of converting from the Heyford to the Armstrong Whitworth

---

* Only four of the seven Heyfords were damaged or destroyed; details are in Appendix D – Author.

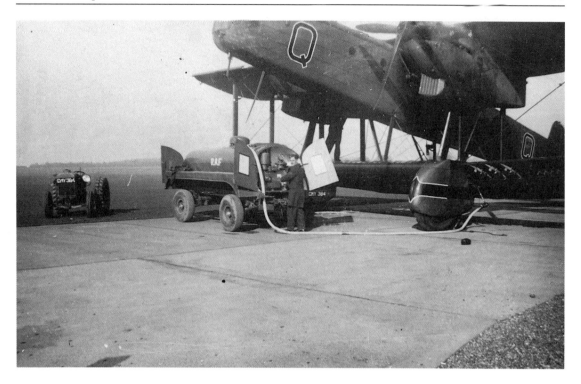

'Q' for Queenie seen at Honington

Whitley, a process that had commenced only the previous month. Conversion was completed by early Spring 1939, the Heyfords being progressively transferred mostly to 97 Squadron based at nearby Leconfield. Although the Squadron had a full complement of the new Whitley quite early in 1939, there was a shortage of flying personnel and I have a recollection of what I then considered an awesome task in my personal responsibility for the minor inspection and servicing of the electrical and wireless installations of two Whitleys and also a Heyford. The personnel state was progressively improved throughout the Summer of 1939 and we were just about up to full strength by the 3rd of September 1939.

'The transition from the Heyford to the more advanced Whitley was something of a problem and the need for specialised conversion training soon became apparent. Incidents about the time of my arrival included a fatal crash of a 77 Squadron Whitley due to loss of height on take off resulting from raising the flaps too soon and a 102 Squadron aircraft belly landing, without casualties, due to failure to lower the undercarriage. There were many other similar incidents throughout the Group.'

With the Squadron fully converted to the Whitley, the pace of training began to intensify. The Squadron's annual armament practice camp in 1939 was far more successful than that of November–December 1936, giving the aircrew very valuable training. In August 1939, with the attempts of the politicians to avert war failing, the Squadron took part in dummy nocturnal raids against the United Kingdom in order to test the Home Defence organisation. The success of such exercises meant that when war

The last and most spectacular accident – Plt Off Clifford's 'S' for Sugar lies broken in a field near Evanton, Scotland, March 1938 (Hall)

A factory fresh Whitley (Hall)

K8951 after a landing accident, Nov 38 (via Thomas)

was declared on the 3rd of September 1939, 102 Squadron and the other Squadrons of Bomber Command's Number 4 Group were the first RAF bombers to be thrown into the Royal Air Force's night offensive, even if at the start, all that was dropped was paper:

One month prior to war, K8957 is seen still wearing its pre-war code letters 'TS' (Jacobs)

Leading Aircraftsman Bill Jacobs

'The morning of the 4th of September 1939 brought great activity in the flights of both 77 and 102 Squadrons and it soon became apparent that we were to do our first show that night. Details of aircraft and crews were posted in the flight authorisation book during the afternoon – Raid DM82. Whitley Mark III serial K8958 coded DY-S. Crew: Plt Off R C Bissett, Plt Off R C Kierstead (pilots), Sgt W Lees (observer), LAC W Jacobs (wireless operator/air gunner), LAC C Killingley (rear gunner). Take off 2359 hours.

'The fuselage forward of the door was crammed with large parcels of leaflets wrapped in coarse brown paper and tied with thick twine. At the evening briefing we were acquainted with the purpose of the mission. Our feelings at not being called upon to deliver anything more damaging than a good supply of paper and stout rubber bands on Germany's industrial heartland were understandably not favourable. However, maintaining strict wireless silence except in any emergency, we were to enter German airspace north of Holland and, avoiding neutral territory, fly southward distributing our leaflets down the Ruhr Valley, into France and home across the Channel.

'By the time we crossed the enemy coast, we were at 15,000 feet and all on oxygen. Visibility was good but ground features were obscured and navigation was by dead-reckoning assisted by wireless bearings obtained by the direction finding loop aerial. Shortly before we commenced leaflet dropping, we observed a beam of light apparently aimed in our direction from a point slightly below and to the right of our nose. We judged it to be airborne and Bill Lees gave it a burst from the front gun. The task of dropping the leaflets was then left to Plt Off Kierstead and myself and what a wearisome business it was. At 15,000 feet the outside temperature was about 15 degrees below zero and we had to disconnect ourselves from the oxygen supply and were soon bathed in sweat from the effort. The parcels nearest the flare chute were discharged first to clear the area but soon the thick brown paper and string became a problem until more space was cleared into which it was stuffed. The parcels aft of the ventral 'dustbin' turret could only be moved with great difficulty over the raised turret and to minimise the effort of moving them to the flare chute, we had to partially lower the turret for a while with the consequent adverse effect on the airspeed and flying characteristics! The whole process seemed interminably lengthy and we were both quite exhausted by the effort, especially at that height. We then found that the turret would not fully retract as the hydraulics had frozen!

'With the dawn, we found ourselves above complete cloud cover. At about 0640 hours, not having had any external check on our dead-reckoning and believing ourselves to be well clear of enemy territory, I broke wireless silence and obtained bearings in quick succession from three of our direction finding stations and these when plotted placed us close to Dieppe in France. Being anxious about our fuel state, we decided to take a look and on breaking cloud found ourselves over the Channel with Dieppe behind us. Plt Off Bissett decided to land immediately on a small aerodrome which seemed to be inactive but the only one that we could see. On final approach, we thought it judicious to unload the guns. I was responsible for two in the ventral turret which had to be lowered to bring the breeches to the unloading position but still being jammed in the half-retracted position, the guns were still loaded when we touched down.

'Looking rearwards, I saw a blue-clad figure being thrown off the leading edge of the port tail plane which apparently was a gallant French sentry who had thrown himself on there in an attempt to arrest our speed. He was fortunately unhurt and by the time we had come to a stop with the nose almost in the boundary hedge, he was strolling nonchalantly towards us with his rifle in the slung position.

'The aerodrome was otherwise deserted until some 20 minutes later when about 12 French Air Force personnel on bicycles arrived from the direction of the town. I then passed a coded message to Driffield informing them of our situation; we had been airborne for six hours and 55 minutes. We then refuelled from small cans which was a lengthy business and three hours 35 minutes later we took to the air again. We arrived at Driffield at 1255 hours after a combined flight of nine hours 20 minutes. Thus ended our first operational flight.'

Leaflet or 'Nickel' raids as they were known were destined to continue for many more months to come so it was inevitable that sooner or later, the Squadron was to suffer its first casualty:

Squadron Leader J C MacDonald

'The meteorological report before take off on our leaflet raid on the 8th of September 1939 gave the wind speed and direction at operational height as about 25 knots from the east. To detail my operation first, I had the luck to have an excellent second pilot and navigator in Fg Off Jock McKay. Our flight plan was to fly due east from Driffield to the Jutland Peninsula, then turn south to the Ruhr where we dropped leaflets, then turned west and headed back to base.

'When still nearly 30 minutes short of our first landfall over the island of Sylt, Jock called out that he could see land. We all thought that this was impossible with the wind speed and direction that we had been given before take off but it was, in fact, Sylt and the wind was coming from the west not the east. Using the new wind direction, we recalculated our course and, after dropping our leaflets landed safely back at the airfield of Manston in Kent.

'My fellow flight commander, Sqn Ldr Murray, had a very different experience which I heard from him when I met him two and a half years later in *Stalag Luft III*. After take off from Driffield, the crew all had a cup of coffee and a chat and then the navigator asked if anyone had made a note of the time they had set course. Guesses varied between 10 and 15 minutes so they settled on 15 minutes for their first turn point, then duly turned south and after dropping their leaflets, they turned west and headed for home.

'After about half an hour, they saw the lights of a large city and assumed it was Paris. Because of the incorrect wind direction and speed and the fact that they had miscalculated the time they set course, they were much further east than they thought and what they believed was Paris was actually Berlin! Soon after dawn, they ran out of petrol and had to force land in a field. When they got out of the aircraft, they saw soldiers approaching and, thinking them to be French, cheered. In fact they were German soldiers – they had landed near Itzehoe in northern Germany and the whole crew spent nearly five years as prisoners of war.'

Sqn Ldr Murray was not the only casualty that night. Another Whitley, flown by Fg Off Cogman, strayed into Belgian airspace. Belgium at that time was neutral and the Whitley was attacked by two Belgian fighters and forced to land at the airfield of Nivelles where the crew and bomber were interned.* Fg Off Cogman and his crew were later repatriated but the Whitley was kept by the Belgians.

After the initial flurry of activity, a long monotonous period of inactivity, which became known as the 'Phoney War' set in but the Squadron was

---

* Both of the Belgian pilots later flew with the RAF – Author.

The first prisoners – Sqn Ldr Murray (centre) and Plt Off Thompson seen with their German captors (Bowyer)

The first death – Sgt 'Acker' Gaut and his wife seen in happier times (Hall)

kept busy with non-operational tasks such as air-firing and practice bombing as well as getting familiar with the new Whitley Mark Vs which arrived in November 1939. There were still several incidents, both operational and non-operational which affected 77 and 102 Squadron but none as upsetting as the accident that happened on the 18th of October 1939:

Flight Sergeant Graham Hall

'Sgt 'Acker' Gaut was the first death during the war for 102 Squadron. He was detailed to fly pilots, ground crew and equipment from 41 Squadron* in Catterick, Yorkshire to Wick in the north of Scotland. He flew to Catterick and despite his protests, three starter trollies were loaded in the back of his Whitley. 'Acker' phoned back to Driffield to protest but was overruled. On take off, the trollies slid back, the Whitley's nose flicked up, the aircraft stalled and crashed. 'Acker', three crew and three passengers were killed, two more were seriously injured.'†

Towards the end of November 1939, the Squadron started flying a new type of mission in addition to the 'Nickel' raids. 'Security patrols' as they were known, were flown off the north German coast against enemy shipping and sea planes and gave cause to be remembered by the crews involved:

Leading Aircraftsman Bill Jacobs

'My first Security Patrol was on the 14th of December 1939 with Flt Lt D W H Owen as captain – Raid DM167 Borkum and Sylt. Duration five hours 10 minutes and nothing observed. My second was on the 20th of December this time with Fg Off R C Bissett brought some relief to the monotony. In a flight lasting seven hours and 5 minutes off Borkum–Nordeney–Sylt we were fortunate enough to spot some shipping activity at Sylt and we deposited our load in a two-run attack, encountering only light opposition from the ground defences. Third patrol on the 9th of January 1940 – nothing observed in atrocious weather conditions necessitating the breaking of wireless silence and considerable direction finding activity on my part.

   'During these patrols we were under strict orders to bomb shipping and aircraft that were sufficiently clear of land to safeguard against bombs falling on land to the peril of the civilian population and perhaps giving rise to reprisal. The sea plane base of Sylt was the exception as there were no civilians on the Island. These missions were dreadfully monotonous and we suffered a great deal of discomfort in the extreme weather conditions and intense cold. The real purpose was not appreciated by the crews who, not surprisingly, thought them a waste of time and a bit of a bind.'

* 41 Squadron were equipped with Spitfires.
† One of the passengers killed was Sgt Pilot A H Harris who only the day before had participated in the shooting down of the first German aircraft to be shot down in British waters during World War II – Author.

The weather during the winter of 1939–1940 was particularly bad and was responsible for the first gallantry awards to the Squadron for the war. Whilst on a reconnaissance flight off Wilhelmshaven on the 27th of November 1939, the Whitley flown by New Zealand Plt Offs 'Lofty' Long and Kenneth Gray was hit by lightning whilst flying at 2,000 feet. With the fabric stripped off virtually all of the port and part of the starboard wings, both pilots struggled to bring the Whitley back home and successfully landed at Bircham Newton in Norfolk. Both were awarded the Distinguished Flying Cross in January 1940. However, shortly after the arrival of 1940 came another unusual and hazardous task. Yet again, Bill Jacobs was involved:

The lightening damaged Whitley of Plt Offs Long and Gray (Bowyer)

Leading Aircraftsman Bill Jacobs

'The 26th of January 1940 dawned bright and sunny with several inches of newly fallen snow on the aerodrome. Soon it seemed that everyone on the Station was gathered outside the hangars and in line abreast about 25 yards wide, rank upon rank, they tramped over the snow to flatten and compress it enough to form a runway. The reason for all of this was revealed to us when we were called to the Operations room at the odd time of mid-morning and told we were to fly to Villeneuve in France and from there to carry out leaflet raids on Prague and Vienna. This would hopefully show the populace that Hermann Göring was misleading them in his claim that the RAF did not have the capability to penetrate so deeply.

Plt Off Ken Gray DFC who was later killed in a tragic accident whilst still with the Sqn (Bowyer)

'I had just been transferred to Sqn Ldr MacDonald's crew and this was my first trip with him. We took off at 1200 hours in clear conditions but we had been warned of worsening weather as we proceeded southwards. We soon got even worse than we expected when we found ourselves in blizzard conditions. Navigational assistance was called for and I tuned to our medium frequency direction-finding system, only to realise with horror that all was not well. Atmospheric noise was extremely bad and my transmissions were so poor that bearings could not be obtained. The cause of this was found to be a fault in the high tension supply to the transmitter so I cleaned it up as best I could which resulted in an improvement allowing us to proceed to Villeneuve.

'Shortly after our arrival, we learned that only four of the Number 4 Group crews despatched had arrived, all others having aborted. The only other crew from 102 Squadron was my old crew under Fg Off Bissett. Our intended stay was three days but weather conditions in that appalling Winter of 1940 virtually froze us to the ground and it was not until the 22nd of February before we were able to do what we came for. Our objective was to drop leaflets on Vienna and a reconnaissance of München.

'In quite good conditions, we were able to pinpoint our route to Vienna which we found clear and not only bathed in moonlight with its famous Danube and other features clearly visible, but also brightly illuminated for our special pleasure. We leisurely deposited our leaflets and turned west for München. The weather now began to deteriorate and we found the Bavarian capital totally obscured by towering cumulo-nimbus clouds. As we were to reconnoitre the city and since we could not see anything but clouds, we decided to go down and have a look. In the next few minutes we were to sample for the first time what must surely be the most terrifying of wartime night flying experiences. Whilst still in cloud and trying to find a hole, we were subjected to considerable turbulence and buffeting. Loud detonations and flashes about us led us at first to believe that we were in an electrical storm until closer flashes and smoke puffs with diffused searchlight beams made our situation quite plain. Down we went through hell and somehow managed to get safely below the cloud and heavy flak. Probing searchlights failed to locate us as we stooged around and avoided the light but innaccurate flak. We had found out that München seemed to be adequately defended and not having a target or anything to drop, we thought it propitious to leave the scene and get home. So heading west again, we began our climb through cloud to the moonlit sky above and in the cloud tops when our watchful eyes caught a glimpse of something shining in the moonlight off the port wingtip and three voices screamed "Balloon cable!" How many we had not seen I shall never know but looking upwards, I could see those ghastly shapes above and before us. The pilot sat there like a block of granite and we thanked God for that moon by which we were able to pick our way through those deadly cables.

'Homing on Villeneuve, we touched down after a flight of nine hours 15 minutes, got the lorry back to our billets and spent most of the day on our straw palliases.'

Bill Jacobs, prepared for the worst!

The war now began to take a turn for the worse. On the night of the 17th of March 1940, the Luftwaffe had accidentally dropped bombs on land whilst attacking warships at Scapa Flow in the Orkney Islands killing one and wounding seven civilians and as a direct result, Bomber Command was ordered to mount a reprisal attack on the seaplane base at Hoernum on the island of Sylt.

On the 19th of March, 30 Whitleys and 20 Handley Page Hampdens were dispatched with 102 Squadron leading. Coincidentally, it was Wg Cdr Burton, the new Commanding Officer of 102 Squadron's first operation with the Squadron who was there when, at 1953 hours, the first bombs were dropped. This was the first real bombing raid for Bomber Command and from now on, their war would be different.

Operational flying intensified in April 1940 as the Squadron directed its efforts towards the German invasion of Scandinavia and on the 19th of April, the Squadron sent a small detachment to Kinloss in the north of Scotland in order to attack the more northerly Norwegian targets. With the war intensifying, it was not long before the first operational deaths occurred when on the 26th of April, Fg Off Horrigan and his crew were shot down in an attack on Aalborg in Denmark. Only one of his crew of five survived to become a prisoner of war.

The Phoney War definitely ended when, on the 10th of May 1940, the Germans invaded France and the Low Countries. Bomber Command was now committed to hindering the German advance by attacking their lines of communication which directly resulted in the first strategic bombing raid against a German industrial target five days later when 102 Squadron took part in the attack on industrial and railway targets in the Ruhr. The war would never be the same again as one pilot who took part in this attack was soon to find out:

Flight Sergeant Graham Hall

'On the 16th of May, my flight commander said it was silly to have two experienced pilots, Plt Off L Miller and myself, flying together so we were each to have a new crew and would have three weeks to train them. On the 19th of May, still with no new crew on Station, I was called up for briefing and told that I would be flying that night against Gelsenkirchen. I asked if it would be with my old crew but was told that a Plt Off Glover, a Canadian pilot, and Sgt Dick, an observer, were now on Station. "Find them and get them to briefing!"

'Plt Off Glover and Sgt Dick did not have time to get themselves a room and unpacked. I did not even have time to see what experience they had and I even had to plan the route and work out the navigation myself. Sqn Ldr MacDonald drove the crews out to dispersal and shook hands with Sgt Rix and his co-pilot Sgt Dean posted in that day from 'Shiny' 10 Squadron at Dishforth. Wishing them luck, he turned to me and said that I would always turn up like a bad penny and because of this he did not wish me luck!

'In the air, I soon found out what little experience my new crew members had but made sure that Sgt Dick could at least fuse the bombs. I was sure that we could get to the target and back – we got there okay and the factory was as plain as a pike-staff. Trouble was Sgt Dick could not identify it, although I did two dummy runs at 6,000 feet. I then made the mistake of putting Plt Off Glover in the seat and told him to fly this course but to jink every 10 seconds. I nipped down the back, showed Sgt Dick the target but when I got back to my seat, Glover was frozen flying straight and level, coned by searchlights and in the middle of a box barrage. One engine was hit and on fire so we jettisoned the bombs in the target area and tried to get clear, which we did. However, we were losing height and when got to Goch on the Belgian border, we were down to 1,000 feet and the fire was spreading. I decided discretion was the better part of valour and gave the order to abandon aircraft. Glover and Dick went out through the bottom hatch and I held on until I was sure LAC McCutcheon, the wireless operator, and Sgt Murray, the rear gunner, had ample time to jump and by then it was so hot, so out of the bottom hatch I went!

LAC Jimmy McCutcheon – POW 19 May 1940 and awarded the DFM whilst in captivity (Jacobs)

'I could see two 'chutes below me and thought that they were Glover and Dick but then I thought I might have left McCutcheon and Murray to go down in the burning plane which I could see go in a couple of miles away. I was picked up after a few hours and found myself at the *Dulag Luft* interrogation centre, where I gave number, rank and name as expected but found myself under interrogation for about 10 days when others passed through in three. They kept asking me what special mission I was on until one morning the interrogator asked where I was when I passed my trade test! Without thinking I said Honington and they then said "You *can* be a Flight Sergeant but we did not know there was such a flying rank. Berlin has just confirmed that if you have passed your trade test, only then can you be promoted to Flight Sergeant!" You see, I was the first Flight Sergeant aircrew to be captured!'

At the start of June 1940, 102 Squadron's attention was directed to industrial targets such as Essen, and then switched back to transport systems in the hope of disrupting the nearly completed German invasion. Then on the 10th of June, Italy declared war on Britain and 102 Squadron found itself taking part in the first bombing mission against the Italian mainland:

Sergeant Bill Jacobs

'Having proceeded to Jersey on the afternoon of the 11th of June 1940, we left that same night for Turin. About two and a half hours out, still climbing to clear the Alps, we entered cloud and soon encountered severe

N1380/DY-R crashed near Hamegicourt, France on the 20 May 1940, killing Flt Lt Owen and all his crew (Jacobs)

Officers of 102 Sqn taken in July 1940
Front left to right: *Plt Off A Z Pengelly (POW 14 Nov 40), Fg Off F H Long DFC (+ 13 Mar 41), Flt Lt J D Warne, Sqn Ldr P R Beare, Wg Cdr S R Groom (+ 21 Nov 40), ?, Sqn Ldr O A Morris, Fg Off J J McKay, ?, ?*
Middle left to right: *Plt Off J Verran, Plt Off G L Cheshire, ?, ?, ?, Plt Off R F Beauclair (POW 27 Jul 40), Fg Off A D Frampton, ?, Plt Off T R Murfitt (+ 24 Oct 40)*
Back left to right: *?, ?, ?, ?, ?, Fg Off R James, Fg Off R A Barnwell (+ 28 Oct 40), Fg Off H M Young (+ 16 May 43) (Verran)*

turbulence. Electrical disturbance was quite the worst any of us have ever experienced and the noise in my headphones was unbearable. Fearing for my wireless equipment led me to disconnect the aerials and in doing so, I suffered some superficial burns to my right hand. It became agonizingly cold and we soon felt the depth of its penetration. The cloud seemed solid and without tops as we struggled laboriously for height. We now heard ominous bumps of something striking the aircraft and soon deduced that ice was being slung off the propellers. The captain asked me to shine the Aldis Lamp along the leading edges of the wings and we could see the ice building up despite the pulsating de-icing boots. The ice formed with such rapidity that soon we could see it building up thickly over the leading edges and we began to wallow very badly. We descended rapidly as low as we dared but there was no improvement in our condition which was now very dangerous. The fear we all shared was aggravated by the extreme cold and it was quite impossible to keep still. The pilot was fighting with the aeroplane to keep it airborne and we were obviously not going to make it this trip so reluctantly decided to abort. We jettisoned our bombs "safe" and staggered back for Jersey where we found that most crews had suffered

the same experience and only a few, miraculously, had avoided the bad weather and bombed their target.'

During the period of the Battle of France, the Squadron had put in a monumental effort. However, even though the losses had been less than expected (only five aircraft lost), the strain was beginning to tell. New crews were being posted in, such as Plt Offs Leonard Cheshire and Jim Verran and they were soon thrown into battle – both arrived during June and in Jim's case, he flew his first mission on the 4th of July. On the same night that Jim Verran flew his first operation, the Luftwaffe paid Driffield a visit by dropping four 100 kg bombs on the airfield. The Battle of Britain was about to start and in little over a month, the Squadron was to experience it first hand:

Pilot Officer Jim Verran

'At about 1400 hours on the 15th of August 1940, we were all dozing in the Ante-Room of the Officers' Mess at Driffield when the air-raid sirens sounded. We had heard them so often before that nobody moved. Then the bombs started to explode and there was a rush for the air-raid shelter near the Mess. A 500 kg bomb dropped near the Mess causing some

A Sqn Whitley basks in the sunshine at Driffield (Verran)

Opposite
Scenes of devastation at Driffield after the Luftwaffe had visited (Verran)

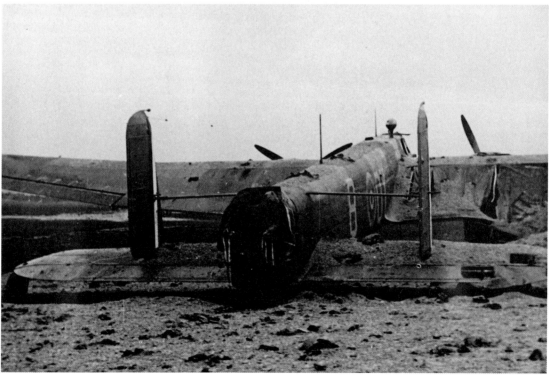

Scenes of devastation at Driffield after the Luftwaffe had visited (Verran)

damage and many of us were blown into the entrance of the shelter. In my case, the loop on the back of one of my tunic buttons was crushed into my chest and a small chip of bone dislodged from my sternum without breaking the skin. None of us were badly hurt.

Scenes of devastation at Driffield after the Luftwaffe had visited (Verran)

'However, two airmen manning a machine gun on the roof of the Guard House were killed, a WAAF and a horse pulling a car or a waggon were also killed. Many aircraft were hit and destroyed as were hangars and other buildings in the airfield complex.'

169 bombs were dropped on the airfield killing 13 personnel, wounding countless others and causing extensive damage to the airfield with many buildings and all five hangars damaged or destroyed. 102 Squadron lost five Whitleys, 77 Squadron lost another five whilst a visiting Whitley from 51 Squadron was also destroyed. One of the attacking Junkers Ju 88 bombers was carrying a war reporter who submitted the following report which is full of inaccuracies and journalistic licence but gives an idea what propaganda was fed to the German public:

Oberleutnant Rupps Krass

'At last, the target – Driffield! Those [RAF] fighters were beginning to get damned uncomfortable. This is it. I wouldn't give tuppence for the lives of those down there. Let's get rid of the bombs. Down they go – the bomber is put into a dive. The speed increases, the wind roars and howls. The hangars rise up to meet us — they are standing still but not for long. The flak guns are shooting out of everywhere but it cannot help them. A shudder — the bombs are gone. Their steel bodies whizz into the depths. Down there, all hell is let loose — steel crashes onto steel and stone, bomb after bomb explodes, tears and destroys whatever is hit. The walls and roofs of hangars fly up like tin sheets and fly through the air. Aircraft on the ground are turned into sieves by shrapnel. Barracks collapse in dust, huge smoke and dust clouds grow like mushrooms out of the ground. Here and there, flames shoot up and there are explosions — field and hangars are raked over and over and still the bombers behind us are dropping their loads. There, what madness is that? Two RAF fighters are trying to take off from the destroyed airfield. They think they will be safer in the air! One is hit during his take-off run — he is blown away, crushed. The other turns over during take off and is on his back.

'Bombs continue to rain down gruesome clouds burst. Ammunition is going up and volleys of fire shoot up like hordes. The flak has been extinguished; their stations turned into craters. Thick smoke fills the air and fire shines through the grey, now gradually disappearing from our view.'

A Junkers Ju 88A of Kampfgeschwader 30 — the unit responsible for attacking Driffield on the 15 August 1940 (via Rauchbach)

The Squadron only flew one more bombing raid, which was against Augsburg on the night of the 16th of August 1940 losing one crew, before moving to Leeming on the 25th of August 1940 because of the damage inflicted on Driffield 10 days before. The Squadron was then informed of the intention to attach eight of their Whitleys and crews to Coastal

Command as a stop gap measure. The twin-engined Blackburn Botha had been declared unsuitable as a reconnaissance and maritime bomber and as there was a surplus of Whitleys and 102 Squadron was temporarily without a home, it got the job whilst 502 Squadron converted from Bothas to Whitleys. Most of the remainder of the Squadron were attached to 19 Operational Training Unit at Kinloss to help pass on their operational experience but, sadly, before all of this happened, the Squadron was to suffer another avoidable loss:

Private Jock Welsh

'On the night of 28th August 1940, "B" Section, 2 Platoon, Silsden "I" Company of the 33rd West Riding Battalion, Home Guard, were on duty at the Silsden Reservoir Post.

'A plane passed over flying in a westerly direction at 2300 hours, flew back again, circled a few times and crashed at approximately 2307 hours, about 500 yards away. We immediately ran towards the plane which was burning furiously and we were about 50 yards away when there were two explosions which I thought were exploding petrol tanks.

In the background Whitley N1385/DY-G, lost with its crew on the night of the 16–17 August 1940 (Verran)

'Private Dobson and myself were first on the scene and managed to get through the petrol, blazing on the ground, to one flyer lying near the trailing edge of the starboard wing and the rear gun turret which had apparently broken off on impact. I sent Private Fort back to the reservoir to telephone Major Driver.

'Ammunition was continually exploding but the flyer was too heavy for us to carry and we could not drag him away because of possible internal injuries. He was badly burned about the face and hands but nothing could be done except try to clean the slight cuts with a field dressing. He appeared to be conscious but we were unable to get any intelligible replies as to whether there were any more still in the plane or whether they were carrying any bombs. He spoke vaguely about Dishforth, Driffield and Leeming aerodromes which I subsequently found were in the same Group of Bomber Command. This was the first intimation we had that it was a British plane.'

Sgt Norman Bott had taken off from Leeming on what was intended to be a routine cross country training flight. He and three of his crew were killed when, for unknown reasons, the Whitley flew into the hillside at Silsden, near Keighley, in Yorkshire. Amazingly, the rear gunner, Sgt Len Smalley, was thrown clear and despite his injuries, was soon back on operations.*

The Coastal Command detachment, led by Sqn Ldr O A Morris, arrived at Prestwick on the west coast of Scotland on the 1st of September and then followed an unexciting period of convoy escort duties, operating both out of Prestwick and Aldergrove in Northern Ireland. Little has been recorded about this period of the Squadron's life as each flight was without incident apart from one. Fg Off Henry Young, an American of American Indian descent, was forced to ditch his Whitley in the Atlantic on the 7th of October when the engines failed. 22 hours later he and his crew were picked up by HMS *St Mary*. This was the first of a number of ditchings for Henry Young who, for reasons that will become obvious, was soon to become known throughout Bomber Command as 'Dinghy' Young.†

However, on the 10th of October 1940, the Squadron moved back to Yorkshire and Number 4 Group and recommenced bombing missions against Germany. This was the start of four and a half years of virtually unbroken operations. Sadly, with the intensification of Bomber Command's war against Germany, the losses soon started to increase for 102 Squadron:

---

* Len Smalley did not rejoin 102 Squadron. He was shot down and wounded again in 1941 and then later that year shot down and taken prisoner of war. He died in 1986 – Author.
† 'Dinghy' Young was killed, as Sqn Ldr DFC and Bar, taking part in the famous 'Dambusters' raid on the 16th of May 1943 – Author.

Sgt Norman Bott (Mrs M E Barnett née Bott)

Sergeant Douglas Mourton

'At the beginning of October 1940, I reported to "B" Flight 102 Squadron which at that time was commanded by Sqn Ldr Philip "Maxie" Beare. I met up with several of the lads that I had trained with but as yet, we did not know the odds were stacked against us. We did not realise that now it was just a question of survival.

'Sqn Ldr Beare gave us our first assignment. Six of us were detailed to be the funeral party at two separate funerals. A couple of nights previously, the Squadron had taken part in a bombing raid and one of the planes that was taking off was shot down by a German intruder fighter and as a result, four of the crew were killed.

'One fellow we buried locally and it was very sad to see the terrible anguish of his wife and parents at the service. The other one we took down to a train to be transferred to his home town for burial.'

The incident that Sgt Mourton refers to took place on the 24th of October 1940. Plt Off A G Davies had just taken off from Linton-On-Ouse for an attack against Luenen in Germany, unaware that he was being watched. Soon after retracting his undercarriage, a Junkers Ju88C nightfighter flown by *Feldwebel* Hans Hahn of *3 Staffel/Nachtjagdgeschwader 2* opened fire on the helpless Whitley. Hahn had taken off from his base at Gilze-Rijen in Holland earlier that evening with the specific task of shooting down RAF bombers as they were taking off to attack Germany. The Whitley did not have a chance and crashed just north of the airfield. Amazingly, Plt Off Davies survived but his crew were either killed in the crash or died of their injuries nine days later.

A Junkers Ju 88 nightfighter, similar to the one flown by Feldwebel Hahn (Warren)

With the tempo increasing as well as the losses, great acts of heroism soon began to occur. On the night of 12th–13th of November 1940, the Squadron was briefed to attack Cologne:

Pilot Officer Leonard Cheshire

'We were off just before midnight and set course for the oil refinery at Wesseling, Cologne. We went straight to the target but unluckily the clouds were there before us and we could not see the ground at all. We circled for 50 minutes hoping that it would clear; then we decided to attack the railway goods yard before that was obscured too. The anti-aircraft gunfire which had been very severe and accurate for the last hour slowed down and it seemed as though we could not miss our new target. The bomb doors were open, the wireless operator was standing by to drop the flare and the bomb aimer started giving the usual alterations.

'Then the anti-aircraft fire opened up intensely again and one burst very close. There was a blinding explosion from the front, the perspex in the front turret was blown away and there was another terrific explosion in the fuselage. The shell had set off a photo flash.

'The explosions had hurled the control column out of my hands and the cabin was filled with dense black smoke. I remember asking the bomb-aimer if he had dropped the bombs but the only answer I got was "I've been hit". Very soon the smoke cleared a little and to my amazement I saw that not only were the engines still there but that they were still running. Then the bomb-aimer came up through the well, his face streaming with what looked like blood. He was holding his head and could not stand upright. I could not possibly help him since it was all I could do to regain control of the aircraft. Suddenly he shouted "Fire!" and staggered towards the tail.

'A little later I looked round and saw the wireless operator coming through the door with flames licking his flying suit – he was on fire himself. The bomb-aimer dashed up to him and beat the flames out with his hands. Then he disappeared down the fuselage again. He seemed to have recovered completely and it turned out that what I had taken to be blood was only oil!

'Then the cabin cleared of smoke and things seemed to be fairly alright except that the aircraft was flying in an erratic sort of way. Back in the body of the machine, the crew were working frantically to get rid of the incendiaries and anything that might explode.

'Then the second pilot came forward and reported that the fire seemed to be under control. On seeing the fire break out he had gone for the fire extinguisher but by the time he had got back again, the wireless operator had pushed the blazing flare down the 'chute and the bomb-aimer was stamping the flames out. The second pilot then went back to the tail gunner cooped up in his little glass turret who had been knocked out by the explosion. He had come to, thinking that the turret had been blown completely off and that it was falling through the sky. It turned out that it was he who had said "I've been hit" and the next thing he remembers is helping to throw out the incendiary bombs and being told to go back for his parachute in case the other end of the aeroplane should fall off.

'During this time, the wireless operator and I were alone in the cabin. He had collapsed on the floor and said "I'm going blind, Sir". His face was burned black and it looked as if blood was streaming though his eyes. When the crew returned, I sent the second pilot back for the first-aid outfit and told the others to look after the wireless operator who at first refused to be helped. He got to his feet and said "I must get to the wireless". As soon as his burns had been attended to, he clambered to his wireless and started to send out messages saying that we were on our way back to base. First of all he had to explain the setting of the dials to the rear gunner and when everything was ready, he had his hand guided to the key. For 40 minutes he stood like that, tapping out his message but the aerial had been shot away and nothing got through.

'We then took stock. We found the front turret holed, both doors gone and a 10 foot hole in the fuselage itself. The fuselage had been twisted which accounted for the wallowing motion of the aircraft but we were able to maintain height and by running the engines carefully could make a decent speed. It took us five hours to get home – there was an 80 mile wind against us.'

For this Leonard Cheshire was awarded the Distinguished Service Order (DSO) a rare award for such a junior pilot whilst the wireless operator, Sgt Henry Davidson, was awarded the Distinguished Flying Medal (DFM). However, many lesser incidents which deserved gallantry awards scarcely got a mention:

Sergeant Douglas Mourton

'A decision was made to bomb the Fiat Works at Turin. Large reserve tanks were fitted into the aircraft and this of course lowered the bomb carrying capacity. Previous operations to Italy had shown that they were always fraught with danger and although the Italian defences were scorned by those more accustomed to flying to the Ruhr, Berlin and the like, the sheer distance to the target, negotiating the Alps and the uncertainty of the weather normally caused many casualties.

'On the 23rd of November 1940, seven aircraft were detailed from our Squadron and once again I was crewed up with Sgt Rix. We set off at 1345 hours and landed at Horsham St Faith near Norwich. Here we refuelled and had a meal of some sort and set off for Italy at 1720 hours. We flew across France and then past Switzerland where it was quite unusual to see all the lights still on amongst the snow-covered mountains. We did not fly over the Alps – we flew through them. We located the Fiat works without any difficulty and dropped our bombs. It was really poorly defended – probably by about two men and a dog!

'On the way back, the meteorological forecast was completely wrong and instead of the skies being clear, it was 10/10ths cloud right the way back. When it was estimated that we were over England, we tried to break cloud by coming down to 500 feet two or three times but we were not successful and now we were hopelessly lost.

'Suddenly, we were hit by anti-aircraft fire and naturally we thought that

Leonard Cheshire's Whitley after returning from Cologne, 12 November 1940 (Verran)

we were over the French coast. We turned north and were hit again and then ran out of petrol. As there was no lay-by handy, the captain gave the order to abandon aircraft.

'The procedure should have been to leave my rear turret and open the escape hatch half way down the fuselage, climb up through it, walk along the top of the aircraft and jump off the end. However, the hatch would not open so I decided to go to the cockpit. It was very hard to squeeze through the overload tanks but I eventually got to the cockpit and there was Sgt Rix still at the controls holding the plane steady because he was unable to find his parachute. I eventually found it for him and he told me to jump so I left the plane as quickly as possible.

'It was a peculiar sensation as you jump and wait for a few seconds, wondering whether you have strapped on your 'chute correctly and when you pull the handle, a canopy flies past you and suddenly your speed is arrested and you float gently down to the ground. Of course, I was wondering where I would be landing – whether it would be France, the Channel or England!

'When I landed, not knowing where I was, I bundled my 'chute up and hid it in a hedge. It was 0400 hours on a bitter November morning and I walked along until, at last, I came to a house. I knocked on the door – no answer. I threw stones up at the window, wondering where I was and in even what country I was in. Soon a head popped out and said "Are you English, RAF or German?". I said "RAF". "Alright," he said, "I'll come down and let you in." I had landed near Midhurst in Sussex and soon I was sitting in one armchair with my legs in another in front of the dying embers of a fire and, of course, I was soon asleep.'*

The first full year of the war was coming to a close. Sadly, the Squadron was to lose its first Commanding Officer in action when Wg Cdr S R Groom, who had taken over from Wg Cdr Burton in mid-May 1940, crashed into the North Sea returning from Duisburg on the night of 20th–21st of November. Neither he and his crew were ever seen again. More Commanding Officers were to follow similar fates in the years to come. Despite the sadness of the previous twelve months, an incident occurred shortly before the years changed which was amusing and luckily did not result in any further loss of life:

Sergeant Douglas Mourton

'I do not recall what the target was on the 21st of December 1940 but one engine failed after we were 30 miles from the Dutch Coast so we turned back. We steadily lost height all the way back and Sgt Rix was just able to pull the plane over the boundary hedge of our airfield. Unfortunately,

---

* Of the seven 102 Squadron aircraft that took part in this operation, three never even cleared the Alps and turned home. In addition to Sgt Rix's Whitley, another force-landed near Brighton whilst a third ditched in the sea south of Plymouth. The pilot of this last Whitley, Fg Off Henry Young, now earned his nickname 'Dinghy' when the crew took to the dinghy and were rescued a few hours later – Author.

Leonard Cheshire's Whitley after its accident on the 21 December 1940 (Verran)

Sgt Rix's Whitley fared better. This was repaired and lost in an attack on Hamburg in March 1941 (Verran)

on the other side there was a parked Whitley and we went right through the middle of it – we cut it in two! Our undercarriage was ripped off and we slid along the ground. We still had our bombs on board and we could not get out of the usual exit so clambered out through the emergency exit on the top of the aircraft in an orderly fashion. Sgt Rix had encountered little trouble until I joined his crew and his last remark to me was "Mourton, you are a bloody jink!". I never flew with him again!'

Plt Off Leonard Cheshire had been watching all of this and mentions it in his book *Bomber Pilot*. The Whitley in which he was flying when he was awarded the DSO had finished being repaired earlier that day and was waiting to be flight tested prior to returning to operational flying. His Whitley was the one unceremoniously sliced in half by Sgt Rix. Mercifully, nobody was injured in this incident which seemed to be the normal state of affairs for the Squadron's operational flying during 1940 – despite the number of operations flown during the year, losses had been relatively light. Unfortunately, this was to change in 1941.

CHAPTER THREE

A Very Dangerous Business —
1941–1942

1941 started badly as within two days, the Squadron had lost its first crew to an old adversary. Fg Off D C Coutts, who had been the second pilot to Plt Off Leonard Cheshire during the raid which resulted in Cheshire being awarded the DSO, was now captain of his own aircraft and crew. However, his tenure as captain did not last long. Shortly after having taken off from Topcliffe on the 2nd of January 1941, the Squadron having moved there in mid-November 1940, to attack Bremen, he had the misfortune of meeting a German nightfighter. *Oberfeldwebel* Hans Hahn was heading for his hunting ground of Bomber Command airfields and hoping to add to his score of one, the 102 Squadron Whitley he shot down back in October 1940. In a short one-sided battle, he shot down the Whitley 50 km east of Withernsea; Coutts and his crew were never seen again.

Unusually, the Squadron was not to suffer any losses until early March 1941. Yet again, the Winter weather had played its part by preventing the Squadron from operating for at least three weeks. However, with the arrival of better weather came more operations and in just over a month, the Squadron lost two flight commanders and the Squadron Commander. In one night, two Whitleys were lost attacking Berlin and before the 24 hours were over, the Squadron was to lose another attacking Hamburg:

Sergeant Douglas Mourton

'On the 13th of March, we were detailed to go to Hamburg. We had a comparatively easy trip. It was a bright moonlit night and as we were approaching Hamburg, we could see another Whitley flying along on a parallel course with us.

'Suddenly, the other Whitley exploded. What had been an aircraft a few seconds before was now a mass of debris falling through the air. It had been hit by anti-aircraft fire, most likely in its bomb bay. There had only been three aircraft taking part from our Squadron and the one that was missing was piloted by my very best friend Alec Elliott. He was the man with whom, before my wife Maisie had come to live with me, I had gone out drinking with every night played crib, day after day, while waiting in the crew room. I had seen him die but it was remarkable that such tragedies did not appear to cause us any distress. It just went to emphasise how lucky we had been to get back.'

As each month passed, the same targets came up again and again – Bremen, Hamburg, Kiel, Cologne. Considering the number of sorties flown, losses remained light but by mid-June 1941, they were starting to creep up:

Sergeant Philip Winter

'I arrived at 102 Squadron on the 14th of May and flew my first trip as seond pilot three days later. We had almost daily briefings and stand downs from then until the 6th of June – very trying, especially when kitted up and ready to go.

'On the 12th of June 1941, I flew my third and last trip. We were to attack a railway marshalling yard at Schwerte. After take off, I was given the controls and remember telling the crew, on flying over Bridlington, that in four weeks time I would be there on my honeymoon. However, over the sea, we began to ice up and the Skipper, Sgt Rees, took over. Ice coming off the propeller blades made quite a din and we used the Aldis Lamp to monitor build up on the leading edge.

'We were clear on reaching the Dutch coast by which time I was map reading in the front turret. As the target approached, it was obvious that we were in for quite a reception – many searchlights and lots of flak. We were soon coned and the bursts of flak were quite close and audible. The turret was holed and one could smell the cordite. I exchanged places with the navigator for the bombing run and whilst on it were coned again but our Skipper decided to hold his course. I shall never forget the violet glow in which we were all bathed and the noise of the bursting shells. Suddenly, there was a burst very close to the aircraft and I felt as if someone had hit my left foot with sledgehammer – no pain, just a stunning blow. The Skipper called us all up and I had to say that I thought I had been hit. The bombs were dropped, the guns were used to fire at the searchlights and we managed to get away. I turned round from the navigator's table and the wireless operator looked at my foot. There was a large hole clean through the ankle so the boot was cut away, a field dressing and tourniquet applied and I was laid down in the fuselage near the Elsan toilet, wondering about the prospect of a wedding in four weeks time. Only after we had landed did I realise how much blood I had lost and to cut a long story short, I never flew again operationally.'

Sgt Winter was one of the luckier ones that night – the Squadron lost two Whitleys on the night of the 12th–13th of June and a further Whitley during a follow up attack on Schwerte the night after. Another Whitley was treated the same way as Philip Winter's but in this case, the damage was to the aircraft and not those inside it:

Sergeant P S Thompson

'We thought that Jerry had been lying "doggo" but must have picked us up on the bombing run because immediately after we had dropped our bombs on Schwerte, we were caught in the searchlights, just one or two at first but soon we were rapidly coned by many, many lights. Then all hell broke loose as they pumped all the heavy flak they could into the coned area.

'Being in the nose in the bomb aimers position, I got what seemed to be the full attention of the searchlights and can only describe it as a feeling of being caught naked in a room when the lights are switched on. The flak was lifting the plane and as it hit, made a noise like gravel hitting metal.

'By now, the Skipper was taking violent evasive action but unfortunately, our tail elevators were hit with the result that we could not maintain height and each time the pilot opened the throttles to gain height, the nose rose steeply and he had to throttle back to avoid stalling.

'By this time, we were down to about 4,000 feet so reluctantly but sensibly, the Skipper gave the order to bale out before it became too late. When I heard the order, I was still down in the nose. In those days, the observer was both the navigator, bomb aimer and front gunner and being out of it all, I was not aware of the damage and was really taken aback to hear the order to bale out! Indeed, my first reaction was to say "Bugger this for a lark!". Nevertheless, it was my job to jettison the front escape hatch so I clipped on my parachute and moved unwillingly to the hatch and was just about to jettison it when I heard the second pilot shout "Hold on!".

'Both pilots had kept their wits about them and one of them had the bright idea of feverishly turning the trim wheel to make the nose as heavy as possible. Luckily, the Whitley flew nose down, so with the nose heavy and a moderate amount of engine power, the old "Flying Coffin" as we called the Whitley, managed to stagger towards home. Being south-east of the Ruhr, we had to fly north-west back over the Ruhr. We dared not deviate too much from the shortest course home because of the damage and we were getting low on petrol. As a result, we were further damaged whilst crossing the Ruhr.

'We now realised that it was no longer Thursday the 12th of June but was now Friday the 13th. Bad omen or not, we survived the Ruhr and on the run up to the coast, the Skipper suggested that we pep ourselves up and counter stress by putting our oxygen masks on. To demonstrate the beneficial effects of oxygen, he took several deep breaths and exclaimed "That's better!". We did not have the heart to tell him that all of the oxygen bottles had been broken by the flak and he was breathing normal air but the thought that he was on oxygen did him good!

'Eventually we crossed the English coast and headed towards Topcliffe. As we could not get the rear gunner out of his turret, it was decided to attempt a landing. The Skipper made a long and careful approach and all seemed to be going well but we had forgotten about the bloody Gremlins. Towards the final stages of the approach, the Skipper tried to ease the nose up prior to landing but could not get the desired response. Wisely, he decided to go round again and when he opened the throttles, the nose just shot up steeply. I could not say what height we reached before it shuddered and began to stall but I reckon it must have been about 1,000 to 1,500 feet. I clearly remember looking down at the ground as the plane flipped sideways, with the starboard wing pointing directly at the ground; I felt quite calm and thought "This is it". Someone said afterwards that they heard the Skipper scream "I don't want to die!" but all I know is that he kept his wits about him and as we were going down, he wrenched the controls over so that instead of plunging violently into the ground, we skidded sideways across the airfield. The tail turret broke away so the rear gunner was the first to escape from the wreckage. Both engines were torn from their mountings and thankfully there was no fire. No one was seriously injured – the wireless operator banged his head on the roof, I got a gash on the palm of my hand where I was gripping a metal tray for support. I also got a bang on my back and a black eye when someone trod on me in their haste to get out!

'The superstitious might be interested to know that the serial number of this plane was Z6565. 13 × five equals 65 and the crash took place at 0640 hours on Friday the 13th of June 1941. Fortunately for us, neither unlucky 13 nor the Whitley's reputation of being a "Flying Coffin" lived up to their reputation. I completed my tour without incident on 102 Squadron as well as a subsequent tour on 76 Squadron.'

So far, the majority of 102 Squadron losses had been caused by anti-aircraft fire. The German nightfighter force was improving rapidly and from the end of June 1941 onwards, started wreaking death and destruction on 102 Squadron crews. One such nightfighter pilot was *Oberleutnant* Helmut Lent. Originally a dayfighter pilot, he had scored seven day 'kills' before his unit was withdrawn and reformed as a nightfighter unit in September 1940. Given command of *6 Staffel/Nachtjagdgeschwader 1*, Lent found great difficulty acquiring the technique of nightfighting and it was not until the

Oberleutnant Helmut Lent (Kettling)

night of the 11th/12th of May 1941 that he scored his first 'kill'. However, by the time of his death in October 1944, he had a total of 113 kills and was one of the most highly decorated and respected of German nightfighter pilots. Unfortunately for a crew of 102 Squadron, they were destined to be one of his first kills:

Sergeant Brian Booth

'On the night of the 27th/28th of June 1941, we set off from Topcliffe with the "met" officer forecasting good weather conditions on the way. As it turned out, we ran into an unpleasant front as we approached the enemy coast. This gave icing conditions at about 8,000 feet which meant that we were unable to climb above or into cloud and were "stooging" along, beautifully silhouetted against the cloud – just a perfect sitting duck. It was not long before we were caught in the cones of searchlights and a fighter came straight in. That was the end; smoke and the smell of cordite and the old Whitley flying at all angles, even upside down! Fortunately Jimmy Cullen, our pilot, was an experienced Skipper and he did a great job getting the old kite to fly straight and level long enough for all of us to get out by parachute. There were no serious injuries apart from poor old Mike Featherstone, the second pilot, who got a bullet in his bum!

'We all landed safely but separately and there I was, all alone somewhere in Germany. I had a feeling that I was somewhere close to the Danish border so as soon as it was daylight, I made for the nearest farmhouse

The Messerschmitt Bf 110 nighfighter (via Rauchbach)

hoping to fall into friendly hands. Unfortunately, I was on the wrong side of the border and before long, the village policeman arrived looking like something out of a comic opera – short and fat with a conical helmet, carrying a revolver nearly as big as himself and my parachute under his arm. Then he uttered those fateful words "For you ze war is over" and marched me off to the local police station holding that large revolver to my back and making me carry my parachute!'

Another German nightfighter pilot who was helping to increase Bomber Command's losses was *Hauptmann* Werner Streib. He was one of the first and scored the first official German nightfighter kill of the war on the night of the 19th/20th of July 1940. He was to score 14 kills during 1941, two of which were from 102 Squadron. The first on the 1st of July, resulted in the deaths of all the crew; the next crew were a little luckier:

Sergeant Basil Cotton

'On the 3rd of July trip, we had been to Essen and were caught in the only efficient German searchlights on the way home. It was not the first time but previously we had managed to get away. A German nightfighter then attacked us very successfully and we had to bale out. I was wounded in both legs and in going through the escape hatch apparently hit my head. I remember descending, being circled by the nightfighter several times, but don't recall any more until I was found lying in a ditch by a large Alsatian dog with three German soldiers. They tried to move me by lifting but I passed out twice so two disappeared leaving one to guard me. The two returned with a German hospital orderly who cut off my flying kit from feet to waist and dressed both legs. He was both very efficient and kind and I was put on to a stretcher and taken to hospital in Krefeld. I was there about four days and during that time I was informed that I had been shot down by *Nachtjagdgeschwader 1*. The German pilot who told me this indicated that he was *Oberleutnant* Prinz zur Lippe-Weissenfeld but whether he was or not, I do not know.* I have since been told that it was the *Gruppen Kommandeur* of *I Gruppe/Nachtjagdgeschwader 1*, *Hauptmann* Werner Streib, who shot us down at Arcen in Holland.'

Sergeant Norman Davies

'We arrived over the Dutch border with no sign of any ground or air attacks. Suddenly, there were four or five flak bursts behind us. They were reasonably accurate – a moment later a searchlight locked onto us; it did not have to search for us as it was so powerful. The colour of the beam was blue-ish – I'd experienced searchlights before but this one was accurate and much more powerful.

---

* *Oberleutnant* Egmont Prinz zur Lippe-Weissenfeld was a rising nightfighter ace flying at that time with *4/NJG 1*. At the time of his death in March 1944, he had a total of 51 night victories. He had been involved in a collision with another aircraft on the 30th of June 1941 so it is possible that Basil Cotton met him in hospital – Author.

'We were only in the searchlight for a minute or two. I centralised the guns and tried to see any enemy aircraft but the turret perspex ruined my vision as it was reflecting the searchlight. Suddenly I saw four to six streams of cannon and machine-gun fire arcing leisurely towards us from dead astern. I opened fire in that direction and swept my guns downwards anticipating that would be the fighter's track. A second later his gunfire swept our aircraft from stem to stern.

'My turret was hit and there were several explosions. Both my hands were hit but I did not notice the pain – I think I was too absorbed expecting another burst from the fighter (the injury to my hands was caused by my own cartridge cases exploding – it took another two years before the bits of brass were finally removed from my hands). I still hadn't seen the fighter and presumed that he had overtaken us and was holding back outside .303 range. I centralised the guns and fired them to ensure they still worked but on firing, I just got one short burst and no more. The turret would not rotate which meant the hydraulics had been fractured, and my intercom did not function so it was impossible to check what damage had been inflicted to the front of the plane. Luckily, the turret doors opened and the manual handle still worked.

'Smoke was now pouring into the turret from fires in the fuselage. I grabbed my parachute, opened the top hatch and leapt into the night. I delayed opening the parachute as I did not want the fighter cutting through me. I watched our aircraft flying onwards, still on a level course. It was a sad and ghostly sight. The searchlight still held onto it and flames were licking the full length of the fuselage. I felt relieved and disgusted with myself. It had been so easy for the nightfighter. He had shot us down with

Sgt Norman Davies (front second from left) together, on his left, his wireless operator Sgt Ken Bowden and his navigator, Sgt Alan Lakin seen as prisoners later during the War (Davies)

so little danger to himself. The searchlight had been his main weapon – all he had to do was shoot the nails into our coffin lid!'

With so many combats and losses, sooner or later 102 Squadron was destined to get its second DSO. This happened on the night of the 14th–15th of July. As Flt Lt George Davies approached the target which that night was Bremen, his Whitley was coned by searchlights and subjected to very heavy anti-aircraft fire. Nevertheless, he continued his bombing run only to be attacked by a nightfighter which killed his rear gunner and badly damaged the Whitley. He then lost control of the crippled bomber which spun from 10,500 feet to 7,000 feet before he could regain control only to be attacked again by another nightfighter. He managed to shake off his attacker then, in the words of the DSO citation, "he attained level flight and with a superlative display of airmanship succeeded in flying back without further damage to the aircraft or crew".

June and July 1941 were to prove to be the most catastrophic so far in 102 Squadron's history. The Squadron lost 13 Whitleys and 40 crew members killed or missing with a further 18 prisoners of war. The Squadron soon got a reputation as being one where crews had little chance of completing their tour and it was about this time that the unofficial Squadron song was composed from which this book gets its title. One incident sticks in one particular Squadron member's mind:

Below and overleaf
*George Davies' damaged
Whitley (Stanley)*

Sergeant P S Thompson

'One afternoon in June 1941 as I was returning to camp, a young pilot arrived to join our Squadron. The Duty Sgt asked me to take him to the Adjutant and I waited while he said a loving goodbye to his parents who had brought him to Topcliffe by car as they lived in Yorkshire. I introduced him to the Adjutant and the flight commander. He was as keen as mustard and when told that we were on ops that night, he volunteered to go as second pilot with a very experienced crew. I spoke to him briefly in the crew room when we were changing into flying kit. He was very excited and I wished him the best of luck.

'That was the last time I had any contact with him as the whole crew did not return from the raid. The next morning, I was told to report to the Adjutant's office. There I met the young pilot's parents who, having said cheerio to him about 1600 hours the previous afternoon, had received a telegram that morning informing them that their son was missing. They were very distressed and could not accept that he had been lost so quickly. Naturally, they wanted more information but there was none to give at that stage. However, they had remembered their son going off with me and asked to speak to me. They were so desperate for any details about their son's short time with the Squadron. I told them all I knew and added that I was sure he was happy to go on the raid and although he was missing, there was a good chance he would survive the war. I hope that I gave them some comfort but I found it rather disturbing. Had I been older and not so used to seeing pals "going for a Burton", I now feel that I might have been able to have given them greater solace. As I left 102 a few weeks later, I never found out what had happened to that young pilot. I hope that he survived.'*

The end of July saw a great influx of new people, many of them Canadians. Prior to this, Officers' and Sergeants' Messes had been like morgues and one could get a seat anywhere in the ante-rooms. Now it was standing room only! The majority of newcomers were straight out of training such as Sgt Tom Vermiglio who arrived from the Operational Training Unit on the 12th of August 1941. However, a number of experienced crews were posted from other Whitley Squadrons to maintain the level of experience. One pilot, posted in with his crew from 78 Squadron, was Sgt Alan Hawkes who arrived at Topcliffe the same day as Tom. Both Vermiglio and Hawkes were to fly their first operation with the Squadron two nights later but in separate crews whilst another observer in a third crew, Sgt Edward Alderton, was hoping that his third trip would be as uneventful as the previous two. Events were soon to prove otherwise for all three:

* It is believed that the pilot in question was Sgt D M Philip who was lost on the night of the 27th–28th of June 1941. The bodies of all five crew members were washed ashore a few days later and buried at Brochswalden in Germany – Author.

Sgt Tom Vermiglio (Vernon)

Sergeant Edward Alderton

'The target on the night of the 14th–15th of August 1941 was Hannover and we were to fly very close to the nightfighter airfield at Leeuwaarden. That night it was flashing a white "W". That was the last entry in my log as then we were hit by a nightfighter which I though to be an Me 110 (I met the German pilot the next day). I baled out at about 3,500 feet and landed in the middle of a field in the North Friesland area of Holland. I crawled into a lean-to shed and slept until 0900 hours on the 15th of August.

'Later I was picked up by a Dutch policeman and taken to the mayor's office. He treated me very well as his son was in the Royal Navy. At roughly 1300 hours, German soldiers arrived and with the rest of my crew, all of whom were safe, we were taken to Amsterdam and put in the civilian gaol. On the wall of my cell I read the following: "Only birds and fools fly and birds don't fly at night!". This was signed by a wireless operator from 102 Squadron shot down three weeks previously. Tom Vermiglio was also there – it was his first op.'

Sergeant Tom Vermiglio

'On the 14th of August I first met my crew. During the day, we had a short flight and then briefing and that evening set off for a raid on Hannover. The raid itself was uneventful but we had crossed the Dutch coast on the way back and were nearing the Frisian Islands when we were attacked by a nightfighter. The first I knew of the attack was seeing tracer coming from below and to the rear but I could not see any aircraft so I returned fire as best I could. As the fighter broke off the attack, it crossed my line of vision and I recognised it as a 110.* It immediately dived as I opened fire again but by now the lining of the cockpit was on fire and attempts were being made to put the fire out. Difficulty was also being experienced with the controls. A second burst of fire wounded Sgt Penn in the foot and orders to abandon the plane were given.

'I escaped over the turret and immediately all was quiet. I saw a flash of flame as the aircraft hit the ground and then I landed. I found myself on a low sandhill-covered island with, as I thought at the time, no way off. On exploration I found two wooden chalets – one named "Chez Nous" and the other "Happy Days". It is remarkable how unimportant details stick in the mind!

'I wandered back to the water's edge. A spotter plane flew over and as the whole situation seemed hopeless, I waved but it passed on without apparent recognition. I then returned to "Chez Nous" and in a lean-to at the back found a sledgehammer. With this I opened the door. Inside I found some matches and lit a fire with wood from the shed. Outside a barrel had been sunk into the ground for a well – the water was alive with mosquito larvae. I filtered some water through the sleeve of my pullover, boiled it well and drank it. I then climbed the ladder into the loft to await

* Both Tom Vermiglio and Edward Alderton were shot down by Dornier Do 215 B-2s which at night looked similar to a Messerschmitt Bf 110 – Author.

Ofw Paul Gildner, the nightfighter pilot who shot down Tom Vermiglio

developments and shortly afterwards, I heard a noise and looked down to find I had been taken prisoner by two German soldiers mounted on horses.

'Despondently and wearily I trudged behind my captors, wading at times up to my knees in water. At last I was so tired and weary that in despair, I sat down. Guns were pointed at me but I, not out of heroism but sheer despair, took no notice. I really did not care whether I lived or died. The corporal ordered the private to dismount and for the first time in my life, I rode a horse and so I completed my journey to their guardroom. The next day I was taken away by boat and train for interrogation. Even if I had been willing, there was little I could have told my interrogators. I did learn, however, that Sgt Penn, although wounded, had survived but the remainder the crew had crashed with the plane and had been killed.

Sergeant Alan Hawkes

'14th of August 1941 we left base for Hannover on our 12th trip. The plane was not climbing well but we arrived over the Dutch coast alright. Plenty of flak about and on the port side, I could see Emden. We planned getting into the searchlight belt at about 0050 hours but they got us after five minutes and held us so I put the propellers into coarse pitch and cut the motors. At 0115 hours I told the rear gunner to keep a look out for fighters but he replied he was unable to see because of the searchlights, about 100 of them by now. A couple of minutes afterwards as we were about to leave the belt, I noticed tracer through the top perspex. I did a diving turn to the left but as we turned, the intercom failed and there was a loud explosion in front of me. The observer reported that the front perspex had been

Sgt Alan Hawkes (pointing) showing local dignitaries around a 78 Sqn Whitley (Hawkes)

blown away so I told him to jettison the bombs. Then the airspeed indicator dropped, the port exactor went unserviceable and the propeller went into fine pitch so I commenced the drill for single-engined flying. The wireless operator reported the rear turret was completely ablaze and the rear gunner burning. The wireless operator couldn't find the extinguisher so I told the second pilot, who seemed to be rather dazed and in a flat spin, to get the extinguisher from the front turret which he did and passed it back. The bombs had gone and we are losing height rapidly. The wireless operator put the fire out but couldn't get the gunner out as the turret was off centre and was also white hot.

'By now we were at 5,000 feet and I was just about able to fly level but the trim tabs were not working. I had great hopes to getting back but they were dashed to smithereens when the port motor started to pack up, the oil pressure dropped and the temperature rose. I throttled right back but the plane juddered and started to lose height quite rapidly. Then the port engine caught fire so I pressed the fire extinguisher button – the flames go out for a second but the engine caught fire again and the flames got bigger. I now had to cut the petrol and the engine packed up altogether. We were now at 2,000 feet and descending. Fire had now got a good hold so unfortunately I had to inform the crew to prepare to bale out. By this time we were at 1,000 feet, the crew had baled out but we were unable to get the poor rear gunner out. I put in "George" hoping he worked though I doubted it. I got into the well and the plane was now at 800 feet. I had forgotten to unfasten my oxygen plug – I started to pull but no good then I realised why not just take the helmet off. I did so and left the plane facing backwards and slid out as easy as anything. I was now at 350 feet. 'Chute opened OK – how easy and comfortable it was! The time was 0145 hours on the 15th of August 1941.

'I looked up and watched the plane diving away. I then looked down and see ground rushing up and boy did I hit with a bump! Everything was deadly quiet. I started walking and came to a road so I started along it going south, I hoped! A motorbike came along so I ducked into a ditch. After it passed, I decided to find somewhere to sleep so I found a field with a hedge of sorts – whistles were being sounded all round me it seemed. I tried to sleep but no chance so at about 0400 hours I started off heading west. I came across a village called Gelbe(?) near Osnabrück so I started to skirt the village but I had the misfortune to run into a Luftwaffe chap.'

In just one night, 102 Squadron suffered five men killed and 11 prisoners of war and, in addition to the three Whitleys shot down over enemy territory, a further bomber crashed on return to Topcliffe. Sadly, losses continued to mount up almost to the end of the year. It started some of the luckier crews thinking:

Sergeant Ed Cooke

'In about October 1941, a few of us were sitting around chewing the cud and one of us wondered what our chances were of completing a tour which was 30 trips or 200 hours. At that time, I had 20 trips to my credit so off

A brand new Halifax starting up at its dispersal at Dalton (Powell)

we went to research the Squadron records and finally came to the conclusion that we had a three percent chance of survival! Most of us after a few trips became fatalists and believed that if there was one there with our name on it, so be it but we were going to do everything in our power to survive. I was lucky. I completed my tour and followed my pilot, Alan Davis, to instruct at 19 Operational Training Unit. When I got there I had found that Alan had just been killed – he had walked into a propeller.'

With the arrival of winter came a few changes. First of all, to the relief of the Squadron aircrew and groundcrew, the tempo of operations lessened, as shown by only eight Whitleys being lost in November and of those, two were not as a direct result of combat; December was better – only one lost. Secondly, the Squadron moved to Dalton in the middle of November as concrete runways were at last being built at Topcliffe. Finally, it was rumoured that the Squadron was getting rid of its Whitleys and converting to the Handley Page Halifax which would mean even less operations as the crews got to grips with their new aircraft. Sadly, despite all of this, some crews would not see the New Year whilst others were luckier as the final two losses of November illustrate:

Sergeant Jock Williamson

'On the 30th of November, the target was Hamburg. The crew were the same as normal apart from Sgt Taylor, the wireless operator, who was standing in for Ed Cooke who was on leave.

'We had a hard time with searchlights and flak leaving the target but we were unhurt and I heard the navigator give a course to the pilot. We were low, between 2,000 to 3,000 feet, and we were all expecting to see the North Sea when the second pilot said "This is Kiel!". Then the Germans sent up two parachute flares and it was like daylight, with light flak coming from all directions. I was firing my guns like mad but they got the port engine and the intercom went dead. I rotated my turret by hand and was coming out of it backwards when the plane took a dive and it crashed into the Kiel Canal. I was thrown back into the turret and expected to drown but I managed to get out through the broken perspex and onto land. Everywhere was on fire so I started running but stopped when I came across the navigator about 20 yards from the plane. He was unconscious and his face badly damaged. All the others were still in the burning wreckage. We had actually crashed 50 yards from the flak battery that shot us down and the Germans immediately started giving medical aid but by that time the navigator was dead.'

Sergeant Robbie Robinson

'Routing back from Hamburg on the night of the 30th of November, the weather was bad and we experienced a bad electrical storm. Sheets of blue flame shot off the tips of the propellers, the ends of the guns glowed with St Elmo's Fire and the windscreen iced up. Little did we know that the storm had affected our compass by 15 degrees so instead of coming back to Dalton over Flamborough Head, we came over the coast at Holy Island! I was in the nose at this time and saw the waves breaking over a rocky coastline which didn't look right to me.

'Soon we realised we were lost and despite doing a square search and descending through cloud every now and again, it was decided to bale out. It was a textbook bale out and as my parachute opened, I heard the Whitley's engines stop. I later heard it had crash-landed itself on a beach.

'I landed in a wood, gathered up my parachute and started walking down the hill. We had thought we were over Eire but on seeing a cottage and, on knocking, being greeted by a Scottish tongue, I felt relieved. I had landed near Dumfries. From then on, I was fêted very well – the best room in the house and the next day, when all the crew had been rounded up, the local vicar arranged a "do" in our honour. We were then all taken to Dumfries, stayed in a local hotel and eventually got back to Dalton three days later. Our first task on getting back was to give the WAAF parachute packer ten shillings each for saving our lives.'

The final words for 1941 come from Sgt Ed Cooke. Ed had been stunned when, on getting back from leave, he had discovered his crew had gone missing. Instead of getting another crew and, as the Squadron had been told in January 1942, 28 Conversion Flight was arriving to convert them to the Halifax, he kicked his heels for the rest of the month. However, there was still the threat of operations, even on Christmas Day:

Sergeant Ed Cooke

'On Christmas morning, we were told that if Jerry didn't operate, so we wouldn't. Christmas morning arrived and the bar was opened at 1000 hours but just before lunch, the phone rang and we were told to report to the flights. So we all mounted our trusty bicycles and headed the one and a half miles from the Mess to the airfield. Of course, everyone was in good voice and as we swung through the gates, Wg Cdr Howard, our Commanding Officer, came out of his office and said "You drunken bunch of buggers aren't going to fly any of my aircraft today!" so we all saluted as we went past him, did a 180 degree turn and headed back to the Mess.'

1942 arrived and five days later the conversion crews from Number 28 (Halifax) Conversion Flight, under the command of Sqn Ldr P B Robinson arrived to form, on the 6th of January, 102 Squadron Conversion Flight. The first Handley Page Halifax Mark I, serial R9390, had arrived on the 3rd of December 1941 with the remainder of the first batch arriving in between the 24th of December 1941 and the 17th of January 1942. However, some crews had already started their conversion training. Plt Off Wally Lashbrook, one of the Conversion Flight's instructors, recorded giving conversion instruction to four 102 Squadron pilots in December 1941. One of these was Sgt Larry Carr who had his first flight on the 22nd of December and flew as first pilot for the first time four days later. By the end of January 1942, Larry had amassed a total of three hours 50 minutes dual, four hours 45 minutes as first pilot and eight hours 15 minutes as second pilot. He had still to fly the Halifax at night.

Despite conversion training, operational flying continued with the Whitleys, albeit at a reduced rate due to crew training and vagaries of the winter weather; the Whitleys were to soldier on for another three months. Sadly, the very day that the Conversion Flight started in-situ Halifax conversion training, the Squadron was to lose its penultimate Whitley:

Sergeant Ed Brain

'The flight was to be a "nursery" for Sgt "Bruno" Hollingworth – his first as captain. Sgt "Jacko" Jackson and myself were loaned for the trip which started with the posting of the "Day's Ops List" in the early morning. Briefing was in the late afternoon and early evening so we did an air test in the morning just to ensure the Whitley was alright.

'As we crossed the English coast, I managed to get an excellent fix and recalculated the wind speed and direction and the final course for the target which was Cherbourg Docks. We had strict instructions only to drop the bombs if we could clearly see the target but that night it was pitch black and we could not see a thing. After "stooging" about for a bit, we had reluctantly decided to bring the bombs back with us when suddenly there was a horrendous noise and the aircraft shook violently. I thought we had been hit by flak (even though it had been very light so far on this night).

The starboard engine temperature was off the clock and had to be shut down so we feared we had a coolant leak.

'We turned for home on one engine and as we crossed the English coast, we were greeted by a cone of three searchlights showing us the way to the nearest airfield. "Bruno" said "They want us to land but I want to make it back to base". No one disagreed so we slowly headed up England, slowly losing height, with only one engine, a full bomb load and decreasing fuel load.

'We then decided to drop our bombs so I went forward into the nose, selected "Bombs Safe", double checked safe and unarmed and opened the bomb doors. I selected open ground in what I thought was a quarry and away they went – no explosion, thank goodness!

'If I remember correctly, "Bruno" then tried to restart the engine as we were getting lower and lower and were a fair way from the nearest aerodrome. We were furiously busy – "Bruno" coaxing the aircraft and engine with Sgt Johnny Hazeldine's help (he was the second pilot); Sgt "Buck" Buchanan was getting bearings and probably sending out "Maydays"; "Jacko", alone in the rear turret, was shouting out town names as we passed over them as by now it was broad daylight. I was busy plotting courses, advising nearest airfields and telling "Bruno" where and what to avoid and was completely engrossed with my navigating when I felt a punch on my arm. It was "Bruno" and he was pointing to the starboard engine which was completely ablaze with 15-foot-long flames. He signalled me to get out.

'I couldn't see the second pilot – he had already gone. I then followed the drill that had been drummed into me and as "Bruno" was without his mask and helmet, I gave the order to bale out. I didn't hear from "Jacko" and assumed he had gone. However, I saw "Buck" on the floor trying to repair his wireless – he hadn't heard me so I grabbed his leg and tugged. He turned and I pointed to the inferno and he jumped up and followed me back to the cockpit. We moved quickly and I went forward to the nose door and as I passed "Bruno", I saw his face was ashen white – he had no parachute and was going to try and crash-land. We exchanged thumbs up and I went to the opening, sat on the edge and dangled my feet in the slipstream, immediately losing one of my flying boots. I checked my harness, grasped the "D" ring and jumped. As I fell, my arms flew upwards and I saw the "D" ring was loose in my hands. I looked at it and thought "Oh my God, my 'chute hasn't opened!" when all of a sudden, I felt as if I had been jerked 10 feet upwards – my 'chute was open! I looked around and then heard "Boom!" and there was an explosion – looking up, the plane was a ball of fire and a partially opened 'chute was streaming from flames – it had to be "Buck".

'Now my 'chute was swinging violently in an arc like a pendulum and I feared it was going to collapse. I looked down at the side of a hill which rushed up quickly and I hit the ground. I had made it.

'"Boom!" again another explosion and a mushroom of smoke. A car was stopped in the road besides the field where I landed – it was a policeman. I gathered my parachute, walked over and got in. My left leg started to shake – I couldn't stop it. I was taken to the police station where I met Johnny and had a cuppa well laced with rum. No, "Buck" hadn't made it, neither had "Bruno". "Jacko" was alright but had injured his foot.'

There is a sad ending to both this story and 102 Squadron's Whitley career. Only one more Whitley was lost on operations and that was on the 26th of January 1942 when serial Z9283 coded DY-F was shot down by a nightfighter off the Dutch coast when returning from Emden.

Conversion training now went ahead at full throttle and for the months of February and March 1942, no operational flights were undertaken. Plt Off Wally Lashbrook notes that during January he instructed six pilots, including Sgt Hazeldine the pilot of DY-F. During February, it was the turn of a further eleven to be instructed, including the new Commanding Officer, Wg Cdr Sydney Bintley, and a further ten were instructed the following month. At this point, it should be mentioned that towards the end of March 1942, the Squadron had the honour to take part in a very special flight:

Sergeant Ed Cooke

A 102 Squadron Halifax starting up at its dispersal at Dalton (Powell)

'Most of March was spent local flying with the exception of practice for a ceremonial flypast for their Majesties which was on the 25th of the month.

We flew over the Officers' Mess at exactly 1400 hours, three Halifaxes in "Vic" formation. Afterwards we gained height and as their car was on the other side of the perimeter track, down we came and flew over them as low as we dared. We received some funny looks on landing but got away with it.'

25 March 1942. Left to right: Wg Cdr Sydney Bintley, OC 102 Sqn, The King, The Queen, Gp Capt Richard Grice, Dalton's Station Commander (Powell)

Sadly, the first Halifax accident occurred on the 14th of April 1942, killing two of the recently converted pilots and a further six crew. Soon, however, most of the Squadron was declared operational and on the 22nd of April 1942, the Halifaxes took part in an attack on Le Havre Docks almost without incident. Five days later, the Squadron was instructed to take part in two attacks – one force directed against the docks at Dunkirk,* the other against Cologne. Two Halifaxes, one from each raid, were lost but, for the first time in this war, four 102 Squadron crew members succeeded in evading capture:

Sergeant F A Barker
'We left Dalton at 2200 hours on the 27th of April to bomb Dunkirk. Whilst

---

* The attack on Dunkirk saw the last Whitley operations flown by a front-line Bomber Command squadron. Only Operational Training Units would continue to use the Whitley for such tasks in the future – Author.

One of the first pilots to convert – Sqn Ldr E D Griffiths, OC 'A' Flight (Powell)

over the target, we were hit by flak. Three of us evaded capture, three of the crew were killed and one taken prisoner.

'I landed in a field just west of Fort Mardyck. I hid my parachute and Mae West in a ditch and after covering them with earth, I sat down and got out my escape kit. It was too dark to see the maps so I started off in a general south-westerly direction. I soon struck the Dunkirk–Gravelines road and followed it until I neared the outskirts of Gravelines where I hid in a small ditch and waited for daybreak. When it was light, I went to a small cottage where the farmer, on being told who I was, gave me a jacket and cap and said he could not shelter me. I then made a detour south around Gravelines and reached the road leading to Bourbourg. I rested all day in a ditch and at night walked south through the fields. In the morning, I reached Watten and lay up during the day near a railway line.

'At dusk, I entered the village and walked through it. Unfortunately, I turned into a cul-de-sac, at the end of which was a factory. I could not turn back as two Germans were approaching so I clambered over a wall and dropped into the grass of a field. I was challenged by a sentry about 30–40 yards away but hoping that he had heard me and not seen me, I lay quite still. He made no further move and after an hour and a half, I crawled away and reached a road which took me into the Bois du Ham. This wood was full of wire and as I could not get through, I turned back to Watten, which I reached at 0600 hours. This time I took the road to St Omer. I continued walking all that day as I had come to the conclusion that to walk at night meant running the risk of losing my way. I had also decided that as I did not know the exact location of the line of demarcation, I would make for Switzerland and so be able to remain in Occupied France all the way.

'I walked through Aire to Lillers which I reached on the 1st of May. I hid in a wood just south of the town where I was found by a Pole. When I told him who I was, he fetched me food and on the following morning took me to a house in Bruay. I stayed here for two days and when I left on the 4th of May I was given a small parcel of food. I continued by side roads as I was told the towns of St Pol, Arras and Douai were being strictly controlled as a result of sabotage there. That day, I passed through Givenchy, Vimy, Arleux, Oppy and Fresnes to Vitry where I spent the night. Next day, I continued through Sailly, Saudemont, Bourlon and Marcoing till I struck the main road south from Cambrai. I followed this for the next few days, passing through La Fere and reaching Soissons on the 9th of May.

'As the next day was a Sunday, I lay up at Rozieries and the following day continued to Chateau-Thierry. I hid near the town for the night and the next day took a train to Paris as I had decided that I could not walk the whole way to Switzerland and would have to risk train journeys for part of the way. I spent most of the day in Paris and in the evening took a train to Vesoul. I travelled by a German leave train which had a civilian carriage at each end.

'From Vesoul, I started to walk again. I followed the road south towards Besançon spending the night at La Malachere where I was given food at a house and allowed to sleep in the hay loft. I was also given a Michelin Guide which proved very useful. My route then followed side roads through Rougemont, L'Isle Sur Le Doubs, Goux and Pont de Roide. From the last-named place, I continued east by footpath across rather rough country till I reached the Swiss border. There is a mile and a half wide strip of "Zone Interdite" along the border but as this was a Sunday, there were a number of people strolling about and I attracted no notice. I followed a footpath which ran through a defile and the actual border, marked only by stones, ran along the top of the almost precipitous slope on the right of this. At about 2200 hours, I clambered up this slope and crossed into Switzerland. I was not quite sure where I was and made north-west in what I judged to be the direction of Rocourt. I reached a road just as a sergeant of the Swiss frontier guard was cycling along. He asked me who I was and on being told, took me to the frontier post.

The guards here were very friendly. They searched me and took all my personal belongings which were later given back to me. I was then taken by motorcycle to Porrentruy where I spent three days in prison. My request to speak to the British Consul on the telephone was refused but on the third day, I was sent to Berne where I was interrogated by a Swiss Intelligence Officer. He indicated that he did not really believe that I was a prisoner of war but as long as I said so it was all right. I was also questioned by a colonel in the Swiss Air Force. I gave him some information about the Halifax as I saw that he had with him a copy of *Flight* which gave him a full description of the aircraft. The only information that I gave away at those interviews was my name, rank and number. I was later repatriated to this country, arriving by air at Whitchurch on the 14th of September 1942.'

Flight Sergeant Larry Carr

'I was first pilot of a Halifax which left Dalton at 2140 hours on the 27th of April 1942 to take part in a bombing raid on Cologne. As the aircraft from 102 Squadron were much faster than the other aircraft taking part, we had taken off later than the others and were ordered to fly high and fast in order to arrive at the target at the same time as the main attack. The French coast was crossed at 12,000 feet and we experienced little flak and my gunners were conscious that this usually meant nightfighters were active. We were on time reaching our turning point at Le Cateau when, shortly after midnight, a Messerschmitt 110 was spotted by the rear gunner.

'The nightfighter made a stern attack and with the first burst, hit the rear turret and injured the gunner. I took evasive action but the nightfighter closed in and set the port wing, engines and fuselage on fire as well as killing the mid-upper gunner and flight engineer. I gave the order to abandon aircraft and those who were still alive baled out; sadly the wireless operator's parachute failed to open and he was killed. I then started to get out – the Halifax was well and truly on fire and as I was leaving, the plane gave a sudden lurch and the port wing and engines broke away from the fuselage. The aircraft then crashed and the bombs blew up in the vicinity of Hamois-en-Condroz.

'I came down by parachute about one kilometre from the burning wreckage at about 0030 hours on the 28th of April. Using a collar stud compass, I set off south. About an hour and a half after I touched down, I met two Belgians who asked me if I was British and if I wanted to get back to England. One of the Belgians took me to his house and gave me a meal and took away everything that might have identified me as a British airman. He also promised to get my parachute and Mae West which I had hidden after landing and to bury them. Next morning, I was put in touch with the "Comete" organisation which arranged for my return to Britain via Brussels, Paris, St Jean de Luz and over the Pyrenees to San Sebastian in Spain. I arrived by ship at Gourock, Scotland, on the 23rd of June 1942. I never again flew operationally.'

Soon the Squadron became fully operational with its new aircraft and it was not long before losses began to creep up. May 1942 was a very quiet month for the Squadron and no aircraft were lost. However, what soon began to happen was that crews were experiencing incidents that almost cost their lives only to survive to be shot down a few weeks later:

Sergeant H E 'Batch' Batchelder

'On the night of 19th/20th of May 1942, we were returning from Mannheim when near Brussels, our port inner-engine failed – number one tank was empty and although the engineer tried to switch to number two tank, he found the cable had been severed and we could not restart the engine. We feathered the engine and trimmed the aircraft to fly on three engines when, approaching the Dutch coast, the rear gunner reported an arrow formation of lights and searchlights pointing along our course. As we crossed the coast, the tail gunner reported an aircraft, possibly a

Damage to Sgt Batchelder's Halifax, 20 May 1942 (Batchelder)

The hunters – pilots of IV/NJG 1 commanded by Hptm Helmut Lent (sitting centre). Oblt Rudolf Sigmund who shot down Sgt Jack Powell is sitting to Lent's left (Greiner)

Me 110, astern. The enemy fighter and my tail and mid-upper gunners opened fire simultaneously while I took evasive action to port as the German's tracer passed to starboard. The German fighter then passed underneath and made another attack from the port quarter – this time I dived to starboard. The battle continued down to 3,000 feet (it had started at 12,000 feet) and the fighter was last seen diving down – both of my gunners claimed to have scored hits.*

'The Halifax had been damaged and I was having great difficulty in maintaining flying attitude with the control column and rudders almost jammed solid. I had to control the aircraft using the trimming tabs and I set course for Horsham St Faith near Norwich. Approaching Norwich, we called up with no response to our first or second calls – there was an air raid alert in the area so now we had to call "Mayday" as we were almost out of fuel and barely maintaining height. Horsham responded, a searchlight pointed the way and the airfield lights were switched on. With the crew in their crash-positions, I selected undercarriage down and the wheels dropped with no indication they were locked down! Not risking a circuit, I landed using the ailerons and trimming tabs and as we touched down, the port outer engine cut.

'On examining the aircraft in daylight, it was found that cannon shells

---

* The Luftwaffe lost two nightfighters on this night. The only Messerschmitt Bf 110 lost, that flown by *Oberleutnant* Fritz Gutezeit of *6 Staffel/NJG 1*, collided with a Short Stirling of 7 Squadron or was the one claimed by Sgt Batchelder's gunners – Author.

had hit the tail severing and jamming the rudders and elevators. The port inner engine (the dead one) had been hit by cannon fire and there were numerous holes in the fuselage. An inspection light which was located about 10 inches from the mid-upper gunner's head had been shot away and another had entered the fuselage just below the rear turret and must have passed between the gunner's legs! None of us had been hurt.'

For this, Sgt Batchelder was awarded the DFM. However, he was only to last another 28 days on the Squadron before he and his crew were shot down and taken prisoner during an attack on Essen on the 16th/17th of June 1942. Another close shave was experienced by Sgt Jack Powell. He and his crew were shot down by a nightfighter flown by *Oberleutnant* Rudolf Sigmund of *II/NJG 2* on the 9th of July 1942 but a month before that, he and his crew were lucky to have survived another encounter with the enemy:

Sergeant Jack Powell

'On the night of the 2nd of June 1942 we were briefed to attack Essen in "Happy Valley", as we called the Ruhr. Over the target we were suddenly confronted with a box barrage of flak and all hell was let loose. We suffered heavy damage but luckily spotted a gap to the south and got away from the trap. We were unaware of the scale of the damage until the landing approach run was made when all control was lost. We hit the ground and as the Halifax was in the act of turning over, its back broke and fell back allowing us all to escape without injury. Wg Cdr Bintley, our CO, was

Plt Off Vic Hunter (Hunter)

watching from the control tower and ran a quarter of a mile to the wreck to help get us out not knowing we were already out!'

The luckiest of all of the early Summer 1942 double crashes was Plt Off Vic Hunter. His first incident was spectacular to say the least:

Flight Sergeant Ed Cooke

'In June 1942, I did four trips to Bremen. On the first one, the target was supposed to be clear but it was cloud all the way from 20,000 feet down to 5,000 feet so we bombed on "Gee". The next was supposed to be cloudy and we were to bomb on "Gee" but it was clear over the target so after bombing we dived for the deck and came back at zero feet as they wanted us to do at the briefing. We saw an aircraft flying between the islands getting everything thrown at it so we sneaked to one side without too much fuss. On arriving back we found that one of the Halifaxes had lost both starboard props hitting the sandbanks between those islands. It was lucky that he had wooden props – one of the few on the Squadron.'

Flight Sergeant Carl Sorsdahl

'On the night of the 26th/27th of June 1942, my usual captain had been taken ill so I was assigned to a new crew captained by Plt Off Hunter. At the briefing, crews were cautioned that because of nightfighter action being taken against bombers leaving the target, crews might consider coming out low to escape detection.

FS Carl Sorsdahl (far right) seen with fellow Canadians (left to right) Sgt F Williamson (pilot), ?, FS F Holmes (+ 3 Jun 42 – pilot), FS D Conter (+ 17 Jun 42 – nav), ?, Sgt T O McIquham (gunner) – early Spring 1942 (Dales)

'On release of bombs on target, Plt Off Hunter put the plane in a steep dive. I was still in the bomb aimer's position – when it was suggested we came out low, I did not expect it to be roof height! I remained in the nose keeping watch for power lines – it was a clear and bright night and I could see all very clearly. We reached the coast more or less on track and I was getting prepared to return to my charts when we spotted some ships and it was decided to investigate. I had just warned Plt Off Hunter that they might be flak ships when all hell broke loose and blinding searchlights made it impossible to see. We hit a sandbank, bounced a couple of times and then became airborne again, after a fashion! There was sand everywhere in the aircraft and we soon discovered that the starboard outer props were shorn. The engine was feathered when we discovered that the starboard inner prop must have also been damaged but the engine just about worked. We managed to climb to about 200 feet but could only maintain a speed just above stalling. I must say that Plt Off Hunter was a capable pilot to nurse that aircraft along and keep it airborne.

'The "Gee" set was not working (it got its power from the feathered engine) and we had lost our trailing aerial so we had no navigation aids. The pilot maintained quite a steady course and we were one and a half hours overdue when the coast eventually appeared and we were right on track. He managed to climb enough to clear the coast and we landed without incident. Plt Off Hunter was Mentioned In Dispatches for his skill. He and his crew did not return from a Hamburg operation shortly after this one. I heard him say he intended to come out low so I guess his luck ran out.'

Sergeant Dick Kinsey

'Sunday the 26th of July 1942 was night ops to Hamburg, bombing at 20,000 feet with the option of coming out at 50 feet. Unfortunately for us, on the way out we hit the coast at Emden, right into the dock area. With cranes and barrage balloons ahead, we pulled up to in between 200 and 300 feet – a prime target for the German ground defence boys. The Halifax was repeatedly hit, resulting in the port engines being taken out. We had no option but to ditch in the Dollart Basin just off the coast.

'I was standing next to Plt Off Hunter when we ditched and as the aircraft came to rest, the water filled the cockpit almost to the top of the canopy. Plt Off Hunter, Sgt Jim Fryett and myself scrambled out and we perched on the top of the fuselage. We expected the aircraft to sink but soon realised that we were resting on the bottom. The navigator had been killed by the flak and the bomb aimer died in the front turret, whether hit or drowned after impact I do not know. As the tide went out, the rear turret was seen to be separate from the aircraft, standing upright with the doors open. The rear gunner had been wearing a flotation suit so he must have been carried away by the tide.

'While perched on the canopy, we could see lots of hardwear flying about and another aircraft appeared at low level and ditched. This was another 102 Squadron crew captained by Sgt Wilson – we met the survivors later that day.

'At first light and with the tide going out fast, we could see the green shoreline and were forced to plod towards it, through the knee-deep mud. Whilst making our way ashore, we met a local shell-fisher using a flat-bottomed skiff. Our Skipper, who had a fair command of German, told him that we were the crew of a German U-Boat which had been sunk by the "verdammt Englanders". He went away quite happily but after we were captured, he returned and threatened our Skipper with his basket of shellfish. I don't suppose he relished being made to look a fool!'

The Summer of 1942 rolled on. August was a quiet month for losses, with only two Halifaxes lost through enemy action, two damaged by enemy action and two involved in accidents. Of the two combat losses, one crew were all killed but the second crew were luckier:

Pilot Officer Monty Lamont

'Our crew was only with the Squadron a month. We were an international crew – Doug McLeod, the pilot, was Australian, Plt Off Murray McCarthy, the rear gunner, was Canadian, Sgt Jones, the bomb aimer, was American, Sgt Richards, the mid-upper gunner, was Australian, Sgt Ray Willshire, the engineer, was British and I was a New Zealander. Our regular wireless operator, Sgt Jimmy Smith, was Canadian but for our last trip we had Sgt Long, another Canadian.

'The Squadron moved from Topcliffe to Pocklington on the 7th of August 1942 and two days later we were shot down. It is not a night I am ever likely to forget. First of all we were briefed for a daylight on Warnemuende but this operation was cancelled when we were in the vans to go to the dispersals.

'Later, we were briefed for Osnabrück that night. As we were taking off, we could see a raid in progress not too far away – our German counterparts were attacking Hull or Grimsby! Soon after we crossed our coast, we were fired on by one of our convoys and although we did not feel we were in great danger, the colours of the day were fired as a precaution.

'The only unusual feature that I remember on the way to the target was that I couldn't get anything but "grass" on "Gee". That had me baffled and I was convinced that I must have done something very stupid. It wasn't until some years later that I read that the Germans first started jamming "Gee" on this night.

'We had no difficulty in finding the target and I do not remember anything else unusual until the aircraft caught fire . . .'

Pilot Officer Doug McLeod

'. . . Moments later, we were hit in the area of the port engine and I told the bomb aimer to let the bombs go and he did so. There was a fire developing in the port inner engine and I cut that motor and tried unsuccessfully to feather the propeller. I turned towards the Dutch coast but we were losing height. We were at 4,000 feet so I gave the order to bale out. I remember Mac saying shortly after "I'm going Tex" (my nickname) and I did not hear from him again nor did I ever see him again. The intercom was quite silent and there was no one about so I took of my helmet, took a quick look at the altimeter which was now reading about 1,000 feet and went out through the bottom front hatch. Away from the target area, the night was dark and I soon landed in a pine forest on the German side of the Dutch border. I have never felt so sick in my heart in all my life not then knowing how my crew had fared and also hearing other aircraft overhead and returning to base.

'All that day and the following night I cautiously moved through wooded countryside towards Holland. Early the next morning, I came to a big canal and as I was attempting to cross it, I was hailed most aggressively by a German farmer who came at me with his pitchfork at the ready. I was turned over to a German officer from a nearby flak battery and later that day I was taken to a German nightfighter base near Lingen where an attempt was made to interrogate me. On the way to Lingen, the little van in which I was being driven deviated off the road and a little later backed into a big dark farm barn and stopped. I thought that they were going to shoot me but instead they asked me questions as to the identity of a dead body clad in full flying gear stretched out over his opened parachute on meadow hay in a German farm wagon. It was the body of Sgt Willshire,

Doug McLeod (far left) and Monty Lamont (second from the right), Offlag XXIB, Schubin, Poland, soon after their capture (Lamont)

my flight engineer. He still had his parachute "D" ring firmly clenched in his hand.'

One of the two accidents had a much happier ending:

Sergeant Eddie Berry

'On the 22nd of August 1942, we were on a training flight for navigators where they were to be instructed on the use of "Gee". The route was Pocklington–Reading–Fishguard– Isle of Man–Pocklington. Whilst on the second leg of the flight, the port outer engine failed. I followed the procedure for feathering the propeller but as this had no effect, it started to windmill at about 3,000 revolutions per minute setting up considerable drag on the port side and causing the aircraft to fly in a circle. I soon realised that it was not possible to keep the aircraft flying for long as the port inner was starting to overheat and we were gradually losing height. I told the crew that I intended to crash-land and that they could bale out if they wanted to; no one wanted to so I told them to get into crash positions.

By this time we were over Builth Wells in mid-Wales and flying in ever descending circles. I chose some suitable fields, about a mile from the edge of the town and remember thinking that there wasn't a soul in sight – by the time we got out of the aircraft, hundreds of people, many of them children, were pouring down the hillside. Afterwards the police told me that they had caught small boys running away with the two guns from the front turret and thousands of rounds of ammunition which had been thrown out of the aircraft as we had slid along the ground. The aircraft had finally come to a halt with the starboard wing up against a tree and the rear turret the other side of a river. The port outer engine was ripped from its mounting, the port inner had caught fire and there was a fire in the fuselage. Bill Pattison, the flight engineer, put out the fires and in doing so burnt a hand. Bill had saved my life as I wasn't strapped in when the engine failed and we were almost on the ground when he managed to get two straps across my body and thus prevented me from being thrown through the canopy.'

September 1942 saw an increase in losses and accidents and during this month another two Squadron aircrew succeeding in evading capture. The following month brought a similar combat loss and accident rate and one accident was to be the saddest of the Squadron's history:

Flight Sergeant Eddie Berry

'On the night of the 23rd/24th of October 1942, we were returning from a raid on Genoa. As we approached Pocklington, we were told that we couldn't land there due to poor visibility and were instructed to go to Holme on Spalding Moor. We landed and after travelling about half of the runway, the port wing struck the cockpit of Halifax DY-Q killing Wg Cdr Bintley and injuring his wireless operator who subsequently died in hospital. It appeared that one of "Q"'s tyres had been punctured on landing and the aircraft had swung off the runway with the cockpit just over the runway. It was a very tragic accident and one which I shall regret for the

One of the more spectacular September 1942 accidents – on the 9th of the month, Sgt Robbie Robinson could not get the port engine to reduce revolutions on landing from an attack on Frankfurt and landed on top of another Squadron Halifax; nobody was injured (Robinson)

The Berry crew, Summer 1942. Standing left to right: Sgt Pattison (engineer), Plt Off Hargreaves (navigator), FS Berry, Sgt Wood (bomb aimer). Kneeling left to right: FS Grimes (gunner) and Sgt Forman (gunner) (Berry)

Squadron officers, Summer 1942. Left to right: Plt Off 'Junior' Smith (+ 10 Sep 42), Plt Off W H Baber (+ 26 Jul 42), Fg Off Peter Gaskell, Flt Lt 'Maisie' Lewis, Fg Off N L Shove and Fg Off Harry Drummond DFM. Lying at the front is Fg Off 'Smokey' Graham (+ 24 Oct 42) (Hunter)

rest of my life – Wg Cdr Bintley had been a very popular CO of 102 Squadron.'

Autumn now moved into winter and the pace of war continued unabated. November 1942 was a quieter month with fewer casualties but December made up for it when seven crews were lost in combat or accident and all before the 12th of the month had passed. 102 Squadron was heading towards its fourth year of the war. More was to come in the way of death and sadness as this final account for 1942 illustrates:

Pilot Officer Don McKim

'On the night of the 2nd/3rd of December 1942, we had just reached our turning point for the bombing run to the target [Frankfurt] and I gave the change of course to the pilot. As we straightened out on the new course, we came out of the clouds into bright moonlight and the bomb aimer reported we were approaching the Rhine and that he could see fires burning in the distance. At that moment, Sgt Edwards, the rear gunner, came on the intercom and said "Dive to starboard, Skipper – we are about to be attacked by a nightfighter!"* Simultaneously, a couple of tracers

* The nightfighter was flown by *Leutnant* Heinz Hadeball of *8/NJG 4* – Author.

streaked in front of me and disappeared into the blanket that we had hung in the well of the front turret so that my navigation light would not be visible outside the aircraft. I remember thinking poor May, the bomb aimer, has had it when he raised the bottom of the blanket and looked at me with a puzzled expression. Fortunately, he had been lying down at his bomb sight and the bullets had passed over his head, smashing the perspex in the turret. Immediately a second and more accurate attack was made – the intercom went out and I was aware that the pilot was shouting something. I got up from my chair and stepped back so that I could look up and see him. He was shouting "Bale out!", motioning with his right hand towards the escape hatch, which was under my seat, and moving the control column back and forth to indicate that the controls had gone. There were fires in the fuselage aft of the main spar.

'I got my parachute and snapped it on. I then folded my chair from over the escape hatch, removed the cover from the hatch with Sgt May's help and out I went. The force of the slipstream caused me to bang my head against the side of the hatch and knocked me unconscious. When I came to, I immediately reached up to pull my rip cord but my chest pack was not there and I remember thinking I am not going to like seeing the ground coming up to meet me! Then I remember floating down with my parachute open above me and the River Rhine below. I then lapsed back into unconsciousness because the next thing I remember is seeing the ground just before I landed.

The remains of Don McKim's Halifax lie in a vinyard at Laumersheim in Germany (Menges)

'I had just gathered up my 'chute and stuffed it into the furrow of the ploughed field in which I had landed when I heard voices so I sprawled down on top of the 'chute. I soon found that I had almost come down on top of a flak battery and the crew had seen my parachute in the bright moonlight. The owners of the voices stopped at a fence row about 150 feet from where I was lying and I suppose because I had not reacted to their shouting, started firing at me. My position was not enviable and I instantly realised that the best thing I could do would be to stand up with my hands raised as quickly as possible, so I did just that. I might add that reaching the decision was speeded up when one of the bullets nicked my Mae West!'

CHAPTER FOUR

'Not so Disastrous a Night?' — 1943–1944

As with previous winters of this war, the weather was an ally by keeping losses for 102 Squadron low in the first month of 1943. Only two aircraft were involved in any incidents of note – one being a training accident on the 4th of the month and the only combat loss on the 26th of the month:

Sergeant Reid Thomson

'I was not the regular gunner for this crew. We were on a special assignment during an attack on Düsseldorf. We had to drop our bombs and wait outside the target area and report on what we saw. One of the crew reported seeing a nightfighter and I saw what at first glance looked like a fighter and shot at it. The bullets went straight through what in fact was smoke looking remarkably like an aircraft!

'By this stage we had been hit by flak but we apparently seemed to be flying with no problems and with the raid finished, the pilot asked the navigator for a course for home. When he received no reply the engineer said that only he and the pilot were still in the aircraft! I then shouted from my turret that I was still in the back. However, we had problems. The pilot headed down the Ruhr and eventually climbed above the cloud, turned round and headed back over the target. I told the pilot that we were lost so when we came over water, the engineer dropped a flame float and we started sending a distress message whilst firing off distress flares. An airfield lit up and as we prepared to land, they started shooting at us so again we climbed back up and headed out to sea.

'The situation was hopeless – we had no idea where we were so the pilot headed back for Holland and told me to bale out when we were over land which I did. Shortly afterwards, the Halifax ran out of fuel and crashed in the sea. I was kept in solitary confinement and when questioned, couldn't even give the Germans the names of the crew. However, they told me that the pilot and engineer were killed in the crash, the observer was killed over the target when his parachute failed to open and the navigator and wireless operator were taken prisoner after baling out over the target.'

During February 1943 the losses started to increase. Some of the crews who had been on constant operations from the Summer and Autumn of 1942 were by now approaching the end of the 'tour'. One such pilot was 22-year-old FS J L Hartshorn who in September and October 1942 had two crashes from which he and his crew had walked away. On the night of the 14th of February 1943, it was not to be third time lucky and perhaps he and his crew knew this:

Leading Aircraftsman Norman Noble

'On the 14th of February 1943, my mate met me at dinner and said he had a date in York and it was his turn to see his "kite" off on ops. Would I do it for him? I said I would and went to dispersal. I didn't realise until the transport arrived that it was FS Hartshorn and his crew who were taking the aircraft.

'This crew were an unusually popular and well known "team". Hartshorn was a Canadian – he was built like a rugby forward and, with the rest of the crew, always together, laughing, joking and leg pulling. They were really popular. The "Skipper" had also met and married a WAAF from Pocklington. However, this night they got off the transport and got straight into the aircraft without saying a word to anyone or each other. I pulled away the starter batteries and after the engines were started, went up into the cockpit with the Form 700 and waited until the pilot had run up the engines and did all the required checks.

Plt Off Malkin's crew pose in front of their factory fresh Halifax (Dales)

'The pilot throttled back the engines and just sat staring into space. I put the Form 700 in front of him but he still didn't move. I gave him the pencil

thinking he probably hadn't one. He signed and gave me back the Form. I had to repeat the procedure twice more for fuel and oil and I gave him a pat on the shoulder and said "See you in the morning!". I don't think he heard me – he was still staring. The rest of the crew were the same – not a word, not a sound and all were staring like zombies. It was an atmosphere I have never forgotten. I was the last person to see that crew alive – they never returned.'

Shortly after crossing the Dutch coast, FS Hartshorn and his crew were shot down by a nightfighter flown by *Oberleutnant* Manfred Meurer of *3/NJG 1*. All the crew were killed and all but one of them were buried next to each other at Nijmegen.

If February was busy, so was March 1943 and again, some crews were hoping to finish their tours:

Sergeant John Hurst

'In order to complete our tour of 30 ops, we, in fact, had to do 36! This was because if you did not reach and bomb the target, that trip did not count despite the fact that one had run the gauntlet of flak and fighters. For instance, on the 9th of March 1943, we took off at 2001 hours to bomb Munich. Well into Germany, we were coned by searchlights the blue master beam got us first and the Skipper took violent evasive action to escape. The Germans were very persistent and the compass and artificial horizon became unserviceable. We jettisoned our bombs and returned to base. Despite landing at 0428 hours after being airborne for eight hours and 27 minutes, this trip did not count as part of our tour.'

Other crews did not even complete one mission against Germany. Sergeant Walter Hedges was shot down by flak* on his first trip over German soil on the night of the 12th of March 1943. Captured shortly afterwards, he spent the rest of the war in captivity. In 1993 he decided to return to where his Halifax crashed, somewhere in the vicinity of Ahaus-Wessum:

Sergeant Walter Hedges – 1993

'I went to Ahaus and in the information office, I was put in touch with the local historian who lived about three miles away at Wessum. When we met, all fell into place as it was to his house that I had been taken after being captured by a local farmer and the crash site was but a mile or so away. He was able to take my wife and myself to the crash site and I was stunned to meet the same Frau whom I had first called on a shade over 50 years ago. Now a mere 95 years old, she had a very grown up family which I had last met sitting around the kitchen stove.'

---

* Although the crew believe that it was flak that caused their demise, they were also claimed by a nightfighter flown by *Hauptmann* Herbert Lutje of *III/NJG 1* – Author.

Sergeant Walter Hedges – 1943

'I landed wonderfully in a ploughed field and I lay down, stretched out and prayed. Nobody came so I sorted myself out. I hadn't even a scratch or fingernail broken. After an hour or so I decided to find the airman's customary farmhouse – I walked what I thought was miles and found nothing. I then came across an old man whose wife gave me milk and he then walked me to another cottage. I was offered more milk whilst five women, four children and four men looked me up and down – the sympathy was obvious. The police then arrived, searched me and drove me away.'

The following month saw the loss of a pilot who had been connected with 102 Squadron for nearly 15 months. In December 1941, Plt Off Wally Lashbrook had helped convert 102 Squadron's Whitley pilots to Halifax pilots. By May 1942, he had been promoted to Sqn Ldr and given command of the 102 Squadron Conversion Flight. In March 1943, he was posted to 1664 Conversion Unit as a flight commander but on the 10th of April 1943, he arrived back at 102 Squadron to take command of 'C' Flight. His command of 'C' Flight would last exactly one week and two ops, even if the second op was completed by plane, parachute, foot, lorry, train and bicycle:

Squadron Leader Wally Lashbrook

'We were returning from an attack on the Skoda Works in Pilsen in what was then Czechoslovakia. We had managed to reach the French–Belgian border without incident despite it being a clear night – too clear. A nightfighter was waiting on the edge of a layer of stratus cloud for us to appear. I had already seen one aircraft shot down nearby but before I could finish warning the crew, the nightfighter came up from underneath. We received a single long burst of cannon fire and the port wing and fuselage were raked, killing the rear gunner and wounding the mid-upper gunner.*

'The port wing burst into flames and looked like a welding torch at full blast and the Halifax started to spiral to the left. As I was unable to control the aircraft with full aileron and full rudder, I told the crew to abandon aircraft. The mid-upper gunner was helped from his turret, a parachute pack clipped to his front harness and he was then bundled out of the rear door. The bomb aimer, navigator and wireless operator went out through the forward hatch. By now, the aircraft was at 3,000 feet – the flight engineer clipped my parachute pack onto me before jumping himself. I let go the controls and the spiral then became a spin making it hard for me to get out – my parachute harness got caught on the trim indicator and when I had unhooked that, my intercom lead got entangled with the

---

* They had been shot down by *Oberleutnant* Rudolf Altendorf, *Staffelkapitän* of *2/NJG 2*. An experienced day and nightfighter pilot, Altendorf had flown day missions in the Battle of Britain before converting to nightfighters, Wally Lashbrook's Halifax was his 17th confirmed 'kill' – Author.

control column! After throwing off my helmet and two unsuccessful attempts at getting out of the spinning Halifax (which was now throwing me around inside the nose of the aircraft), I managed to lean half-way out of the escape hatch and pull the ripcord. To my amazement and relief, this did the trick and I popped out literally like a champagne cork. The Halifax crashed 100 yards from me as I hit the ground a few seconds later. I baled out last from about 1,000 feet and came down first. I landed about 0405 hours on the 17th of April on high ground just north of La Fagne, Belgium, between the Bois de Chimay and the French frontier.

'My parachute was entangled in a thorn tree and, after pulling it down, I rolled it up and ran through the nearest gate into a field until I reached a marsh, where I stamped the parachute and harness into the mud. After running along the marsh I found I was still wearing my Mae West which I then hid under a thorn bush. After continuing north for about half a mile, I saw two people approaching. They were about 10 yards from me but I threw myself flat on the grass and they walked past me towards the burning aircraft.

'To avoid passing the aircraft, I walked two kilometres east and then turned south. I realised I was leaving a trail in the dew and walked for 400–500 yards on a woodcutters' track. After leaving this path, I hopped across a grass field and looking back could see no tracks. I then followed a stream into a wood. One half of the wood had been felled and I hid myself here under two heaps of branches, arguing that any search for me was more likely to be made in the unfelled part of the wood. I was then about three miles south-east of the aircraft.

Sqn Ldr Wally Lashbrook (sitting centre) with members of the Conversion Flight. Sitting far left is Plt Off Graham Williams GM, Wally's rear gunner killed on 17 Apr 43 (Lashbrook)

'I remained in hiding from about 0600 hours till 2200 hours, drying my shoes and socks and checking the contents of my pockets and my escape kit. During the day, I heard Germans shouting but did not see any of them. I set off south-west by the compass from my aids box, keeping to the woods all night. At 0500 hours on the 18th of April, I went through a small village and seeing the word "Burgomeister" on a doorplate, concluded I was in Belgium. At a farmhouse near the village, I stole some milk from a churn at the door but was disturbed by a barking dog. I kept along the road, walking in the fields undercover of a hedge, to another small village, where I hid in a loft from 0600 hours till about midday, where I watched the villagers returning from church.

'I then skirted the village and headed south and south-west. About 1500 hours, I came on a farmer milking a cow in a field. I made signs that I wanted milk but he signalled me away. To be sure of getting clear of him, I continued for two or three miles till I got into a big wood. In this wood, south of Momigmes, I crossed the frontier into France. There was an anti-tank ditch, trenches and a concrete blockhouse in this area but I saw no sign of any guard or patrol.

'After crossing a small river, I met an old man and woman who brought me a bottle of beer and a sandwich but would give me no further help. I then reached a railway line, along which I walked till within sight of Hirson. I then made a detour around Hirson to the east and eventually reached the Hirson–St Michel road which I was unable to cross before dark because of the number of people about. After crossing the road, I walked south to Bucilly across country. After crossing the river Thoo by a footbridge, at about 0500 hours on the 19th of April, I met a Frenchman whom I told I was a British airman and asked him where I could get food. He said any of the houses in the village would give me some so I called at the first house at the edge of a wood near Iviers. Here I was taken in and given a meal, allowed to shave and put to bed.

'That afternoon, my host brought me civilian clothes and buried my uniform in the wood (I was wearing ordinary shoes when flying). He also brought me additional food and vitamin tablets. Next morning, he and I got a lift by lorry into Montcornet whence we went by train to a station which was probably Samoussy, east of Laon. We travelled third class and I gave him 150 francs for my fare to Rheims. My host's ticket was for Samoussy and from there, after visiting a friend of his, we went separately to another station, probably Eppes, south-east of Laon. Here we joined the express for Rheims.

'In Rheims, we travelled by bus to a house where a young man lived who put me in touch with an organisation. My subsequent journey was arranged for me.'

Safe in the hands of the French Resistance, 50 days after baling out of his Halifax, Wally Lashbrook arrived in Spain, arriving at the British Embassy in Madrid on the 10th of June 1943. He at last could relax only to find that he began suffering from back pain which was later attributed to his landing after baling out from the Halifax. Furthermore, on his return to the UK he discovered that he was the victim of an all too often pay anomaly. At the time his aircraft was shot down, he held the war acting rank of Sqn Ldr and was paid accordingly. However, as soon as he crossed into British territory, he was demoted to his substantive rank of Flt Lt and his pay was reduced on the grounds that he was 'no longer filling a Sqn Ldr post'. Many other aircrew who were taken prisoner also suffered similar 'anomalies' and even today are still fighting for the back pay which they, rightly, still believe is owed to them.

While Wally Lashbrook was evading the Germans, 102 Squadron was still maintaining its fight against them and still losing many valuable crews. However, on the 5th of May 1943, a crew which had the misfortune of ditching in the North Sea became the first recipient of what was the RAF's brand new survival aid. The following is taken from the official report:

'While over the target, Halifax DY-V of 102 Squadron [flown by FS J Bowman] was hit by flak rendering the starboard engine unserviceable. As height was lost to 14,000 feet, evasive action was taken and the incendiary containers were jettisoned. None of the crew were wounded. The Dutch coast was passed at 8,000 feet but in the neighbourhood of three degrees east, the starboard outer engine failed. At approximately 0308 hours, the port outer engine failed and height was lost at about 1,500 feet per minute.

'At 4,000 feet, the whole crew were ordered to ditching stations which they took quite correctly except that the captain was unable to fit his Sutton Harness. The pilot's exit and both mid-upper exits were opened while the security of the lower exit was also checked. At 0313 hours, SOS was transmitted with speed, course and height while the Identification Friend or Foe had been changed to "3" at 0310 hours. The aircraft was fixed in position 53 deg 35 N, 01 deg 32 E but no aircraft acknowledgement was received of this fix. "Gee" was unserviceable and the wireless operator clamped down the [morse] key.

'The aircraft approached the water at 45 degrees across and down the swell with the wind on the starboard bow. Flaps were lowered as appraoch was made at 127 miles per hour with the port inner engine at full revolutions. At about 50 feet, the aircraft was held off and she struck the water aft of the trailing edge at an approximate speed of 75 miles per hour. The impact was not violent but the bomb aimer was thrown from his ditching station and hit his face. He was holding a torch in one hand and therefore may not have been holding on sufficiently hard. The water level was soon up to the rest position and the crew hastily evacuated the aircraft . . .'

After a few problems, the crew successfully boarded their dinghy and waited to be rescued, hoping that their SOS had been heard. It was about three hours later that the dinghy was spotted by a Lockheed Hudson which immediately reported their position. The official report continues:

'At 0747 hours, Hudson coded OS-W of 279 Squadron, carrying an airborne lifeboat Mark I, took off [from Bircham Newton in Norfolk] in company with Hudson OS-Y. At 0820 hours, both these aircraft were over the dinghy and smoke floats were dropped. The dinghy crew had never heard of the airborne lifeboat and were curious about the peculiarly shaped Hudson flying above them. Their astonishment was great when the bottom of the Hudson fell off and they saw that it was a boat, even noting that it had propellers protruding from the bottom.

'The lifeboat left the aircraft satisfactorily from 800 feet. One parachute developed slightly before the others but the general parachute development appeared most satisfactory. The rocket drogue did not fire and the self-righting chambers failed to inflate. The boat descended in a slightly bow down attitude at a noticeably low rate of descent but due to the fact that the parachute slings were fitted the wrong way around, the craft struck the water in an attitude much too near horizontal and the impact appeared to the crew to be considerable . . .

'The distressed crew boarded the lifeboat with ease in spite of having been wet, cramped and seasick for the last five hours; two of them were also injured. The injured bomb aimer lay down on the forward self-righting chamber which had not inflated and thus concealed the forward equipment hatch, the presence of which the crew were ignorant. Furthermore, only the aft self-righting chamber was half-inflated by hand. The engineer and navigator (who had yachting experience) started the engines and noted the smoothness of their running. At the same time the captain shipped the rudder . . .'

Later that afternoon, after a series of trials and errors, the crew were picked up by a high-speed launch and landed at Grimsby. After recovering from the deprivations of their enforced boating trip, they submitted a very detailed report on the 'Airborne Lifeboat' thus helping improve future rescues and making fellow aircrew aware of what to expect.

Nine aircraft were lost during the month of May 1943 and five during the following month. However, as Bomber Command's night offensive intensified during the Summer of 1943, losses again began to creep up and crews found themselves unluckier than the crew who received the first airborne lifeboat as the following reports show. The first is translated from an official Dutch police report:

'On the night of Wednesday the 13th and Thursday the 14th of July 1943, at approximately 0133 hours, the air-raid sirens sounded at the State Coal Mine Hendrik; the alert lasted until 0237 hours. At approximately 0203 hours, a combat took place above the grounds of the coal mine and part of an aircraft, the tail assembly, fell in the grounds of the mine. The coal-mine police took the necessary action.

'In the tail turret, the remains of a crewman were found. Immediately, a Roman Catholic priest and a doctor were called. The remaining part of the aircraft and the four engines had fallen 500 metres further away on German soil. German authorities had taken the site under protection and Dutch people were not allowed to cross the border. We were later told that there were four dead crew members in the wreckage. German soldiers

searched the area since they assumed that the plane had a seven-man crew. Dutch police and staff from the coal mine also searched the area but without success. Therefore they concluded that the aircraft carried a five-man crew. The coal-mine police were ordered to guard the tail turret and the remains of the dead gunner. A German officer visited the site and instructed the police that no one was allowed to touch the body or steal any parts of the wreckage.

'On Saturday the 16th of July 1943, at approximately 1700 hours, a couple of officers and enlisted men from the Venlo nightfighter base arrived and removed several instruments from the aircraft which carried the following codes – DY-X JB894. Despite instructions not to touch anything, we have done our very best to identify the dead crew member. On his left ring-finger he wore a golden monogram ring carrying the initials "W.R."; this ring will be sent to the next of kin of the dead man. He also carried a picture of himself as well as two small photographs of girls dressed in uniform.'

The body in the turret was that of Sgt John Raw whose body was buried on Dutch soil a few days later. Of the remainder of the crew, one was taken prisoner and the bodies of five, not four, crew members were found in the wreckage and buried on German soil. Eleven days later, the Squadron suffered its next loss:

Pilot Officer F G Smith

'The night of the 24th/25th July 1943 is a night I will always remember. Sixteen minutes after bombing [Hamburg] and on our way back to base, the Identification Friend or Foe started bleeping. The mid-upper gunner reported that it was alright; it was one of our own bombers about 2–3,000 feet above us. Someone remarked over the intercom that the bastards were dodging the issue and disobeying orders. However, some seven minutes later, the Skipper yelled out over the intercom "Get out quickly, blokes!". Nonplussed, I quickly asked over the intercom "What the hell for?". He shouted back "We're on fire, you bloody fool!". I immediately pulled back the heavy black curtain which shuts off the navigator's cabin and was almost blinded by a brilliant white light positioned, it seemed, just by the aircraft's main spar near the flight engineer's position. I immediately grabbed the secret codes written on rice paper and ate it, stuffed my log into my battledress, grabbed my parachute and unwisely only attached it to one of the two hooks provided. I then grabbed the pilot's 'chute and remembered that the bomb aimer had left his 'chute by the bomb-aiming device. I grabbed his 'chute, intending to throw it over the spar to him and held it in my left hand. In my right hand I held aloft the Skipper's 'chute when there were lots of bangs and the 'chute was knocked out of my hand into the bomb bay, causing me to fall down. Scrambling along the floor, I hurriedly picked up the 'chute when the aircraft went into a steep dive, a very steep dive, which pinned me to the floor. After some seconds, it seemed like an age, I shouted 'Pull her out, Tom – you'll have the wings off her!". As there was no reaction, I again shouted over the intercom and after what seemed an age, the aircraft pulled out of her dive. I said "Blimey, Tom – about time too!". I picked up his 'chute and it was when I was on my feet that the aircraft went into a spin. I fell to the side, then the roof, then the side again and again and again and again. The curtain was on fire, burning debris fell into my cabin and onto me and my clothes started burning. Every time I was spun to the roof, I saw the escape hatch quick-release handle and I tried, desperately tried, time and time again to grab the handle but every time I grabbed it, I was thrown the other way and it fell back into its slot. I then prayed for my wife, for my mother and then to die. I prayed hard to die, thinking my family would be proud the way I was facing death bravely and being burnt alive. Funny, eh?

'Suddenly, there was a flash and then it was dark, cold and above me there was a black circle with thin silver lines (this was my parachute and the stars were the silver lines). I thought I was dead, having prayed so very hard to die. I then wondered whether I was in heaven, paradise or hell. Having never been to those places before, I reasoned with myself. I realised that I was cold because my shoes and socks had been blown off, half my trousers were either torn or burnt off. My face was damp because of blood and burns. My neck was entwined in my harness. Never having pulled a rip cord before but having twisted the quick-release button on the parachute harness many times, I proceeded to do that latter which meant that I would have fallen out of the harness. I realised what I was doing, stopped and slowly twisted the button back into the locked position, then reached up and pulled down my 'chute, which was on one hook only, pulled the "D" ring which came away in my hand and let the 'chute go. Nothing happened. I pulled the 'chute down again and this time ripped away at the cover to try and open it, removing most of my fingernails in the process. Suddenly, the 'chute tore past my face and remained in a small ball. I reached up, pulled the cords apart and suddenly there was a "bloop", then another and another and another and another and then silence, utter incredible silence. I gave one huge sigh of relief, one deep, very deep, breath and then "bang!". I had landed very heavily in a cornfield. Balancing on one leg, I hurriedly said part of The Lord's Prayer and looked around and saw three fires which I presumed was the aircraft. So, dragging one leg, I pushed my way through the ripened corn towards the flames to save the crew not knowing I was the sole survivor.

'I found it painful walking through the corn with bare feet, not knowing that I had three severed muscles in my right leg below the right knee, the cartilages were torn and sticking out, all my ribs on the left side were broken and cutting my lung (hence the blood coming out of my mouth), my stomach torn away from my pelvis, my kidney had burst, my ankles damaged and swollen, fractured skull, fractured spine and my arms and hands were damaged and swollen. Despite this, I made Spain my objective, only a few thousand miles away. Off I went, flying helmet around neck, oxygen and intercom wires trailing behind. The footpath through the corn had a restricted view and around the corner, unannounced, came a German guard with a rifle on his shoulder, then two more, one of whom spoke to me. I replied "Ja, Englische flieger" and kept on walking, waiting for their bullets to hit me and not knowing I was surrounded on all sides. Then the first German shouted and they took their rifles off their shoulders. I was in the bag.

'I realised afterwards that the bangs I heard were bullets hitting the aircraft and knocking the Skipper's 'chute out of my hands. These bullets must have hit the Skipper who fell forwards over the joystick and put the aircraft in a steep dive. He could not answer my intercom calls because he was dead. The dive then forced his body back which caused the aircraft to go into a spin. The Halifax then blew up and I must have been blown out at the same time.

'What caused the aircraft to catch fire? My belief is that the aircraft which was flying above jettisoned his bombs on us and the burning bomber was then attacked by a nightfighter. Unknown to the bomber pilot, he had caused the death of six RAF aircrew.'

Another Squadron bomber was also possibly caused to crash as a result of what today has been termed 'friendly fire'. This happened within the next 24 hours:

Sergeant Tom Wingham

'On the 26th of July 1943, a Squadron aircraft, engaged in an attack on Essen, had signalled an early return. Fighter Command claimed a Dornier 217 [a German twin-engined bomber but with a tail similar to the Halifax] off Flamborough Head. Some time later, weeks I think, fishermen trawled up two bodies in the area. Watches on the bodies had stopped at the same time as the shooting down of the "Dornier". At that time, we were all convinced they had been shot down by Fighter Command. The Squadron Bombing Leader, Doug Moon, was one of the bodies recovered; he was

The Dornier Do 217 a great friend of mine.'

The following report was submitted by an RAF nightfighter Squadron operating off the Yorkshire coast on the night of the 24th/25th of July 1943:

Wg Cdr Coventry (left), 102 Squadron's 9th CO of the War, killed in action 13 Jul 43 with Gp Capt North Carter (Station Commander RAF Pocklington) and Sqn Ldr J E H Marshall

'First aircraft had a contact at about four and a half miles to the right and below at 0047 hours. A visual was obtained at 2,500 feet above and ahead of a Dornier Do 217. Strikes were seen on the starboard engine and wing root. Our aircraft fired several short bursts and the enemy aircraft, well alight and losing height, was last seen flying very rapidly on a north-westerly course. A further contact at four and a half miles and above. Enemy aircraft took mild evasive action. A visual was obtained at 1,500 feet and recognised as Dornier 217. The fuselage was seen well alight and bits flying off hit our aircraft. Enemy aircraft turned to port losing height and was watched going into the sea where it exploded.

'Second aircraft headed for gunfire in the Humber area and a contact was made at 7,000 feet altitude, range three and three quarter miles to starboard and below. Visuals on the exhausts at 3,000 feet and a proper visual was obtained at 800–1,000 feet dead below. Enemy aircraft jinked and contact was lost. Visual was then regained and contact held at 1,000 feet range. The aircraft was identified as a Dornier 217 and our aircraft opened fire at 600 feet astern. Strikes were seen on the fuselage and return fire was experienced from the upper turret. Enemy aircraft then burst into flames, disintegrated and went straight into the sea.'*

* The German bomber unit briefed to attack Hull that night lost two Dornier 217s to nightfighters and a further one to anti-aircraft fire. Fighter Command claimed three Dorniers destroyed and two damaged – Author.

August 1943 would be another busy month with 14 Halifaxes either lost or badly damaged in combat and accidents. Two of them were, in retrospect, spectacular accidents – one on take off and one landing; the honour of the first accident went to the officer soon to take command of the Squadron:

Wing Commander Stanley Marchbank

'At Pocklington, one of the runways ran within the danger zone of the Flying Control Tower and therefore a deep trench had been dug in front of it, the purpose of which was to wipe off the undercarriage of errant aircraft driven by a squadron commander. I am almost sure that at the time we were equipped with Halifax Mark IIs which had the unmodified tail fins. Later on, with the Mark IIIs they changed the tail fins in order to give greater lateral control, particularly at low speeds.

'On the 23rd of August 1943, we were tasked to attack Berlin. On take off, I opened the throttles and almost immediately, power decreased on the port side and try as I might, I could not correct the swing. In no time, one wheel was on the grass and we were heading for the Control Tower. Off came the undercarriage and the aircraft slithered to a halt not far short of the building. I seem to remember that under these circumstances, and I hope I am correct, the first chap out had to be the pilot through an escape hatch in the top of the cockpit near his seat. The rest of the crew followed me very smartly but the bomb aimer caught his flying boot on something and fell on his head; he was the only casualty.

'The aircraft by now was on fire and we all high-tailed it across the airfield as fast as we could and at a suitable distance, we threw ourselves

Wg Cdr Stanley Marchbank (in cockpit) with his crew (Marchbank)

to the ground and waited for the big bang. The bombs being unfused, when the inevitable happened, I recall it was more of a "whoosh" rather than a crack – the trip was going to be a long haul so the bomb load was only about 4,000 pounds and I think we had overload tanks in the bomb bay. Anyway, innumerable windows were removed and no good was done to buildings, in particular the Flying Control Tower. Those inside had exited in no time at all, the roly-poly base navigation officer going out through a window and try as he might afterwards, he could never repeat the feat! There is an apocryphal story that Air Cdr Gus Walker, minus his spaniel, was leading the pack when he realised the dog was missing and turned to Wg Cdr Operations and said "Nip back and get George for me to which the reply was "If you want George, bloody well go and get him yourself!". Being a dusk take off, we were not seen to get out of the aircraft and were given up for dead! When we wandered back across the airfield and turned up out of the gloom, people were astonished. All I then remember is being taken to Sick Quarters and given a cup of tea. I assume all flying was stopped but I know that Pocklington was operational the next day. Being war, there was no time for a court of inquiry!'

The second accident was just as spectacular but in this case occurred on

Sandy Powell (3rd from the left) and crew in front of a new DT-K (standing in such a way to obscure the H2S radome) (Powell)

landing. Yet again, the unlucky Control Tower was involved as well as the people within it:

Sergeant Sandy Powell

'We took off from Pocklington at 2110 hours on the 27th of August 1943 as part of a force of 674 aircraft detailed to attack Nuremberg. This was our 15th operation in Halifax serial DT702/DY-K, an aircraft to which we had become quite attached. On the way home, we were diverted to Westcott in Berkshire due to bad weather at Pocklington. The next day, we took off at 1030 hours but due to continuing atrocious weather conditions, we were diverted to Snaith in Yorkshire, taking off from there at 1545 hours. On final approach to Pocklington, the ferocious winds were playing all sorts of tricks with air currents and only the superb handling of the aircraft by the pilot enabled us to touch down on the runway before being immediately hit broadside by a violent gust of wind of a terrific force. With no brakes, DY-K for "King" swung off the runway until the man-made trench surrounding the Control Tower removed the undercarriage and we finished up with our wing tip literally inches from the Control Tower windows causing confusion and a mass exodus of personnel in all directions. To add to our embarrassment, a brand new Halifax landed and taxied up to the Tower. This was piloted by an Air Transport Auxiliary lady pilot who gave us a wry smile as she passed by.'

September 1943 was a quieter month as far as the Squadron was concerned but one of the two crews lost that month had some unusual and different experiences compared to those taken prisoner both before and after them. On the night of the 6th/7th of September 1943, Munich was the target. For some of those RAF crews shot down and taken prisoner in the target area, unusual experiences awaited:

Pilot Officer George Butcher

'I cannot remember for the life of me where we stayed in Munich but wherever it was, it was my first experience of a unisex loo! I also remember that we travelled to the city centre in a bus powered by a wood-burning device, guarded by Waffen SS. They were very affable and kept saying words to the effect that "Orders are orders" – we were bewildered as to the reason why Göring now wanted to show us the cultural damage we had done! I cannot say I remember much apart from the Opera House with its marble steps and statues of the great, including, I think Shakespeare. I must say the place was a bit of a burnt shell which probably accounted for the tears in the eyes of the *Oberstleutnant* in charge of the guards.

'Shortly after, we were visited by six or so Luftwaffe fighter pilots who were a jolly crowd. They had brought some scotch along to make a party of it but the officer in charge of us refused to let them bring it in which they [the German fighter pilots] considered to be the German equivalent of a piss poor show! Most of them had been shot down at one time or another, one of them two days before our meeting. They said they always carried an overnight bag with them with their shaving kit, pyjamas, etc. just in case.

Above
*A 102 Sqn Halifax
successfully lifts off from
Pocklington (Wroughton)*

Left
*Sgt Hugh Moore, one of
the survivors of the
Halifax lost over Muenich
on 6/7 Sep 43. Photo
was taken at Dulag Luft
after his capture (Moore)*

They spent a very cheerful hour with us and we departed, if not the best of friends, at least respecting our adversaries.'

Another member of the same crew, having been captured by a soldier home on leave, was surprised by the compassion shown to him:

Sergeant J S Kirkby

'I awoke lying on a sack of straw in an oxen waggon. Someone had placed a warm coat over me. An elderly man was approaching, complete with a Tyrolean hat and lederhosen. He had brought some lunch – cheese sandwiches and bottles of milk. His daughter gave me her lunch and I scoffed the lot.

'I must have looked a mess – blood on my face and unshaven so I had a general clean up and felt much better. The father asked me if I liked beer – I nodded and he disappeared into the inn across the road and came back with a couple of mugs of beer. We later had a meal of sliced potato but by now, I couldn't eat, being in pain from the bruises I got on landing by parachute. The soldier must have reported my capture because it wasn't long before a policeman turned up, took his hat off and offered me a cigarette, which I declined. He indicated that I should go with him but as it had started raining, and only having one boot, I didn't fancy the walk. He accepted this and left me in the charge of the soldier. I stayed with them for the rest of the afternoon and then the soldier changed into uniform, got two cycles out of the shed and indicated that I take one. His mother had packed some sandwiches and apples into a bag for me and I wished them all goodbye. The father then asked me to sign the back of a calendar and to leave my home address which he then covered up. After the war, this was the reason why I got a letter from the soldier, whose name was Benedikt Gehr, and who by then was the village policeman. We then cycled to the village of Pensburg where I was handed over to the SS. That was when the rough stuff started.'

The next two incidents, a combat loss at the end of September and a freak accident at the start of October, were both, unusually, as a result of something happening to the aircraft's engines:

Sergeant Alec Taylor

'During the bombing of Hannover on the 22nd of September 1943, my aircraft was coned and whilst the Skipper was making strenuous efforts to escape the beams, the starboard inner engine over-revved. Whether this was caused by flak or nightfighter, we were not aware. The engine would not feather and eventually, the propeller came off and scythed through the nose of the Halifax. The fuse panel was blown out and all electrical equipment in the aircraft failed.

'The navigator plotted a course for home and with the aid of a torch held by me, the pilot was able to turn onto this. However, a fire broke out in the damaged engine and we were ordered to bale out. I was caught in the vicinity of Hameln three days later and eventually taken by the Germans

to see what they assumed were the remains of my aircraft. They were in fact correct as a flying boot, belonging to our rear gunner, was lying beside the aircraft and his body was visible, protruding from the rear escape hatch. As I had lost a boot on the way down, I wore that boot for the duration of my internment.'

Noel McPhail's Halifax after its successful landing at Pocklington, 3 Oct 43 (McPhail)

The next engine-related incident had a happier ending:

Flight Sergeant Noel McPhail

'During the bombing run over Kassel on the night of the 3rd of October 1943, we experienced several bursts of flak under our aircraft. On crossing the British coast and with the airfield in sight, I altered the pitch of the propellers when a blade became detached leaving two blades behind. The resulting vibration was terrific and within eight seconds, the port inner engine left the airframe damaging the propeller on the outer engine as it fell away. At first I thought we had a mid-air collision and after a difficult circuit of the airfield, we made an emergency landing without incident.'*

Once again summer rolled into autumn which soon became winter but Bomber Command's offensive continued unabated. 102 Squadron was to lose another 13 aircraft before the arrival of 1944 and it is fitting to mention just three incidents out of these 13. First of all, the two losses over the city of Kassel on the night of the 22nd/23rd of October 1943 and in particular the story of the man who caused the author's interest in 102 Squadron. His demise is best described by others – his crew and a young German schoolboy:

* For this feat of airmanship, Noel McPhail was immediately awarded the DFM – Author.

Flight Lieutenant 'Ned' Kelly

'We bombed as usual but while I was holding the Halifax level for the photographs, Jerry Jerrum, the engineer, told me to feather the port inner. He had been watching the temperature go right off the scale. I did that and we hared off into the darkness, trimming out the dead engine as best we could whilst still weaving. After I considered we were relatively safe, I flew straight and level to get a better trim and it was then that the nightfighter caught us.

'He came from behind, raking the fuselage and setting the port outer engine on fire and the wing alongside that engine. The hydraulics also went, the bomb doors opened and Johnny Wroughton was wounded. I made the decision that I couldn't keep the Halifax airborne so I ordered the crew to bale out before the fire made the aircraft uncontrollable. I have frequently wondered if I made the right decision but I still feel it was the only one to make . . .'

Pilot Officer John Fell

'I was completely enclosed in my blacked out compartment and saw no evidence of an attack. Over the intercom, I heard worrying talk but it was not until the pilot repeated "Parachute, parachute, bale out!" for the second time that I jumped to it. The navigator sat over the escape hatch and had to get up, ditch the hatch and drop out before other members of the crew could escape. This I did in a hurry and as I left the aircraft, I felt a whoosh of flame pass above me . . .'

Flying Officer Johnny Wroughton

'I next remembered floating gently down; at least not even floating down at all, only one of suspension and later, when an air current hit the parachute, only one of nausea. The target was still visible, burning brightly and, less brightly, the wreckage of the aircraft. I noticed that the ground was coming up quickly, so quickly that I scarcely had time to relax before hitting it. "It" was a ploughed field and I sat in the midst of the furrows and looked around me. My backside was hurting now as was the whole of my left leg.* It was very dark but faintly I could see a barn, about 100 yards away. I stood up and found it very uncomfortable, but I piled up my 'chute and harness and started walking. The barn was locked so I went on walking until I came, at the end of a willow-edged road, to a level crossing with its gates lowered. The crossing keeper saw me and when I told him what I was, he brought me some water and rang the local hospital. An Opel ambulance soon appeared from the darkness and I was piled into the back, to sprawl as best I could on a metal seat. After a ride of 15 minutes, we came to a village and eventually to a high ironwork gate by a hospital . . .'

---

* Later it was discovered that he had suffered a bullet wound to the left calf and another to his buttock – Author.

Günter Brandner

'I was only 10 at the time but it was the first time the war had come to our village of Niesen. On the night of the 22nd of October 1943, we could see the bombers flying away from Kassel when one, virtually a ball of fire, appeared flying in descending circles. We were afraid that it would land on our village but eventually, getting lower and lower, it landed itself one mile north of the village. The next day there was little left of the bomber – the tail lay broken off and the four engines were found nearby. The rest of the aircraft had burned itself out but the main wheels were recovered and used on a farm trailer for many years afterwards.

'Soon after the crash a wounded airman was captured near to the crash site and brought to our family inn. All the village turned out to see this airman whose wounds were bandaged by my grandfather. The local policeman was very aggressive towards this British flier but the rest of the village, led by a soldier who was home on leave, told him to leave the flier alone. My grandfather drove an Opel ambulance and probably took this airman, John Wroughton, to the hospital at Warburg.'

About the same time, the Halifax that was destined to be the second 102 Squadron casualty of the night had been found by a German nightfighter. Again, the story is better told by those who were involved:

Hauptmann Rudolf Altendorf

'On the 22nd of October 1943, I had taken off from Brandis airfield at 1944 hours in a Messerschmitt Bf 110 on a "Wilde Sau" night mission to Kassel. At approximately 2104 hours, I saw at 18,300 feet three four-engined bombers. Of these, one went off to the left and one to the right. I followed the remaining enemy aircraft which I identified as a Halifax. At about 2108 hours, I opened my first attack from astern after which the enemy turned south and then back on a course of 360 degrees. At 2110 hours, I attacked him again at 16,000 feet from below and a distance of 160–260 feet. The enemy aircraft caught fire at once along the entire fuselage and an intense fire was seen on the starboard wing. The bomber fell into a spin, a burning part broke loose and the aircraft hit the ground in two burning parts at

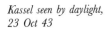

Kassel seen by daylight, 23 Oct 43

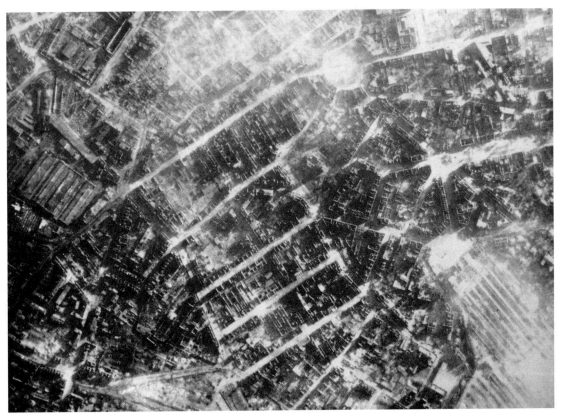

Sqn Ldr Alfred Abels (Abels)

Silixen, 27 kilometres east of Herford. Above the crash site, I fired four green flares.'*

Obergefreiter Walter Meier

'On the night of the 22nd of October 1943, I was at home in Silixen. As there were loud noises from aircraft starting at 2000 hours, I went outside to watch. At 2100 hours, I cannot give the exact time, I observed very high above me tracer fire and soon afterwards saw a bright fire coming down very fast. I assumed instantly that it was a burning aircraft. It crashed about two kilometres south of Silixen and I observed three or four green flares being fired above the crash site. The next morning, I went to the crash site. It was cordoned off by police. The shot down plane was badly damaged but it seemed to be a Halifax.'

Squadron Leader Alfred Abels

'We were shot down by a German nightfighter which had two cannons mounted at 45 degrees which made it easy for him to shoot us down from underneath our fuselage. After we were hit I unclipped my oxygen, with a view to going back to find out what was going on, when the aircraft went into a spin and I was forced into the nose of the plane. Then there was a big bang and I found myself flying through the air with no aeroplane. My parachute was at the end of its rigging lines and I had to haul it back in before I could pull the rip cord. Soon after I landed in a small field with two Germans talking on the other side of the hedge.'

Sergeant Stan Fautley

'In 1991 I returned to Silixen where Freddie Abels, Jim Walton and myself came down on the 22nd of October 1943. From the back of our host's house, I could see the top of the hill up which I walked that night and at the top of the hill, the wood in which I had hidden. 'On the following day, I was taken by car to the wood and there met a group of middle-aged men. They had all been schoolboys in 1943 and they showed me the spot where our Halifax came to earth.

I was told that the nose had come down about 50 metres from the main fuselage and that the rear gunner, Ken Sewell, who had been shot in the head was still in his turret. The mid-upper gunner, Bill Spencer, was out of his turret but was found dead in the fuselage. Dennis Brookes, the pilot, was found still strapped to his seat and clutching the joystick. The dead flight engineer, Dick Sykes, still remains something of a mystery. His body was found close to the nose with his parachute attached to his body but with the opened canopy still in the nose. I now think that when I saw him run down the steps into the nose, he either attempted a quick escape and pulled his rip cord too soon or it had been pulled open by snagging on

---

* Rudolf Altendorf was the same pilot who had shot down Sqn Ldr Wally Lashbrook's Halifax on the 17th of April 1943. This kill was Altendorf's 25th of the war and the flares were intended to help confirm the 'kill' – Author.

something. I was told that his body was face down with his arms across his face which probably meant he was alive immediately prior to impact. Someone told me "He was very young" – at 20, he was the youngest member of our crew.

One of the men who had taken me to the wood apologised for, at the time, stealing a bar of chocolate which could well have been one of mine which I had left in my wireless desk drawer. Another man told me that for about 14 years, a scarf had hung in the high branches of a tree.

'Two days later, a villager came to see me and brought me a cushion from one of the seats in the Halifax. His father had kept it in the cellar for the past 48 years and it was still in very good condition. It was probably the cushion from my seat although it could have been from the navigator's seat.'

The final story of 1943 is that of Noel Pearce. Probably the last 102 Squadron casualty of that year, his Halifax was shot down and he was taken prisoner near Berlin on the 29th of December 1943. In 1947, he returned to Germany in the hope of finding the graves of his crew. He had heard that a new cemetery was being constructed near Berlin and arrived on a Saturday night intending to visit the cemetery on the following Monday:

One of 102's most successful crews captained Sqn Ldr Ted Millson (3rd from left) (Millson)

Noel Pearce (sitting left)
(Pearce)

Flight Sergeant Noel Pearce

'On the Monday morning, it was pouring with rain and in fact continued all day. So bad was the weather that I decided to visit the cemetery on the Tuesday. The following day, I had to make my way across Berlin by tram and train as it was quite a distance from where I was staying, near the Olympic Stadium. I arrived just after lunch and went into the office by the main gates which was manned by two Germans. I gave them the number, rank and name of the rear gunner, Terry O'Hare, and I asked them if they could show me the plot where his grave was. One of them said certainly and got a register off a shelf (there were about eight volumes) and when he found what must have been the right page looked at me quite strangely. He said "We have just brought him in now to be buried!" and he then told the other chap to take me to plot so-and-so immediately.

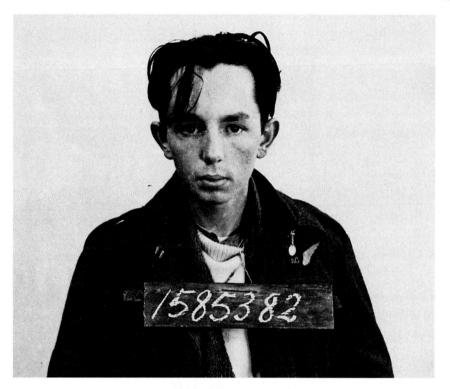

'and they shall not grow old' – Sgt Ron Bryant POW 25 Nov 43 (Bryant)

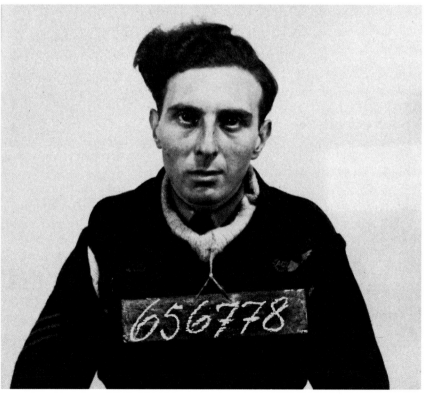

Sgt Don Veale photographed after his capture

'We moved off sharpish and got there just in time to see the coffin being lowered into the grave which was rather strange as I was able to see the plaque with Terry's name on the coffin lid. It was while I was there that they filled in the grave and I took some photos. One of the Germans went away and got some flowers and branches from a hedge and made a sort of wreath and laid it on his grave.'

It was a quiet start to 1944, with the only mission during the first three weeks being a 'gardening' trip for ten crews on the 6th of January 1944. The first major operation was planned for the night of the 20th of January 1944; the following day it was recorded in the Operations Record Book 'This was an exceptional night of misfortune and unlikely to be repeated':

Sergeant Don Veale

'I was busy dropping "window" and jamming enemy radio messages to their nightfighters (we had a carbon granule microphone situated in one of the engines. I had been given a number of frequencies to monitor and when I heard Jerry transmissions, I "back tuned" my transmitter and tried to jam the frequency by broadcasting our engine noise). On the bombing run, I always stayed on the intercom whilst looking out of the small window in the wireless cabin – the cabin was underneath the pilot and we all regarded ourselves as "Pilot's Bottom Armour". The mid-upper gunner reported the starboard outer engine was on fire – Jerry had put a load of heavy flak over the aiming point target indicators knowing that we had to fly through them. The Skipper aided by the second pilot (it was his first trip) operated the Graviner extinguisher in the engine and he dived in an attempt to put the fire out. We lost about 3–4,000 feet doing this and having put the fire out and just about to set course when the rear gunner reported an unidentified aircraft following us. Next thing, we were attacked, caught fire amidships and were told to bale out.

'We were still over the target so having destroyed the Identification Friend or Foe transmitter, Fishpond and various other items, such as eating the secret codes which were on rice paper (they tasted horrible!), I pulled the blackout curtain aside to find the Skipper, navigator and second pilot had already gone. The fire was blazing and what with the engines and the fire, it was extremely noisy. I saw the bomb aimer coming out of his position and looking to the rear saw that the engineer was headed my way. I stood up just as the aircraft lurched and went into a spin. I grabbed the escape hatch coaming and pulled myself through.

'After getting out, it was very quiet and I could see the flak coming up and our "blockbusters" going down. These bombs made a noise similar to the "shush" of compressed air in a Tube train. I had sprained my ankle, lost one of my flying boots and broken my nose. I finally landed or rather got hung up between two trees and, having punched my quick-release button, dropped down. I found that I was in a park from which I quickly moved but shortly afterwards was caught burgling a house. I was handed over to the police and ended up in the police station at Neuenhagen where

I objected strongly to being put in a cell – I was not a criminal but an RAF senior non-commissioned officer.'

Don Veale was one of the lucky ones. No less than seven of the sixteen aircraft which took off failed to return. Five crews were lost over the target, one crew became lost on their return and baled out and a further Halifax ran out of fuel and crash-landed near Norwich. Another Halifax was set on fire through being attacked by a nightfighter but managed to return to base. The cost in human terms was 16 crew killed or missing, 22 prisoners of war and one wounded. Bearing in mind that one crew aborted shortly after take off, the Squadron suffered a 47% loss rate of the 15 aircraft that attacked the target. The reason for all this carnage? The German nightfighter controller had managed to feed his fighters into the bomber stream early where they inflicted heavy damage both before, during and after the attack. A total of 35 RAF bombers were lost that night, by far the heaviest losses being from 102 Squadron which caused the Squadron diarist to refer to this night as one of misfortune [and] unlikely to be repeated.

The following night, the target was Magdeburg:

Sergeant Stan Adams

'Suddenly there was a terrific bang and rattling noise accompanied by shuddering. It was obvious that we had been hit further back in the aircraft so I immediately pulled my intercom switch down to hear what had happened. The first words to greet me were from the pilot saying "OK lads, abandon aircraft, abandon aircraft". I sat there stunned for a second or two. There was no time for any assessment of damage or discussion between us. The pilot knew straight away that there was no chance and that we still had a full bomb load on board. The bomb aimer and navigator both stood up, lifted their seats and started to tussle with the escape hatch. I vaguely remember the pilot asking the engineer to pass him his parachute and both told me that they were alright. I heard nothing from the rear and mid-upper gunners. Having moved forward to attach my parachute, the navigator and bomb aimer had by that time pulled the hatch cover into the aircraft and had thrown it forward – pushing it out could have got it wedged in the hole. I then saw both of them slip through the hatch into the cold night air just as a sudden movement from the aircraft threw me over the open hatch, wedging me by my left leg in the hatch and the rest of me being pinned along the bottom of the outside of the fuselage by the slipstream. The slipstream took one flying boot and the two socks I had on that foot clean off! I managed to check the 'chute was safely clipped on, grabbed the "D" ring, tucked my body around and dropped clear of the aircraft. I waited a few seconds before pulling sharply on the rip cord – there was a sudden jolt and I felt my right leg and foot go as cold as I left – the other flying boot and socks had gone!

'It was pitch black and I seemed to be falling so fast that I began to wonder if the parachute had opened properly but peering up, I could see the outline of the big white canopy assuring me that everything was alright. Whilst still above the cloud, there was a terrific flash below me which lit up the cloud, making it look like a big white carpet. I did not know what it was but as we had a full bomb load aboard, I feared that it could have been our plane. Going through the cloud made me very damp and cold; it was eerie. Breaking through it, I saw a light which seemed to be going round me. My mind was working overtime – it must be a fighter and he must have seen my white canopy! I wonder if he is going to attack me? Craning my neck around, it dawned on me that it was a flare or fire in the distance and that it was me that was turning. Could it have been my Halifax? Looking down, I could still see nothing but total blackness. I hadn't a clue as to how or where I would land so I put my legs together and prayed for it to be a soft landing. The thought of some of the places that I could drop on was frightening and whilst still peering down, I hit the deck, travelling backwards, and found myself being dragged along the ground. It was very soft ground – a ploughed field I think. How lucky can one get!'

The Ellis crew shot down on 21 Jan 44; back row left to right: Bill Millar (POW), Syd Fraser (missing), Len Wilson (+), Joe Payne (POW). Front: Stan Adams (POW), Harold Ellis (missing) and Reg Symcox (missing) (Adama)

Shortly afterwards, Stan was captured together with the only other crew members to get out – the navigator and bomb aimer. Ironically, after a forced march from his prisoner of war camp, on the 2nd of May 1945, he was liberated in the same area as he had been captured.

Of the 15 aircraft detailed to attack Magdeburg, one returned early and four were shot down with the loss of 18 crew members killed or missing

Flt Sgt Dai Pugh (Pugh)

and 10 prisoners of war. This time the diarist wrote that 'it was not so disastrous a night' compared to the one before. Yet again, the German controller had vectored his fighters into the bomber stream before it had crossed the German coast and this time helped inflict 57 losses on Bomber Command. Added to this, most of the bombs dropped by those who made it to the target fell outside the city.

The Squadron was to fly one more mission before the month was out – only the fourth for the month. On the night of the 28th/29th of January 1944, the target was again Berlin and of the 17 aircraft from the Squadron briefed to attack, seven turned back because of the weather, one bomber returned on three engines and with a wounded mid-upper gunner, one was shot down by flak over the target and one ditched in the North Sea on the return leg. The captain of the ditched aircraft was FS Dai Pugh – only he, his wireless operator and rear gunner survived to be rescued nearly three days later – three others drowned and the navigator died of exposure in the dinghy. The three survivors had suffered so badly with exposure and frostbite that they never flew operationally again and were in fact discharged from the RAF with War Disability pensions.

So ended the most disastrous month in the Squadron's history. In four operations, they had lost 39 crew killed, 39 prisoners of war and five wounded. This amounted to 13 aircraft and equated to a 26% loss rate for the month, a loss rate which just could not be sustained; it was as if the words of the Squadron song of 1941 was coming true again – it certainly looked as if it was suicide being on 102 Squadron!

The following month Squadron losses during Bomber Command's continuing battle for Berlin took place on the 15th/16th of February 1944 when two crews were lost including one flown by 22-year-old Plt Off Ananda Kularatne – 102 Squadron's only Ceylonese casualty of the war. Three nights later, two more crews were lost in a raid on Leipzig, a raid which cost Bomber Command 78 aircraft. Two crew members involved that night have vivid memories of the attack:

Sergeant Monty Clarke

'Although many years have passed since that fateful night of the 19th/20th February 1944, I can still vividly remember that operation to Leipzig as, to put it mildly, it was a cock-up, mainly due to the wrong meteorological information. I can clearly remember everything from starting in the morning to the time I hit the deck in Germany. I would add that I was able to evade capture for seven days, hiding by day and travelling by night, but due to the atrocious weather conditions – deep snow, blizzards, freezing winds, badly frostbitten toes and hardly being able to walk, I had to give myself up.'

Flight Lieutenant Noel McPhail

'We were apprehensive about this trip which started just after take off and continued until we landed. Over the North Sea, the navigator said the forecast winds were wrong and he was finding tail winds which were directly opposite to the forecast winds. Even before we reached the enemy

coast, we were well ahead of time due to a 100 knot tail wind. I decided
to do several dog legs to lose time but the trouble was many other bombers
had decided to do the same and the skies were full of a large number of
aircraft all on different courses instead of a steady stream. After a number
of near misses, I put on my navigation lights together with my upward and
downward identification lights until the enemy coast was reached.

'When we were well into Germany, the navigator said that he was
finding winds of 150 knots – it was hard to believe as we had never
experience or read of such strong winds. We had been briefed to be in the
last wave of the attack and by now, we were very early and it was suggested
that we orbit before the final leg to Leipzig but with an increase in fighter
activity, I decided to abandon orbiting and to bomb blind before zero hour
using H2S.

'I turned on to the final leg which was a run of about 80 miles. We were
at 24,000 feet – the highest we had ever reached on ops as normally our
ceiling was 20,000 feet. We decided to bomb from 18–19,000 feet in a
shallow dive and going like the clappers. At this height we were very cold
and this nearly cost us our lives.

'The navigator said he had a good radar picture of Leipzig and we
commenced the bomb run. He told me to alter course by 10 degrees to
port and, as I commenced the turn, two lines of tracer and cannon fire

*Flt Lt Noel McPhail
(McPhail)*

passed under the aircraft but very close; if we hadn't altered course it would
have hit us. I screamed "Fighter! Speak somebody!" but got no reply. I
guessed that the fighter must have been below us at five o'clock and so I
commenced evasive action with a violent diving turn to starboard. As we
went into the turn and dive, we were hit in the starboard aileron and wing
tip which made control difficult but not impossible. The rear gunner had
seen the fighter and spoke to me but his microphone had frozen up. He
fired his guns but they had not been oiled with anti-freeze oil and had
jammed because of the extreme cold when the breech blocks tried to go
forward. I told the bomb aimer to drop the bombs because of the control
difficulties but he said he had nothing to bomb because the target had not
been marked. As he said this, a pathfinder marker went down and, elated,
he said we were in a perfect position to bomb – directly above a hole in
the cloud. We dropped our bombs and returned without incident.'

Above
*The Mark III
(Wroughton)*

Opposite above
*The three types of Halifax
flown in 1943/4: the
Mark II series (Bryant)*

Opposite below
*The Mark II Series IA
(Millson)*

In all 78 aircraft were lost on the Leipzig raid. Four were lost in collisions whilst orbiting in order not to be over the target ahead of time and about 20 were shot down by flak. Yet again, the German nightfighter controller got it exactly correct; nightfighters inflicted such heavy losses on the Halifaxes in particular that two Marks of Halifax, the Mark II and V, were withdrawn from operations over Germany. As 102 Squadron was equipped with the Mark II, their part in the Battle for Berlin, to the great relief of the crews, was over.

For the rest of February 1944, the Squadron took part in 'Gardening' trips, losing only one aircraft in the process, whilst March 1944 saw the Squadron concentrating on 'Gardening' trips and, for the first time in many months, targets in France. Again, it was a very quiet month with only one Halifax, that flown by FS James Garside, lost without trace during an attack on Laon on the night of the 23rd/24th of March 1944.

April 1944 saw the end of the Battle for Berlin and the start of bombing missions in preparation for the invasion of Europe. Targets were in France and Belgium, the destruction of which would hamper German attempts to counter any invasion. Added to this, the 'Gardening' trips continued and the only losses during the month were one on such a trip and one in an attack against Aulnoye in France. May 1944 continued with the same type of missions the only difference being that by the 15th of the month, crews had finished converting to the Halifax Mark III and could thus be

Fg Off Arthur Painter, navigator of the 'Gardening' loss on 23 Apr 44. He and his crew had survived a crash during the disastrous Berlin raid of 20 Jan 44 (Painter)

recommitted to attacking targets in Germany. However, it was on an invasion-related target the Squadron had its only combat loss of the month and its first Halifax Mark III:

Pilot Officer Austin Huycke

'On the 27th of May 1944, three groups of 25 aircraft took off from Pocklington to attack a German Panzer division at Bourg Leopold in Belgium. We were in the second group and took off around midnight. It took two hours to reach the target and there were a lot of searchlights and flak but we accomplished our mission. Our return was smooth until we were over the North Sea when we were intercepted by a German nightfighter.* All of a sudden, the plane was filled with smoke and fire but I just about had control of the aircraft so I turned back for the Continent. The two gunners had been killed but the rest of us were able to parachute down about a mile inland.

'At daybreak I met up with the flight engineer and we went to a farmhouse where a Dutch farmer took us to members of the underground. We spent a week in a forest and were then taken to an apartment in Antwerp where we heard of the invasion on the radio. However, we were captured by a German agent while we were in civilian clothes and with no identification. We were incarcerated for two weeks under terrible conditions – the cell was infested with bed bugs and our only food was cabbage soup twice a day. We must have convinced them that we were Allied aircrew because we were, finally, taken to a Dulag Luft and then onto a prisoner of war camp.'

On the 6th of June 1944, Allied forces landed in Normandy and 102 Squadron's targets of the previous two months continued unchanged. However, during a bombing raid over northern France, the Squadron experienced what can only be termed as an "accidental bale out". On the 15th of June 1944, the Squadron attacked German troop and vehicle concentrations at Evrecy where Plt Off A H Munroe's Halifax had been damaged by flak causing the intercom to fail. The pilot's ensuing instructions were misunderstood by the navigator:

Sergeant Roy Harris

'I baled out at 0300 hours and came down in a field. I walked for about an hour and a half in a north-westerly direction and then, as it had began to get light, I hid up in a hedge, staying there until 2330 hours. During the day, I heard some French women talking but saw no one. I lived on the contents of my escape box but was unable to get any water.

'At night, I again started walking in the same direction but I soon became so exhausted that I felt like giving myself up. However, I recovered and hid up again, sleeping in a hedge until dawn. I was very thirsty when I awoke

---

* This Halifax was possibly a victim of *Hptm* George-Hermann Greiner, *Staffelkapitän* of *11/NJG 1* who got his 30th and 31st victims, both Halifaxes, in the Antwerp area at 0228 and 0239 hours – Author.

Sqn Ldr David Fisher (Fisher)

but it rained during the morning and I licked the water off the leaves. During the day, I saw some troops but, judging from the shape of the steel helmets and green blouses they were wearing, I took them to be German. I watched them go to a pump and wash so when it was dark, I managed to fill my water bottle from this pump and after I had put some water-purifying tablets in the bottle, I drank the water. I tried, unsuccessfully, to listen to the troops talking and went back to the hedge.

'Early next morning, I crawled up close to a camouflaged lorry and hid about 10 yards away from it. About 0730 hours, I heard the troops get up but still could not hear what they were saying. However, about an hour later, I heard a voice shout "You've got to dig that goddam trench!". I then came out with my hands up and gave myself up to American troops.'

While Sgt Harris was hiding in the French countryside, the Squadron had flown its first mission against Germany for nearly four months. On the night of 16 June 1944, the Squadron had taken part in an attack on the synthetic oil plant at Sterkrade. Unfortunately for Bomber Command, the bomber stream passed very close to the nightfighter beacon at Bocholt and it was this beacon that had been chosen by the nightfighter controller as a holding point for his fighters. 31 bombers were lost with 77 Squadron losing seven and 102 Squadron losing five. One of the losses was a particular blow to the Squadron and its morale; Sqn Ldr David Fisher had been posted to 102 Squadron in April 1944 – he was a particularly experienced and popular officer having flown a full tour with 77 Squadron, for which he had been awarded the DFM, a tour with Number 1652 Conversion Unit, for which he had been awarded the DFC, and a short time with 466 Sqn before being posted to 102 Squadron. He was just 19 when he started his first tour and was two months off his 22nd birthday at the time of the Sterkrade raid:

Flying Officer Bryan Purser

'My crew, captained by Fg Off Bill Graham, was coming to the end of its tour in June 1944. During our time with the Squadron, we had seen heavy casualties and few crews were completing their tours. Most of our contemporaries had gone missing and our loss of friends and acquaintances seemed endless. Secretly, I think we all asked ourselves "How can one hope to survive?"

'The arrival of Sqn Ldr Fisher and his crew revitalised the Squadron. Here was a young, well-decorated crew starting yet another tour – "Some do survive!" was a common comment. When he and his crew failed to return, the effect was devastating and I cannot think of any other missing crew causing such an effect on those still around.

'We were not operating the night that he and his crew disappeared but I have vivid memories of that day. I recall, as if it was yesterday, seeing him queuing for a cup of tea in the ante-room of the Mess prior to leaving for briefing. Later on, I stood at the take off end of the runway and recall waving to his rear gunner as he swung his turret sideways for take off. This was a technique unique to Sqn Ldr Fisher as he felt it helped to counteract the violent swing the Halifax had until the speed increased and the pilot could get his tail up. His last take off was as immaculate as usual.'

Raids now switched back to the invasion area, concentrating on flying bomb sites, railways and troop and armour concentrations both by day and by night. Sadly, Squadron casualties were to continue right until the end of the month as these accounts show:

Sergeant D Cunningham

'On the 24th of June 1944, we had a daylight sortie to Noyelles. Our usual aircraft was unserviceable so we took Fg Off Jim Weaver's Halifax coded DY-X as he and his crew were away on leave.

'Shortly after crossing The Wash, we suffered an engine malfunction and we lost speed. By the time we had reached the French coast, the engine had been feathered and we ran up to the target on our own, well after the last wave had dropped their bombs and in spite of being told by the Master Bomber to abort, we decided to press home our attack . . .'

Flying Officer Pete Bailey

'Passing near Abbeville, we were caught by heavy flak. Later inspection revealed about 140 holes. One splinter passed between the wireless operator's feet, through his chart table, through the cockpit floor above his head, between my feet, giving me a glancing blow to the forehead before going out through the windscreen. The starboard outer engine was knocked out with a damaged fuel line and we were escorted back by Spitfires and landed at Ford airfield in Sussex.

Fg Off Pete Bailey (centre standing) and his rear gunner Sgt Cunningham (standing far left) (Cunningham)

'DY-X was repaired and later returned to the Squadron as a spare. The Weaver crew were very proud of this aircraft and had impressed on us to handle it carefully. Having re-established contact with this crew after 50 years, they still bear a grudge about this incident but are now on speaking terms!'

Sergeant John Watkins

'On a daylight trip on the 25th of June 1944, I saw a 102 Squadron Halifax disintegrate over the target. I thought it had been hit by another aircraft's bombs but had in fact collided with a Halifax of 77 Squadron. The navigator of the Halifax was on the same navigator's course as myself and he got such high marks that they kept him in Canada for a spell as an instructor. He did his first op around the 23rd of June 1944. Back in flight planning, his navigator's desk was next to mine and when I got back from the daylight op on which he went down, I noticed the navigation log from his first op was open on his desk. In it, the Navigation Leader had written "Good show. Keep this up and you'll have no problem in completing a tour".'

John Watkins was destined to fly only another one and a half operations before he too became one of 102 Squadron's losses. On the night of the 28th/29th of June 1944, the target was a night bombing raid on the railway yards at Blainville:

Sergeant John Watkins

'At about 0030 hours en route to Blainville, we were attacked from below by a nightfighter. The aircraft was a flaming mass in a few seconds; the rear gunner reversed his turret and got out safely and I got out through the hatch under my seat. There were no other survivors.

'I woke up in a field surrounded by a herd of curious cows. Both the sock and boot off one foot were missing. After hiding in some woods until dawn, I set course in a westerly direction, on and off fields and country paths and after half a day was fortunate to be spoken to by a lady working in the garden of a farm. She gave me civilian clothes, had my identity verified by the local Resistance and hid me in a barn. The next day I was given a bicycle and told to follow a guide, also on a bike. We rode through the nearby town of Crepy-en-Valois to Levignez about 40 kilometres north-east of Paris. I was hidden in the woods along with a Canadian pilot, an Australian navigator and four Americans. After three weeks, we moved to Parmain on the outskirts of Paris, split up and I went by train right into Paris. By the 10th of August, the tension, excitement and atmosphere in the city was incredible; we all knew that the Allies had broken out of Normandy but no one knew for sure just how close they were to Paris. Anyway, six of us (two RAF, one Canadian and three Americans) were taken by our guides to the Gare d'Austerlitz and went by train to Etampes. I learned many years later that we were being taken to the Fôret de Freteval near Chateaudun where 200 Allied aircrew evaders were gathered. However, plans for us came adrift after two days because the whole area was full of retreating Germans and some of them had billeted themselves in the "safe house" that we were heading for!

'The next day, we got caught in a firefight between counter-attacking Germans and ill-armed local Maquis and when all French males between eight and eighty were arrested, so were we. Things then got a bit sticky when the German army handed us over to the SD* who took us to Chartres. Somehow, the Luftwaffe got to hear about us being in SD custody and as they were preparing to evacuate, the Luftwaffe grabbed us. As our guide had managed to slip away in the confusion when we were first captured, we were accepted as a bunch of wandering evaders. After a few days in the "cells" at the Gare de L'Est in Paris, we were put on one of the last trains to leave before the Liberation and after a lot of straffing by Typhoons and the like, ended up at Frankfurt and the Luftwaffe Interrogation Centre five days later.'

Of the eleven Halifaxes lost by Number 4 Group in the attack on Blainville 102 Squadron lost five with the cost of eighteen dead and eight prisoners of war. However, due to the chaos currently reigning in the German held part of France, nine Squadron crew members managed to evade capture. Never again would 102 Squadron lose so many men and aircraft in one night.

Attacks, related to or connected with the German defence in northern France, continued throughout July 1944. Losses had been very light for the first three weeks of the month but soon began to creep up again:

Flight Sergeant Harold Brabin

'Our 16th trip was against Le Hauts Boissons on the night of the 23rd of July 1944. This trip was code-named "Operation Cobra". The plan was to use bombers to saturate an area so that ground forces could break through into Brittany. Bomber Command and the Americans had specific targets and were required to be very accurate or to bring the bomb load back. Targets were tank and troop concentrations, artillery and the job of cratering the ground so that German tanks could not make flanking attacks. For this we also used fragmentation and anti-personnel bombs. On this trip, the crew who shared our hut were shot down as we were flying next to each other – the German fighter turned on us but we were able to drive him away with some very effective fire. All the other crew were lost apart from Bob Seth, the rear gunner, who found himself in the sea about 50 miles from the British coast in the pitch black night. Luckily for him, a destroyer had caught sight of him parachuting down and 20 minutes later, he was picked up.'

The next night, the target was Stuttgart in Germany. Being back over Germany was not popular and the thoughts of one crew and their subsequent experiences went only to enforce what they and others felt:

---

* SD – *Sicherheitsdienst*-Security or counter espionage/terrorism service of the SS – Author.

Fg Off Rabbitt and his crew at the end of their tour. Back row left to right: Fg Off Rabbitt, Plt Off B G Spiller, Plt Off D G Young. Front: WO Harold Brabin, Flt Sgt W Ollerton, Flt Sgt N T Starmer and Fg Off A J Allen (Ollerton)

Flight Lieutenant Jim Weaver

'The Squadron Commander suggested we follow the plan in the briefing, heading towards Mannheim so that their fighters congregated there and then at the last minute turning for Stuttgart, or, as he said, "You might be awarded a medal but your Mother would be the one who gets it'. It was a tough target and we were under no delusions so off we went on what proved to be our most memorable evening.

'En route, there was enemy activity on our port beam, where the diversionary attack was taking place over Mannheim, and when we got over Stuttgart, it was obvious that we were not very welcome. Fighters, flak, searchlight, flares – all the elements to make one reflect on the comforts of home or being back in the Mess.

'It was a nice run up to the target with instructions from the Master Bomber, then "Bomb doors open!", "Left, left", "Right, right", "Steady", "Bombs gone!". The Halifax jumped up, relieved of its burden and now there was the long 25 seconds while the photo was taken and then "Bomb doors closed". This whole procedure was not long in time but seemed to be the most intense part of the trip, especially over the more heavily-defended targets.

'Leaving Stuttgart, it gradually became quieter but exceptionally dark when suddenly, all hell broke loose. Tracers and cannon shells were tearing into the tail assembly and port wing. Almost simultaneously, I reacted with a dive to starboard, away from the tracers as, obviously, the fighter was astern. I shouted to the rear gunner "Paul – get that guy!" – it was a Junkers

Flt Lt Jim Weaver's Halifax after its return from Stuttgart, 25 Jul 44 (Weaver)

88 astern, below and to starboard. The defensive action we took brought him up in full view of the rear gunner who shot him down, seeing it break up with a fire and explosion around one of its engines.

'The Halifax was responding well but as we levelled off, we saw that the port engine was on fire. It was extinguished by a few dives which took our altitude from 19,000 feet to 7,000 feet. We were badly off course, heading for Switzerland with the port engine not functioning very well and with a damaged port fin, rudder, elevators and aileron, we could not climb but were maintaining height. There was flak ahead and the bomb aimer went into the nose to more or less guide us around it. However, shortly after he had moved from the nose to help the navigator with his "Gee" fixes, we were attacked again but this time from ahead and below. Where the bomb aimer had been lying, there was a row of bullet holes!

'The fighter disappeared and eight and a half hours after leaving Pocklington, we arrived back. The landing was difficult and power had to be used to counteract the severe side-slip to port but after a ground loop caused by a shot out tyre, we were back on terra firma. We were very late and it was assumed that we had got the "chop" so we had a great reunion with our ground crew and other Squadron friends who were waiting for us.'

Even the daylight trips to France, which were usually without incident, had their moments. On the 28th of July 1944, one crew was on its 19th trip – the V1 launch site at Foret de Nieppe:

Flight Sergeant Harold Brabin

'The Wing Commander began his briefing – "A piece of cake, gentlemen. It's just over the French coast. The aim is to help our brave soldiers by bombing tank and troop concentrations and supply centres for the V1 launches. Today we are full of surprises – two Mosquitoes will lead this raid of over 1000 aircraft. The Mosquitoes will be equipped with 'Oboe' and will fly towards the target in a circle and controlled by radio beacons in Britain. When they are over the target, the radio signals will stop and they will drop flares. You will bomb the flares. Now that's simple, isn't it?". He then told us that as his crew were inexperienced, we would have the honour of leading the attack as our Squadron was leading the Group.

'We took off and tacked on behind the Mosquitoes with the rest of the formation behind us. Flying perfectly straight and level, we made a wonderful target for the German flak guns at Ostend and we were hit repeatedly with many of the holes, in the fuselage, big enough to jump through! In fact Don McLean was thinking of doing just that when Bas Spiller called to him "Hold on! You've got your 'chute on upside down!". Immediately afterwards, Bas was hit in the leg by a piece of flak. I tore open his trousers and held my thumbs near to the wound to try and stop the bleeding as it was too close to the groin to use a tourniquet. Sandy Concannon then came down from his turret with a large sheath knife in his hand – poor Bas wondered what he was going to do with it! He then cut off the trouser leg (which was soaked with blood) while I kept up the pressure on the vein for the remainder of the trip.

'We were near the target so we hurriedly dropped our bombs, as did the two aircraft behind us as they had been told to drop when we did. Because of the wound to Bas and the damage to the Halifax, we waggled our wings and headed for home, handing over the lead to the Wing Commander. However, we had to make several attempts to get out of France as each time we approached the coast, we were driven back by a wall of flak. Eventually, we found a relatively quiet spot, put our nose down to increase speed and managed to cross with only a few more holes.

'On the way back, we saw an American P-38 Lightning and fired off a distress flare. He escorted us back to the Flying Fortress base at Great Ashfield. Bas was taken to a hospital at Ely and on inspecting our poor Halifax, we counted 80 holes in it!'

August and September 1944 continued much the same as previous months with objectives ranging from continued support for the advancing Allied ground forces to the usual targets in Germany. Losses were light – three crews lost in August 1944 and two in September, although one of these was a loss as a result of an accident. However, in mid-September 1944, Bomber Command was released from Supreme Headquarters Allied Expeditionary Force control and allowed to bomb targets not directly related to the war on the ground and, on the 25th of September 1944, 102 Squadron started doing something that had nothing at all to do with bombing!:

Flying Officer Alan Arthurson

'During the Arnhem push, we were transferred to petrol delivery duties flying 200 five gallon jerry cans of petrol to Melsbroek airfield near Brussels. We were to keep below radar height at 1,000 feet so many return journeys were made formatting with other crews and being so low, at times we passed either side of large buildings and even saw cars being blown over by our slipstreams! On one of these flights, as we left the plane to unload it, the mid-upper gunner found himself off-loading the jerry cans to his brother who was then driving them towards the front line. On another day, just after landing, a German fighter roared over the 'drome and shot down an army reconnaissance plane which crashed just outside the perimeter.'

About eight days later, these petrol flights stopped. Number 4 Group had flown 435 sorties without mishap, delivering 325,000 gallons of much-needed petrol. 134,000 gallons were delivered by 102 Squadron alone before it re-started bombing raids against Germany in what was to become Bomber Command's operational climax. With German night and day fighter effectiveness decreasing, numbers of crews and aircraft increasing and bombing accuracy improving, 102 Squadron continued to fly operational missions up to the end of the year. Losses did decrease – no operational losses in October, two operational losses in November (and one of those was a result of "friendly fire") and two in December 1944, the lot of a crew on 102 Squadron was improving to such an extent that they started participating in day as well as night attacks on German targets.

Fg Off Hislop and his crew pose during a lull during petrol delivery duties (Coope)

However, before what was destined to be the last year of the war started, a number of crews still had experiences that they would never forget:

Flight Sergeant Harold Brabin

'On a raid to Bochum on the 9th of October 1944, over the target we were suddenly blinded by a searchlight, then another and then a third. We had been coned. This called for quick thinking as we only had a few seconds before we could expect a shell to explode in our bomb bay – few aircraft escaped once coned. The pilot threw the plane into a steep dive and kicked the rudder pedals at the same time. We gathered speed quickly and turned the opposite direction whilst in the dive. We managed to lose all but one of the searchlights but we were now affected by the extreme "G" forces and could hardly move. Don McLean was in the co-pilot's seat and was able to use the joystick to help the pilot pull the plane out of its horrifying dive by putting his feet on the "dashboard" and pulling with all of his might. Their combined strength pulled us out and the remaining searchlight lost us. Bill said "I'm just a frustrated fighter pilot at heart!" – my heart was thumping whilst my mind was calculating the odds against us in that death dive. We did not need a shell to hit us if we were going to self-destruct!'

Another crew had a similar lucky escape. This time it was not a case of self destruction but another of 'friendly fire':

Flying Officer John Holmes

'On the 31st of October 1944, I was detailed to fly with Sqn Ldr Jarand's crew as bomb aimer. The target for the night was Cologne.

'Over the target, we made a normal run up and I released the bombs. After the distributor arm had completed its passage, I turned towards the bomb panel to press the jettison bars across and from that point, I can remember no more. Two hours later, I opened my eyes and found that I was on the rest bed in the middle of the aircraft. The navigator was leaning over me and said that we were preparing to land at Pocklington!

'I learnt later that we had been hit by a load of incendiaries dropped from an aircraft flying above us. One of these incendiaries had smashed through the perspex nose of the aircraft and hit me on the head, laying me out cold. The mid-upper gunner had also been hit when an incendiary smashed through his turret.'

The only true combat loss of November 1944 occurred on the 2nd of the month. Shortly after the war, a former – 102 Squadron member tried to find out what had happened to this Halifax and its crew:

Sergeant D Cunningham

'From information I had received from the War Graves Commission, I learned that DY-U for "Uncle", captained by Fg Off Redmond, had crashed on top of a pillbox between two small villages of Zimmerath and Bickerath, just north-east of Aachen. At that time, civilians were discouraged from visiting Germany except those that were working for the Control

Sqn Ldr Jarand's Halifax after being damaged by someone else's incendiaries, 31 Oct 44 (Holmes)

Commission. However, rightly or wrongly, I entered Germany posing as a representative of the War Graves Commission.

'I arrived at Cologne in the late evening and spent some time searching for accommodation as 80% of the city was in ruins. Early the next morning, I caught a train to Aachen and then caught a bus to Rurberg, arriving there in the dark at around 1900 hours and stayed in a Gasthaus run by the local schoolmistress. I explained to her in broken German that I was trying to locate a missing bomber that had crashed nearby. She remembered two incidents – one being a Halifax which crashed into the lake immediately behind her house and another which had come down a few miles away.

'In the morning, the Burgermeister arrived and he and his assistant took me to the site. "U" for "Uncle" had crashed on a strongpoint and had finished up some 30 feet below the ground. The locals gave me some scraps of metal from the wreckage. The Burgermeister told me that five bodies were recovered and buried in one grave. The navigator had baled out and was the only survivor. For many years I was unable to trace the seventh member of the crew and only recently did I find out that he had baled out and his body was not found until nearly a month later.'

The final account for the year is that of Sgt Arnie Coope. For him December 1944 had been a quiet month of 'run of the mill' ops without incident. Both he and the rest of the Squadron were looking forward to Christmas when to his surprise, on Christmas Eve the Squadron was tasked with a daylight attack on Muelheim. Their normal aircraft was unserviceable and they were given a new one. On start up, one of the engines was found to lack power but after a short discussion, the crew decided to go ahead. After crossing the enemy coast, it was found that the Halifax could not keep up with the rest of the formation and soon was lagging behind:

Sergeant Arnie Coope

'We were about four minutes out from the target, I had opened the valve allowing nitrogen gas to flow into the now empty fuel tanks as this would lessen the risk of fire. I had also turned on full tanks of fuel – four in each wing – to ensure that there was no danger of running out over the target. Until then, we had seen little flak and we were flying along quite happily when suddenly there was a tremendous thump and the aircraft shook. There was a babble of voices wondering what had happened and after I had collected myself, I looked around to see that the starboard inner engine was on fire and I guessed that we had been hit by anti-aircraft fire.

'The aircraft began to roll and began filling with smoke. The Skipper was trying to hold the aircraft steady and I yelled to him that I was going back to see if I could do anything. We still had the bombs on board and decided to jettison them but the Skipper reported that he was unable to do that. There was a chance that I might be able to release the bombs manually but when I reached the position, I saw that the covers had been blown away and that there was too much smoke and flame around the bomb bay.

'The mid-upper gunner, who had obviously seen what was happening, was already out of his turret and stood beside me in the crew rest area. The smoke was thickening with the flames getting higher and, after a few more seconds of commotion, the Skipper gave the order to abandon aircraft. I clipped on my 'chute and made my way to the rear entrance hatch. The mid-upper gunner was standing besides the already open door and after asking about the rear gunner, who had already got out via his turret, I motioned that it was time for us to go. On looking down, the ground seemed miles away and although neither of us fancied the jump, it was "Hobson's Choice". I grabbed his hand and shook it, put one of my hands onto my harness and dived out head first.

'I never remember pulling the rip cord but I do remember a jerk and then I was floating in the sky. As I hung there, I counted five more parachutes in different points of the sky. The Halifax could be seen going down in flames and then I saw the starboard wing break away and the rest of the aircraft just exploded and fell in burning pieces. Sadly the Skipper did not get out and although the bomb aimer got out, he was never seen again.

'As I hung suspended, frightened and all alone, I watched the rest of our bombers complete their mission and head back home for the Christmas festivities and at this stage I looked at my watch – it was only 1430 hours.

'As I neared the ground, I could see people converging towards where I was expected to land and I got the distinct impression that I was shot at several times. I thought that I had better do something about this so jerked around in the harness and just hung limp until I hit the ground with a thump. I was immediately surrounded by a very hostile crowd who were not about to offer me the hand of friendship. Before they could do something to me, soldiers arrived and with pistols drawn, marched me to the local "nick". So began my life as a prisoner of war.'

Sadly, the crowd were hostile and it is believed that more than one member of the two 102 Squadron crews shot down that day were lynched by an angry mob. On this sombre note, 102 Squadron finished its fifth year of war; only one more crew member was wounded before the start of 1945, a year which would prove to be one with many changes for those who were destined to survive it.

CHAPTER FIVE

War and Peace 1945–1946
and 1954–1956

Bomber Command's policy of attacking oil and transportation-related targets continued apart from the occasional switch to lesser targets such as those that were jet aircraft or U-Boat related. As with the previous winters of the war the weather hampered many operations and, towards the end of January 1945, was particularly severe. Despite this, casualties started early when on the evening of the 1st of January 1945, a Halifax landing from an attack on Dortmund hit a house just short of the runway killing one crew member and injuring all of the remainder. Four nights later, the Squadron suffered three more losses on what was to be the worst night for the Squadron in 1945:

Pilot Officer David Dale

'On the night of the 5th of January 1945, our target was Hannover. On our final approach to the target a few miles north of the city, we were hit by flak which set our starboard inner engine on fire. As soon as this happened, I clipped on my chest-type parachute on which I was lying in the nose of the bomber (I had it under me as part protection from any stray flak coming up from below). I had clipped one side on when our plane flipped over and went into a dive. The centrifugal force was so great that I couldn't move a finger and to this day, I can recall my exact thoughts – "Oh shit, all this training and now it's all over!"

'However, when we were down to 21,000 feet, the plane blew up and I was knocked unconscious as I was blown out of the side of the nose. All I can remember is hearing a thump and moving towards the bombing panel switches; when I came to, I was falling with the wind whistling around my jacket collar. I managed to clip on the other side of the parachute and then pulled the "D" ring. My immediate thought at that instant was "It's broken!" because I gave it one hell of a tug but then I looked up and saw the most glorious sight – a trail of beautiful white silk unfolding and then I was floating down, watching the explosions on Hannover.

'I landed about 10 minutes later on frozen ground, soon realising that I had lost my boots. The drill upon landing was to try and bury the parachute but this was impossible. As I had landed a few feet from a burning pile of debris (which could have been our plane or one of the 30 or so that went down on that night), I threw the 'chute on the fire

and took off in the direction of Holland. I didn't get far before I was captured.'

A similar experience was had by the bomb aimer of another 102 Squadron aircraft lost that night. Pilot Officer Ted Boorman's Halifax was on the final run to the target but was set on fire by a nightfighter. After a struggle, he managed to get away from the stricken bomber and, sorting himself out, opened his parachute. Shortly afterwards, he landed in a snow-covered field:

Pilot Officer Ted Boorman

'At the bottom of the field was my Halifax, DY-Y, well alight with explosions occurring all the while and parachutes hanging outside the fuselage – I was the only survivor. German soldiers were walking around, inspecting what was left of our burning aircraft. Some while later, they left

Sgt R O Jones, Flt Sgt J F Valery, Flt Sgt W K Quill, Capt R W F Heiden, Plt Off E M Boorman, Sgt A I Johns and Sgt P Morgan. Ted Boorman was the only survivor after being shot down on 5 Jan 45 (Boorman)

and I decided it was time to move and start walking home! Having no flying boots, I took the inner Kapok lining from my Mae West and tied two pieces to my feet. After trying to bury the remains of my parachute, as instructed, I gave up as the ground was too frozen and a pen knife was not the ideal tool for digging.

'Looking back, it now seems quite amazing that an RAF officer could walk down a main road away from a city that had just been bombed and was well alight but I did. All sorts of vehicles and ambulances roared past to or from the stricken city and nobody took any notice of a lone figure in flying kit plodding along the road!

'I decided it would be prudent to leave the main road and hole up for a while but the farm dogs at the first farm I approached did not give or sound a very good welcome. Moving along the main road, at the next intersection I turned off and immediately walked into a group of locals standing under a tree and was taken prisoner.'

The war was now drawing to a close for 102 Squadron and between the middle of January and May 1945, only another five aircraft were lost in action – one more in January, two in February and two in March. Despite this, the Squadron continued to undertake day and night bombing raids and even the easier 'Gardening' trips to prevent the escape of German shipping and submarines. It should be stressed that despite the end of the war being in sight, 46% of the total tonnage of bombs dropped by Bomber Command during the conflict were dropped between September 1944 and May 1945. Sadly, of those on the Squadron at the start of the last four

Opposite above
Another crew lost during Jan 45 was that captained by Sqn Ldr Jarand (4th from right) (Jarand)

Opposite below
Sqn Ldr Jarand was flying this Halifax (then re-coded DY-Y) when it was shot down near Wolfshagen on 16 Jan 45; all the crew were killed (Graham)

months of the war, 26 would fail to see peace being declared. Some were luckier as these last accounts of being shot down during World War Two show:

Sergeant Bill 'Ginge' Ollerton

'On the 7th of February 1945, we were briefed early for a daylight raid on Goch in what was an Army support operation. However, there was cloud cover over the target and we were stood down. Later, we were briefed for a night attack and took off at 1912 hours.

'On the run-in to the target, we were ordered to abort* but we continued on our track, through the target area, before turning for home. The sky was a picture despite no moon and on the second dog-leg, the silhouette of a Junkers 88 was spotted on the port quarter. The Skipper was informed but the rear gunner could not confirm what I had seen. However, I resumed my search and again saw a Junkers 88 on our port beam high up and at extreme range. The pilot said to prepare for evasive action and a corkscrew to port was carried out six times – the pilot's skill doing this with a full bomb load was superb, especially as there were other bombers in the area. Although John Grist reported seeing sparks shoot through the bomb bay, there were no reported strikes and we proceeded to get back on course.

'During a starboard search, I noticed that the starboard wing was on fire and even though we tried to put it out, orders were eventually given to abandon aircraft.'

Flight Sergeant John Grist

'I followed Ginge out and presume I was knocked unconscious by the tail plane as I have no recollection from the time of leaving until about five seconds before hitting the ground. Even when I was on the ground, I had a total memory loss for about 15 minutes. However, when I had recovered, I saw that I had landed in a clearing on the edge of pine woods. With my button compass, and using the sound of gunfire in the distance, I headed for what I thought was the front line as I thought I was on the wrong side of it. I cut up my parachute and bandaged my right foot as I had lost the boot during the descent and stuffed the rest into my battledress for warmth. Several people passed by and I lay low and I could hear traffic not far off so went through the woods to see what was there. I lay in a ditch and watched vehicles passing, all of which seemed to be our types but I was not sure. However, I moved to a crossroads and eventually a car headlights lit up a sign which read "Salvage Dump" and I knew I was safe.

'I tried to stop a few vehicles who were suspicious but eventually stopped a motor cyclist who hid in the bushes waiting for me to identify myself as he thought I was a German parachutist! Happy that I was not German, he stopped a lorry which took me to Eindhoven hospital where I had some

---

* The raid was in preparation for the attack of the British XXX Corps across the German border and Goch was one of the German defensive points. The Master Bomber had commenced the attack but aborted when smoke totally obscured the target – Author.

cocoa, a welcome bath by a nurse called "Sunshine" and I spent what was left of the night in hospital. The next day, I was driven to Eindhoven airfield where I met three other members of my crew and we were flown to Pocklington via Down Ampney in Gloucestershire.

'There is a postscript to this story and a happy one for me. The remains of my parachute are now a christening gown for my grandchildren.'

What happened to the crew is best described by 'Ginge' Ollerton:

Sergeant Bill 'Ginge' Ollerton

'I had landed in a small field and I walked to a nearby farmhouse over whose front door was draped a parachute. Inside were the navigator and wireless operator, the latter having landed on the roof and crashed through into the bedroom of a young girl who was asleep in bed! They were alright and we were cooked breakfast – I didn't like the bacon because it was too fatty! The girl whose bedroom was destroyed by the wireless operator was soon to be married and we gave her our parachutes to make a wedding dress. The bomb aimer and rear gunner had landed in trees and had damaged their backs. On arriving back at Pocklington, we were told the sad news that our Skipper had been killed – burned to death in the crash. He was a gentle man and my friend.'

The end of the war was now a matter of time. Re-equipped in mid-February 1945 with the Halifax Mark VI, which offered better engines and a greater range, the offensive continued both day and night. Still, the Luftwaffe had a few more tricks up their sleeves. On the night of the 3rd/4th of March 1945, German nightfighters took part in Operation *Gisella*

Opposite
The Halifax Mark VI
(Wright)

Bill Smith (centre) and
his crew shortly before
Bill's death on 6 Feb 45
(Ollerton)

– attacking the bombers as they returned to their bases. Losses on both sides were high but 102 Squadron managed to get away unscathed:

Sergeant Bill 'Ginge' Ollerton

'Kamen was the target which we clobbered with no enemy activity at all. It was all very easy until we crossed the English coast on our return – then all hell broke loose! Aircraft were flying against the mainstream and the cry of "Bandits! Bandits!" revealed all – the Luftwaffe were attacking aircraft in all stages of airfield approaches. Consequently, no airfield would switch their lights on! There was plenty of confusion and pandemonium and the "mayday" channels were overworked. Eventually we got a "mayday" slot and landed on an approach funnel of three lights and a runway of three lights. Then an equally dimly lit black and white control van took us round the perimeter on our last drops of fuel.'

Just over a month and a half later, little did one crew know when they took off on their 43rd trip on the 25th of April 1945 that this would be their and the Squadron's last operational flight of the War:

Flight Sergeant Harold Brabin

'Wangerooge was an island at the mouth of the Elbe River near Hamburg on which were coastal gun batteries to protect naval ships and installations in the Heligoland Bight. They had been particularly destructive to our bombers so we were all delighted to hear that there was to be a massive daylight raid on this target. The flak that greeted us was very concentrated as usual but as our bombs reached the target, the anti-aircraft fire slowed and eventually stopped. We were well back in the stream in a good position to see the effect the attack was having. I had been instructed to operate a huge movie camera but I found it too heavy to handle and when I told this to the Skipper, he told me to forget it. The Photographic Section people made some caustic comment when I got back on my lack of strength but I was not too concerned.'

At 0001 hours on the 9th of May 1945, the war in Europe ended. Two days before, 102 Squadron had been withdrawn from Bomber Command and had been assigned to Transport Command. The only bombs that their Halifaxes would now carry were the ones that were being dropped in the North Sea, 'no longer required as being surplus to requirements'. A total of about 14,118 tons of bombs and 1,865 mines had been dropped by the Squadron over the past five years and eight months. But the losses had been high, as illustrated by the list in Appendix D of this book, and earned the Squadron the honour of having the third heaviest losses in Bomber Command, the heaviest losses in Number 4 Group (shared with 78 Squadron), the highest percentage losses in Number 4 Group and the highest percentage losses for any Whitley Squadron. However, its story was by no means over and if the previous five and a half years had been regarded by some as suicide, the fun now started to creep back into flying with 102 Squadron.

For the next few months, the Squadron spent its time on such relatively mundane tasks as ferrying trips, bomb jettisoning duties over the North Sea and what were known as 'Cook's Tours' of German cities that were once the Squadron's targets. The occasional accident occurred but only one was fatal. This much easier life-style could not continue for long and on the 8th of September 1945, the Squadron left Pocklington for Bassingbourne in Cambridgeshire and started to convert to the Consolidated Liberator VIII four-engined transport. The move from Pocklington must have been both sad and hard and is best summed up in the words of its former Base Commander:

Group Captain Gus Walker

'In September 1945, Pocklington bade a sad farewell to 102. After four years of hard and bitter endeavour, the Squadron had become so much an integral part of the community – the very nerve centre of its little world – that the departure left a gap and a feeling of sadness and loss which provided a fine testimony to the prestige of the Squadron. Despite all the anxious moments suffered by the local people – and there were many such! – the Squadron truly won its way into the hearts of those Yorkshire folk.'

Below and overleaf
One of 102's 'Cook's Tours' to Cologne (Wright)

Another Squadron member has an even greater affection for Pocklington as it was there that he met his wife to be, whom he married on the 21st of July 1945:

102 Squadron was home to many nationalities Flt Sgt L O Lynch (back row second from left) hailed from Jamaica and completed a tour with Flt Lt Dinty Moore (back row fourth from right) and his crew, Summer 1944 (Etherington)

Flight Sergeant Bill 'Ginge' Ollerton

'Perhaps it is a little vain of me to talk about Pocklington because I only lived there for a year. However, it was part of my life and I value with great pride my time with 102 (Ceylon)* Squadron. It was a happy place to be, given the problems sometimes created by the very nature of our duties.

'Two of the aircrew members were talented pianists who were regularly called upon and could perform anything from classical to jazz music. Our Mess Staff usually mixed-in socially with these sing songs and Mess occasions (Lilian Jones later to become Lilian Ollerton was one). Of course, this worked both ways. When the chaps arrived late for breakfast, I don't think anyone was turned away. This pleasant atmosphere prevailed from top to bottom – the RAF at its best.

'My first crew were adopted by a Pocklington family with whom we visited the local dances and the "Cross Keys" pub, always going back for tea or coffee. The welcome was spontaneous just like a home from home – a marvellous family.'

* The addition of the word 'Ceylon' was granted to the Squadron by the Air Ministry following the inhabitants of that Island adopting the Squadron and requesting their savings should be put towards its maintenance. Whitley serial T4260 coded DY-S, lost on operations on the 15th of April 1941, carried the inscription 'Ceylon' on its nose and Ceylonese aircrew flew with the Squadron – Author.

Opposite above
*The only photo of a 102
Sqn Liberator (Thomas)*

Opposite below
*The first 102 Sqn
Reunion. Left to right:
Sqn Ldr A R Middleton
DSO, DFC, Flt Lt Dave
Hewlett and wife, Tom
Wingham and Ron
George (Wingham)*

In October 1945, conversion training started on the new Liberators which were now emblazoned with the Squadron's new code of "EF", the old "DY" code never being used again. Only one accident occurred before the Squadron started participating in the Transport Command Repatriation Scheme flying regularly to such exotic names as Karachi, Cairo, Castel Benito, Mauripur, Habbaniyah and Shaibah. However, it was soon obvious to the Air Ministry that the number of Squadrons in the RAF just couldn't be maintained and shortly after moving to Upwood in Huntingdonshire on the 18th of February 1946, 102 Squadron was renumbered 53 Squadron; logbooks from this time still bear the stamps of '102 Squadron' with the '102' crossed out to read '53'. The frequency of transport flights soon began to decrease and eventually, on the 14th of June 1946, 53/102 Squadron was disbanded.

The Squadron spirit still lived on. A Squadron Association was formed and on the 10th of May 1947, its first Reunion and Dinner Dance was held at the Cafe Royal, the first President being none other than Group Captain Gus Walker. Some at this Reunion might have thought that the Squadron, as an operational flying unit, would never reform or fly again. However, for some unknown reason, 102 Squadron was linked with 49 Squadron (an Avro Lancaster and later Lincoln Squadron which was based at Upwood shortly after 53/102 Squadron's disbandment) from the 1st of February 1949 until the 19th of October 1954. The day after this link ended, 102 (Ceylon) Squadron was reformed a second time.

Flight Lieutenant Ken Lang

'Following a substantial increase in Soviet tactical air power in Eastern Europe, it was decided to increase the offensive capability of the Second Tactical Air Force (2TAF). As an interim measure, pending the introduction of the English Electric Canberra Marks B(I)6 and B(I)8, there was little option but to establish a four-squadron wing with the Canberra Mark B.2. To assist in its strategic effectiveness, the Wing would be based as near as possible to the east/west border at Gütersloh in Germany.

'The reason for selecting 102 Squadron as one of the four seemed to be more of numeric convenience rather than to resurrect its nostalgic past. 102 Squadron was, therefore, one of three consecutively numbered revived Squadrons, the others being 103 and 104 along with 149 Squadron (my old B-29 Washington Squadron) to form Number 551 Wing under the operational control of Headquarters Number 2 Group.'

Ken Lang brought one of the first Canberras, serial WD948, from Binbrook in Lincolnshire to Gütersloh on the 4th of November 1954. WD948 was an ex-101 Squadron Canberra B.2 which had been on 101 Squadron, the RAF's first Canberra Squadron, since June 1951. In June 1954, 101 Squadron started converting to the Canberra B.6 and 102 Squadron was now getting its cast offs!:

Flying Officer David Weir

'When the aircraft did start to arrive, they were a mixed bag of old chuck

One of 102 Sqn's Canberras (Thomas)

outs from UK squadrons who were converting to the Canberra Mark B.6, and a few brand new ones from the factories of A V Roe and Shorts of Belfast (we used to say that you could tell a Shorts Canberra by looking at it – they were the ones with the ship's rivets!). The aircraft disappeared for a week or two while the ground crew took them to pieces and tried to put them together again. However, on the 8th of November 1954, I see from my logbook that the first flight for the new 102 Squadron was accomplished by Sqn Ldr Martin (pilot), Fg Off Bob Latchem and myself as the two navigators. It was an air test and lasted an hour and 20 minutes.'

Air tests and the dreaded Squadron Commander's checks were the order of the day for the first few months of the Squadron's existence and it was not long before the first 102 Squadron Canberra accident occurred:

Flying Officer David Weir

'Following each air test, there was a Flight Commander's check for the new pilots followed by a Navigation Leader's and Bombing Leader's checks for the navigators. On the 19th of November 1954, Plt Off Ken Speer was being checked when the landing gear on his Canberra wouldn't deploy. What is not told is that the leather straps of the navigator's bag (navbag) were used to provide a shoulder harness for the check pilot who in this case was Sqn Ldr Martin. The Canberra B.2 only had a lap strap for the 'jump' seat and this was thought to be inadequate for a wheels up landing by an inexperienced pilot and there was no way that the check pilot could get into the operating pilot's seat! In the event, all went well and the landing was quite smooth – all the Squadron, if not the Station, had turned out to watch so it was just as well. The navbag straps did their job – maybe they were not necessary – but there was no quick release. As Bill Martin

*Opposite
Plt Off Ken Speer's Canberra after its accident, 19 Nov 54 (Speer)*

struggled to free himself when the aircraft came to rest, Ken Speer just obeyed his own order to abandon the aircraft and left by the quickest route. This just happened to involve using the 'Boss' as a footstep on his way out! Definitely not the way to further your Service career!'

By Christmas 1954, the Squadron had settled down and was soon in the routine of bombing practice (visual and radar), continuation training and cross country training flights. Those fortunate to be posted to 102 Squadron soon began to enjoy themselves:

Flying Officer John Bosworth

'Gutersloh at that time was quite a wild place – four Canberra squadrons and a Fighter Reconnaissance Squadron, 79 Squadron, which used to fly around north-west Europe in its Meteor FR.10s and later Swifts at 10 feet above ground level!

'There was very little command and control by modern standards and the situation was further complicated by the fact that the Wing was partially in 2TAF but in some ways was a detached Wing of Bomber Command. The end result was that we more or less did what we liked. The individual squadron commanders, ours was Sqn Ldr W E 'Bill' or 'Pincher' Martin, probably had more power and freedom of action than an Air Officer Commanding would have today! The majority of aircrew were single men living in the Mess and most were straight from the Canberra Operational Conversion Unit at Bassingbourne. To give you some idea, we had a Flt Lt pilot posted to the Squadron that we had to give to 104 Squadron next door because they needed a Flt Lt to be a Flight Commander.'

Flying Officer John How

'We were quite a young Squadron – all Fg Offs except for the Squadron Leader, Flt Lts Ken Lang and Ray Hillary as "A" and "B" Flight Commanders, Flt Lt Tom Davy as the Navigation Leader and Flt Lt Robbie Gammams as the Bombing Leader. Spare time in the crew room was spent studying for promotion exams which we all took en masse and passed!

'Life was quite full – we learned to drive Land Rovers and three-ton trucks with convoy runs to Winterberg in winter (skiing) and the Möhne Dam in summer. Gütersloh town had a very good officer's club and also a hotel where families could come for a short stay – married quarters were lacking and German houses had to be requisitioned. Some officers lived as far out as Bielefeld but eventually married quarters were built but by that time the Squadron had disbanded!'

'If life on the ground was fun – the Squadron maintained its wartime reputation of being a very social and convivial outfit – the same could be said of life in the air:

Flight Lieutenant Ken Lang

'The four Squadrons had settled down to the usual pattern of familiarisation, continuation training, high level cross-country navigation exercises and general handling (simulated radar) bombing practice at the German and UK bombing ranges. These bore little resemblance to the intruder role we expected to fulfil but we nevertheless enjoyed our task and the inter-squadron rivalry soon began to show itself as the chasing of flying hours above the target line. The dropping of 25 pound practice bombs on the Nordhorn Range then followed which were interspersed with Bomber Command exercises with such exotic names as "Kingpin", "Carte Blanche", "Beware" and "Fox Paw". These exercises were mostly at night with the occasional bombing attacks on the UK east coast ranges.

'Some relief came in March 1955 when I was required to take a VIP to Rome and Cyprus. On arrival at the Italian capital we were met by a member of the Ambassadorial staff and escorted to our hotel from where we were collected and taken to a cocktail party at the Embassy. On our return, the VIP asked the driver to divert to an address from where a lady acquaintance was collected. Unfortunately, en-route a small Fiat car

102 Squadron, late 1955 (Weir)

appeared from a side street and drove straight into the side the Ambassador's Rolls. A crowd soon gathered and amidst their shouting, I was asked to quickly remove the lady from the scene into a nearby bistro whilst the incident was sorted out. Later that evening, Tom Davy and I had a meal in a rather smart little Italian restaurant where, sitting a few tables away from us, was the deposed ex-King Farouk.

'Back on earth from our brief spell in higher places, the next day we were in those of a different kind flying to Nicosia. After the VIP had finished his business, we set off back to Gutersloh but on the way, my passenger asked if we could return to Rome. Having cleared it with air traffic control, we found ourselves back in the hotel and spent the next day enjoying some of the sights of that magnificent city. I never did find out what my passenger did!'

Flying Officer David Weir

'A reward for passing stages of the Bomber Command Classification System* was to be sent on a "Lone Ranger" flight. This involved flights to exotic and far flung places – Gibraltar was a favourite, Luqa in Malta another and the Canal Zone airfields less so. They were a welcome break from routine and authority. 102 Squadron's aircraft were frequently in those places. Fg Off Mike Wakeford's crew with Fg Off John Bosworth as navigator and Plt Off Brian Smith as navigator/bomb aimer got the best.

* Crews were considered fully combat ready after the requisite training and rated 'Combat' or 'Combat Star'. The first 'Combat Star' crew on 102 Squadron and, in fact, on Number 551 Wing was Plt Off Brian Trigger's crew whose navigator was Fg Off David Weir and navigator/bomb aimer was Fg Off Bob Latchem – Author.

They went to Nairobi for a few days and became 102's "furthest south". As the Mau Mau rebellion was then at its height, they were issued with side arms and ammunition for this flight and looked very wild western when fully kitted up!'

Although 102 Squadron was lucky not to lose any crews or aircraft during this period of its history, some crews came close to an accident:

Sergeant Dickie Dykes

'No 102 Squadron aircraft were lost in accidents and I can only recall a nose-wheel collapse on landing at Gutersloh which was easily and speedily remedied. Serious damage did result on one or more Canberras owing to the disintegration of the turbo-starter on start up. This was a consequence of the highly stressed single poppet valve sticking in the "open" position.'

Flight Lieutenant Ken Lang

'During the late summer/early winter of 1955/1956, all Germany Canberras were grounded. This was as a result of a failure of the aircraft's tailplane actuator. This unit was operated by a trim switch on the pilot's control column and following several unexplained accidents when the aircraft suddenly dived into the ground for no apparent reason, it was eventually traced to the switch sticking after the pilot had operated it in the nose down attitude. This resulted in the actuator running its full length of nose down travel from which the aircraft could not be recovered. Although 102 was fortunate not to lose an aircraft that way, we were all relieved when the fault had been rectified.'

Other crews did have some 'near misses':

Flying Officer David Weir

'In the Spring of 1955 we were recalled early from a bombing detail at the Nordhorn Range because fog was closing in. Soon, all of north-west Germany was covered in "clag" and as we had been visual bombing at 17,000 feet, we were a bit low on fuel. When we got to Gutersloh, it was under thick fog right down to the deck. I can remember that all the local airfields were as bad if not worse and we didn't have enough fuel to get to any of them anyway! There was no Ground Controlled Approach at Gutersloh and an Instrument Landing System for the RAF hadn't been thought of. We tried BABS, a primitive but quite useful landing aid (navigators interpreted the acronym to read Blind Approach Beacon System) and we also tried a radio assisted descent through cloud (a bit of a misnomer as we were in cloud!). We even tried visual low level circuits – all were failing, although we sometimes saw an approach light or a hangar roof. Desperation was setting in – fuel had nearly gone, just one more try and then it was time to hit the silk and we were not looking forward to that. Then the anti-climax – we saw enough of the runway to land – no question of "Below Limits" – we just landed.

'Fuel seemed to be a particular bug with our crew. Another incident involved a bombing exercise in which we found we were leaking fuel at a rate of about 1,000 gallons per hour when the total tank capacity was 1,750 gallons and we were well out over the North Sea when the problem was

Fg Off Brian Trigger's crew after a bird strike (Weir)

identified. We diverted to Soesterburg in Holland, landing with dry tanks after one hour and 20 minutes. Put like that, it doesn't sound much but at the time it was quite a drama.

'Apart from bird strikes, my only other incident involved dropping six live 1,000 pound bombs. We normally flew bombing exercises with six sand-filled 1,000 pounders. However, this day we had six live ones to drop on the Sandbanks Range. We told them to expect a big bang after we passed over the range and although we didn't see the bombs leave the aircraft, the bombing control showed the bombs gone when in fact they had not. No one told us so we wondered why there was a small reception committee waiting for us when we got back to Gutersloh. It transpired that four of our bombs had "hung up" and were still on board, fused and potentially dangerous. What impressed me was that the armourers had brought the canvas stretcher arrangements they used to catch the 25 pound practice bomb "hang ups" when the bomb doors were opened. I still wonder what they expected to happen if one of the live bombs had dropped or where I would be now!'

The winter of 1955 was a particularly severe one. Attempts to keep flying involved the whole Station clearing snow the best they could. As well as using snow ploughs and shovels, attempts were made to blow or melt the snow using the heat and thrust from the Canberra engines. This was tedious and ineffective and ceased when fuel became in short supply. Added to the grounding of the Canberra fleet with the tailplane actuator problem, the Squadron was not fully operational again until June 1956 when the normal pattern of events continued as before. Flying had now become more exciting with the introduction of day and night low level sorties – these trips were flown at 500 feet and navigated mainly by map, and some times ending with a dive bombing attack on the Nordhorn Ranges. Life was good:

Flying Officer David Weir

'When the Canberras were grounded, we were kept occupied with more cultural visits (cultural visits normally meant trips to the local breweries and beauty spots), short detachments to other units as observers and trips on Army exercises. Living in Germany was pleasant on the Squadron and conditions were good at Gutersloh, although we did seem to have a lot of parades. Local leave was encouraged by the addition of 10 days extra local leave allowance. Most of us got around and about quite a lot and although there were still shortages and rationing in the UK, we were largely free of such problems in 2TAF.'

However, all good things must come to an end:

Flight Lieutenant Ken Lang

'We felt we were at last becoming a more practical element of 2TAF but alas it was soon to change. On the 2nd of June 1956, my first son was born but this joyful event also unhappily coincided with the departure of Sqn

One of 102 Sqn's last duties – the Queen's Birthday Flypast at RAF Marham in July 1956 (Bosworth)

Ldr Bill Martin to be, much to his disgust, Commanding Officer of the Nordhorn Ranges. Around this time, President Nasser of Egypt decided to nationalise the Suez Canal and Number 551 Wing was put on standby. However, we were not required and on the 25th of July 1956, Number 551 Wing was disbanded.'

On the 1st of August 1956, 103 and 104 Squadrons were disbanded with 149 Squadron disbanding on the 31st of the month. Temporary command of 104 Squadron was given to the former Commanding Officer of 104 Squadron, Sqn Ldr Ted Stephenson, but on the 20th of August 1956, Number 102 (Ceylon) Squadron officially ceased to exist as a flying Squadron. Its crews went to form the new 59 Squadron, reformed on the 1st of September 1956 or, as one Squadron member remembered, dispersed to all corners.

Postscript

On the 1st of August 1959, 102 Squadron was reborn for the third and last time. This time the Squadron was not equipped with aircraft nor did it have any aircrew on flying duties. 102 Squadron was reformed as one of the Thor missile squadrons and was based at Full Sutton in Yorkshire, very close to its spiritual home of Pocklington. Sadly, most of this part of the Squadron's history is still surrounded by mystery and even some degree of secrecy and a little under four years after its reformation, the Squadron was disbanded for good.

102 (Ceylon) Squadron still lives on. Following the successful first annual Reunion in 1947, the 102 Squadron Association still flourishes and will probably continue to do so until there are no more Squadron members left. Each year, it holds its Reunion in the Pocklington area and is attended by men and women still proud of their association with 102. Some who attend the Reunion come from as far afield as Australia, Canada and the United States of America, proud to be wearing the 102 Squadron badge on their ties and blazers. Reunions normally last two days, ending with a church service at Barmby Moor and march-past; talk during the two days is always of flying, the Squadron, Pocklington and absent friends.

If you ever visit Barmby Moor Parish Church, be sure to seek out the 102 Squadron Book of Remembrance, dedicated to the 1,027 aircrew and groundcrew, some as young as 19, who gave their lives both in the First and Second World Wars. It is sobering to think that so many young men died so that today, we do not live under a fascist dictatorship. When this figure of over 1,000 deaths is compared to the total Bomber Command death toll of about 55,500 you can probably now realise what all the bomber crews and especially what 102 (Ceylon) Squadron did for us today and the price they had to pay.

With the benefit of hindsight, it is easy to criticise the tactics adopted not only by Bomber Command but also the other Commands. But try to put yourself in the shoes of a 22 year old Whitley or Halifax pilot who was trying to do his job, night after night, pitting his wits not only against the Luftwaffe but even the weather, potential mechanical problems and the gunfire or bombs of his own side. Both he and his crew were trying to bring an end to another pointless and futile war by the only way they knew – it was a means to an end. Many enjoyed not what they were doing to Germany but the flying, the camaraderie and operating as a team. As one former aircrew member says today:

'I really did enjoy ops – that is not a line shoot – I really did. The adrenalin flow was terrific and nothing has matched it since. Civil flying is very tame.'

However, he was one of the lucky ones. What did a Squadron member, irrespective of his role in the aircraft, think as he saw friends die night after night thinking that he could well be the next to die? Hopefully this book has shown that being on 102 (Ceylon) Squadron, or any other Bomber Command squadron for that matter, could be fun but was also deadly serious.

Suicide but Fun? Sqn Ldr John Marshall and crew, Summer 1943 (Kelly)

No 102 (Ceylon) Squadron Bases

17 Aug 17 – Hingham
24 Sep 17 – St André-aux-Bois
28 Sep 17 – Le Hameau
3 Oct 17 – Treizennes
5 Mar 18 – Le Hameau
10 Apr 18 – Surcamps
19 Sep 18 – Famechon
19 Oct 18 – Hurtebise Farm (north of Famechon)
23 Oct 18 – Le Targette
27 Oct 18 – Bévillers
14 Dec 18 – Serney
26 Mar 19 – Lympne (disbanded 3 Jul 19)
1 Oct 35 – Worthy Down
3 Sep 36 – Finningley
7 Jul 37 – Honington
11 Jul 38 – Driffield
18 Apr 40 – Kinloss (detachment)
4 May 40 – Driffield
25 Aug 40 – Leeming
1 Sep 40 – Prestwick
10 Oct 40 – Linton On Ouse
15 Nov 40 – Topcliffe
15 Nov 41 – Dalton
7 Jun 42 – Topcliffe
7 Aug 42 – Pocklington
8 Sep 45 – Bassingbourne
18 Feb 46 – Upwood (disbanded 28 Feb 46)
20 Oct 54 – Gutersloh (disbanded 20 Aug 56)

No 102 (Ceylon) Squadron Commanding Officers

11 Sep 17 – Maj H Wylie
20 Mar 18 – Maj F C Baker
1 Oct 35 – Wg Cdr F O Soden DFC
13 Mar 36 – Sqn Ldr C F Attwood
21 Jan 37 – Wg Cdr L M Isles AFC
14 Jul 38 – Sqn Ldr R R Nash
1 Oct 38 – Sqn Ldr C F Toogood
5 Feb 40 – Wg Cdr E Burton
16 May 40 – Wg Cdr S R Groom (missing in action 21 Nov 40)
1 Jan 41 – Wg Cdr F C Cole (missing in action 8 Apr 41)
21 Apr 41 – Wg Cdr C V Howes
5 Oct 41 – Wg Cdr L W Howard
27 Jan 42 – Wg Cdr S B Bintley AFC (killed in accident 23 Oct 42)
26 Oct 42 – Wg Cdr G W Holden DFC
20 Apr 43 – Wg Cdr H R Coventry (missing in action 13 Jul 43)
15 Jul 43 – Wg Cdr F R C Fowle
21 Sep 43 – Wg Cdr S J Marchbank
14 Jul 44 – Wg Cdr L D Wilson DFC, AFC
14 Jan 45 – Wg Cdr E F E Barnard
27 Mar 45 – Wg Cdr D F Hyland-Smith
20 Oct 54 – Sqn Ldr W E Martin

APPENDIX C

102 (Ceylon) Squadron Air Combat Victories

Date	Captain/Gunner	Type	Details
19–20 May 42	Sgt H E Batchelder	Bf 110	Holland
30–31 May 42	Sgt T O McIlquham	Fw 190	5.10N, 6.20E
5–6 Aug 42	FS F H Schaw	?	Near Münster
28–29 Aug 42	?	single engine	La Panne
6–7 Dec 42	Flt Lt B K Lindsay Sgt R F Lilleywhite Sgt T J McLean	2 Ju 88	Ac damaged in combat W7919/DY-N
20 Dec 42	Sgt R A Grimes Sgt J J McArthur	single engine	W7935/DY-P
14 Feb 43	WO B J Lewis	Ju 88	W7936/DY-C. Over Holland
11 Mar 43	Sgt W A Griffiths	single engine	DT739/DY-P
16–17 Apr 43	Fg Off E S Kelly Sgt D E Cosford	Bf 110	JB782/DY-W. 49.10N, 09.02E, 0022 hrs
29 May 43	Sgt T Syer	Ju 88	W7927/DY-S. Near Aachen
25 Jun 43	Flt Lt H S Hartley	Ju 88	W7920/DY-D
27–28 Aug 43	Flt Lt E S Kelly Sgt T H McCarthy	Bf 110	JD276/DY-Z. 49.41N, 00.59E
31 Aug 43	Wg Cdr S J Marchbank	Me 109	Damaged. DT435/DY-V
6 Sep 43	Flt Lt A Gibson	?	JD469/DY-U
23 Sep 43	Sgt N McPhail	Ju 88	Probable. JD415/DY-W
27 Sep 43	FS R Ellis	Ju 88	HR927/DY-N
27 Sep 43	Flt Lt B G Glover	single engine	2056 hrs
3 Nov 43	Sqn Ldr A E Millson	Ju 88	Damaged 1950 hrs. HX182
11–12 Nov 43	Flt Lt B G Glover	Me 210	Probable 2355 hrs. HX182
19 Nov 43	Flt Lt D H Phillips	Ju 88	Probable 2015 hrs. Destroyed 2006 hrs. JD469/DY-U
19 Feb 44	Flt Lt D W Moore	Me 110	LW331/DY-D
21 Feb 44	Sqn Ldr A E Millson	Ju 88	0335 hrs, LW288/DY-L
23 Jul 44	?	Ju 88	0140 hrs, MZ300/DY-C
24 Jul 44	Flt Lt I Weaver	Ju 88	0220 hrs probable. MZ745/DY-Z

APPENDIX D

102 (Ceylon) Squadron Losses

1917–1918

Date	Ac & Serial	Mission	Crew	Details
6 Oct 17	FE2b A5680	Ops	2/Lt R H Richardson – P – POW 2/Lt C E Carroll – O – POW	Serial possibly A5630
10 Oct 17	FE2b 4967	Ops	Lt D G Powell – P – POW Lt R F Hill – O – POW	Serial possibly 4969
21 Oct 17	FE2b A5678	Ops	Lt E H Kann – P – + 2/Lt H D Barbour – O – +	Shot down behind enemy lines, deaths confirmed by Germans
27 Oct 17	FE2b	Ops	Capt I A J Duff – P – W (Flt Cdr)	
29 Oct 17	FE2b	Ops	2/Lt C L Shaw – W	Wounded in ankle
31 Oct 17	FE2b	Ops	Lt A R Robertson – W	Slightly wounded
7 Nov 17	FE2b A5577	Ops	Capt E E Barnes – P – + (Flt Cdr) Lt E D S Casswell – O – +	
26 Nov 17	FE2b	Bombing Douai	Lt H Hammond MC – P – W Lt H Howard – O – uninj.	Pilot wounded in left arm by MG fire; ac landed by observer behind British lines
2 Feb 18	FE2b B451	Ops	2/Lt B C W Windle – P – POW 2/Lt S G Williams – O – POW	
21 Apr 18	FE2b		2/Lt A Waterworth – P – inj.	
16 May 18	FE2b	Ops	2/Lt S C Mimmack – P – inj. Lt A E G Bailey – O – inj.	Believed crashed on return from ops at Surcamps
26 May 18	FE2b	Night bombing	2/Lt F W Butt – P – died of inj. 2/Lt F N Philips – O – W	
1 Jun 18			Lt N Smith – inj.	
27 Jun 18	FE2b		Lt G E Reynolds – P – died of inj.	
21 Jul 18	FE2b	Bombing Fremicourt	Lt J A Hoogterp – P – E Lt E C Harris – O – E	Hit by fire in radiator and force-landed near Thiepval
24 Aug 18	FE2b	Ops	Lt C StC Stayner – P – W	

8 Sep 18	FE2b	Ops	2/Lt G A Brown – P – W 2/Lt M E Brown – P – W	Suffered engine failure and crashed near Surcamps, 0500 hrs
15 Sep 18	FE2b	Attacking trains near Beauvois	Capt R T Jones DFC – P – W	Pilot hit in in head by MG fire and force-landed near Doullens
	FE2b A5610		Lt C B Naylor – P – POW 2/Lt H Mercer – O – POW	
29 Sep 18	DH9?	Ops	2/Lt H F Shrimpton – P – W	Believed that ac type should read FE2b
4 Oct 18	FE2b	Night ops	2/Lt G L Shephard – P – inj. 2/Lt A Bairstow – O – inj.	
5 Oct 18	FE2b D9920		Lt L J Forrest – P – + 2/Lt E H Canning – O – +	Died of wounds
27 Oct 18	FE2b	Ops	2/Lt C A Grant – P – W	
4 Nov 18	FE2b		Lt A F Corker DFC – P – inj. 2/Lt V Nutter – O – inj.	Accident due to bomb exploding prematurely

1936–1940

Date	Ac & Serial	Mission	Crew	Details
12 Dec 36	Heyford K4864	Returning from Aldergrove	Sgt S Williams & crew uninj.	Crashed due to icing near Gainsborough, Lincs.
	Heyford K6900	Returning from Aldergrove	Sgt V C Otter – P – I Sgt D G Church – 2P – + LAC Clements – Fitter – + AC2 Bodenham – WOp – +	Crashed due to icing near Hebden Bridge
	Heyford K4874	Returning from Aldergrove	Flt Lt C P Villiers – P – crew uninj. Plt Off Tomlin LAC Keyes AC D Mackan	Crashed due to icing near Oldham, Lancs. Crew baled out
	Heyford K6898	Returning from Aldergrove	Plt Off M G W Clifford – inj. Remainder of crew uninj.	Attempted to force-land at Disley, Cheshire; overshot and turned over
16 Dec 37	Heyford K5183	Training	Plt Off T A Bunting – P – crew uninj.	Crashed on landing at Honington
24 Mar 38	Heyford K6860 S	Bombing exercise	Fg Off M G W Clifford – P – crew uninj.	Suffered engine failure at 300 ft after take off, crash-landed 5 miles SW of Evanton, Scotland, hit corn stack, slewed and undercarriage collapsed
17 Nov 38	Whitley K8951	Training	Plt Off J K Cannon – P – crew uninj.	Landing accident, ac damaged
22 Nov 38	Whitley K8946	Training	Sgt G W Harding – P – crew uninj.	Hit obstacle on landing

28 Nov 38	Whitley K8949	Training	Sqn Ldr R R Nash – P – crew uninj.	Landed with wheels up
8 Sep 39	Whitley K8950 DY-M	Pamphlet raid Ruhr area	Sqn Ldr S S Murray – POW AC1 S A Burry – POW WO C A Hill – POW AC1 P F Pacey – POW Plt Off A B Thompson – POW	Shot down by flak and crashed near Itzehoe, Germany
	Whitley K8985 DY-J	Pamphlet raid Ruhr area	Fg Off W C G Cogman – interned Plt Off A W Mack – interned Sgt G J Henry – interned AC1 A Steel – interned Cpl S R Wood – interned	Forced down by *Sous Lt* A Jottard and *Sous Lt* J Offenberg of *le Escadrille, 2eme Regiment d'Aeronautique*, Belgian Air Force at Nivelles airfield, Belgium
15 Oct 39	Whitley K8958	Training	Plt Off R C Bissett – P – crew uninj.	Force-landed 2 miles north of Driffield due to technical trouble, 1505 hrs
16 Oct 39	Whitley K8943	Ferry flight	Sgt R T Langton – uninj. Plt Off A H Hewitt – inj. AC2 D Parr – inj.	Undercarriage collapsed on landing at Aston Down, 1300 hrs
18 Oct 39	Whitley K8996	Move of 41 Sqn	Sgt H J Gaunt – P – + Plt Off R A M Luckman – 2P – + AC2 C Paterson – WOp – + AC1 J B Clark – +	Crashed on take off from Catterick killing Sgt A Vincent, Sgt A H Harris and AC1 H Jones and injuring Sgt D E Gibbs and Cpl W Jenkinson of 41 Sqn
27 Nov 39	Whitley N1377 DY-P	Wilmshaven	Plt Off K N Gray – P –crew uninj. Plt Off F H Long – N LAC F Hollywood – WOp Sgt F J Bass – O AC2 G Main	Hit by lightning and landed at Bircham Newton. Pilot and nav awarded DFC
2 Apr 40	Whitley N1368 DY-K	Low bombing practice	Plt Off K N Gray DFC – crew uninj.	Crashed on landing at Driffield, 2240 hrs
26 Apr 40	Whitley N1383 DY-H	Aalborg	Fg Off O G Horrigan – P – + Sgt V H Barr – P – POW Sgt N Haithwaite – WOp – + AC2 C C Whitley – + Sgt J F Hayes – O – +	Shot down by *ResFlakabt 603* and crashed Store Vildmose, 10 km SW of Bronderslev, Denmark, 0245 hrs
29 Apr 40	Whitley N1241 DY-C	Oslo–Fornebu	Fg Off K H P Murphy – P – POW Sgt C Warner – 2P – POW Sgt J F Graham – O – POW Cpl D Magee – WOp – POW LAC J Elwood – AG – +	Shot down by *I/Flakregt 611* and crashed near Sylling, 27 km west of Oslo
1 May 40	Whitley N1500	Transit Kinloss to Driffield	Plt Off K N Gray DFC – P – + Sgt J H Hopper – P – + AC1 A W H Hart – WOp – + AC1 H Buttery – + AC2 G Main – + (died 25 May 40) AC1 J A Hewitt – inj. AC1 F Wallwork – + (died 6 May 40) Sgt F J Bass – O – +	Flew into Hill of Foudland, 6 miles SE Huntly, Aberdeenshire/Bains Hole, Insch, 1059 hrs

19 May 40	Whitley N1376 DY-O	Gelsen-kirchen	FS E L G Hall – P – POW Plt Off J T Glover – 2P – POW Sgt D L Dick – O – POW LAC J McCutcheon – WOp – POW Sgt A Murray – AG – POW (+20 Nov 40)	Hit by flak over target, crew baled out and ac crashed near Gennep/Venzelderheide, Holland
	Whitley N1417 DY-B	Gelsen-kirchen	Fg Off W C G Cogman – P – E Plt Off L Miller – 2P – POW AC2 E H Bros – WOp – POW Sgt K V Thrift – O – + LAC J R Nicholson – AG – POW	Crashed Milheeze near Deurne, Holland, 2300 hrs. It is believed that Fg Off Cogman evaded and boarded SS *Aboukir* at Zeebrugge. This ship was then torpedoed on 27 May 40 and Fg Off Cogman reported missing
20 May 40	Whitley N1380 DY-R	Ribemont	Flt Lt D W H Owen – P – + Sgt D H J Barrett – O – + Plt Off D F S Holbrook – P – + LAC R J Newberry – WOp – + AC2 M D Dolan – WOp – +	Crashed Hamegicourt, Senercy, 13 km SSE of St Quentin, France, 2330 hrs
22 May 40	Whitley N1528 DY-E	Euskirchen	Plt Off G H Womersley – safe Plt Off R F Beauclair – safe Sgt J Derbyshire – safe AC2 A Sedgley – safe AC1 H F Hurt – safe	Abandoned near Metz, France 0100 hrs
19 June 40	Whitley N1499 DY-M	Bottrop	Sgt S E Masham – P – + Sgt C Hanlon – WOp – + Sgt C M Clayton – 2P – + Sgt D W Dawson – O – + Sgt H A F Giblin – WOp – +	Shot down by flak and crashed near Neunkirchen, Germany (crashed either at 0048 hrs at Moers or 0106 hrs near Dortmund)
6 Jul 40	Whitley N1523 DY-B	Kiel	Plt Off J M Lewis – P – POW Sgt L Askham – POW Sgt J Fisk – POW Sgt S Fieldhouse – POW Plt Off D F M Mackarness – POW	Shot down by flak north of Kiel. Pilot killed by train 18 Aug 43
13 Jul 40	Whitley N1502 DY-E	Emden	Sgt R T Langton – P – crew uninj. Sqn Ldr C S Byram – P Sgt C P Coad Sgt G Gibson Sgt C Wood	Ditched 38 miles east of Cromer, 0425 hrs
27 Jul 40	Whitley N1377 DY-B	Mannheim	Plt Off R F Beauclair – P – POW Plt Off J C W Bushell – POW Sgt E A Galloway – POW Sgt C Wood – POW Sgt K J Reid – POW	Shot down by flak and crashed near Spijkenisse, 15 km SW of Rotterdam, 0030 hrs
15 Aug 40	N1378/DY-Q, N1413/DY-K, N1420/DY-S, P4945/DY-L, P5022/DY-B – all destroyed in air attack on Driffield by *Kampfgeschwader 30*.			
17 Aug 40	Whitley N1385 DY-G	Augsburg	Plt Off M H Rogers – P – + Sgt M W J Pollard – P – + Sgt S G Jermond – O – + Sgt J Patterson – WOp – + Sgt W F Haywood – WOp – +	Shot down by flak and crashed on the Hochlichspitze Mountain, Walser Valley, Voralberg, Austria, 0030 hrs

28 Aug 40	Whitley N1489 DY-C	Cross Country to Isle of Man	Sgt N K Bott – P – + Plt Off A W Fletcher – P – + Sgt C W C F Harrison – + Sgt A Steel – WOp – + Sgt L G Smalley – AG – inj.	Crashed Hayhills Farm, Silsden, 4 miles NNW of Keighley, Yorks, 2307 hrs
7 Oct 40	Whitley P4995 DY-P	Convoy Patrol	Fg Off H M Young – P – crew uninj. Sgt R Collier Plt Off Forsdyke Sgt Burns Sgt Hird	Suffered engine failure and ditched in Atlantic, crew rescued 22 hrs later by HMS *St Mary*
20 Oct 40	Whitley P4933 DY-F	Luenen	Plt Off K T Hannah – P – crew safe Sgt A L Chapman Sgt J A Clemett Sgt G F Almond Sgt G Robson	Became lost in bad weather and suffered radio failure. Crew baled out and a/c crashed at Bullatree Farm, Maltby, 0530 hrs
24 Oct 40	Whitley P5073 DY-D	Berlin	Plt Off A G Davies – P – safe Plt Off T R Murfitt – P – + Sgt I C Scoular – O – + Plt Off T E Lee – AG – + 2 Nov 40 Sgt A S Wilson – WOp – + 2 Nov 40	Shot down taking off from Linton On Ouse by *Fw* Hans Hahn, *3/NJG 2* at 2202 hrs and crashed near Tholthrope, 2210 hrs
26 Oct 40	Whitley T4136 DY-H	Stettin	Plt Off J S G Crawford – P – crew safe Plt Off E R Osborne Sgt W Livesey Sgt G E West Sgt R Adams	Engine failure and crashed Ebberston, 6 miles ESE of Pickering, Yorks, 2348 hrs
28 Oct 40	Whitley P5082 DY-L	Bremen	Flt Lt R A Barnwell – P – M Sgt H E Danks – M Sgt F J Abrahams – M Sgt T H Pegram – M Sgt M Rose – M	Ditched 20 miles east of Aberdeen
6 Nov 40	Whitley T4135 DY-S	Merseburg	Fg Off D U Lowson – P – crew safe Sgt K H Smith Sgt L Hogarth Sgt D A R Tallis Sgt D Whitehead	Airspeed indicator failure and crashed at Linton On Ouse, 2335 hrs
12 Nov 40	Whitley P5005 DY-N	Cologne	Plt Off G L Cheshire – P – uninj. Plt Off D C F Coutts – 2P – uninj. Sgt H Davidson – WOp – W Sgt Roberts – uninj. Plt Off R C Rivaz – uninj.	Damaged by flak and fuselage stripped. Pilot awarded DSO
14 Nov 40	Whitley P5097 DY-Q	Berlin	Sgt J J Gale – P – crew uninj. Plt Off W L Ellingham Sgt W E Hool Sgt D A R Tallis Sgt N R Skinner	Damaged by flak and crew baled out. Ac crashed Kings Lynn, 2215 hrs

	Whitley P4936 DY-M	Berlin	Flt Lt A Z Pengelly – P – POW Sgt J F M Moyle – POW Sgt C P Followes – POW Sgt H Radley – POW Sgt T Michie – POW	Shot down by flak
21 Nov 40	Whitley P5072 DY-P	Duisburg	Fg Off A M L Selby – P – M Wg Cdr S R Groom – P – M Sgt T D Elliott – M Sgt L Hogarth – M Fg Off E D Stevens – M	Lost over North Sea approx. 0634 hrs
24 Nov 40	Whitley P5074 DY-Q	Turin	Sgt D A Rix – P – crew uninj. Plt Off D A Thomas Sgt J Billington Sgt D Axten Sgt D R Mourton	Became lost on return and ran out of fuel. Crew baled out and ac crashed at Elsted, West Sussex, 0405 hrs
	Whitley T4216 DY-F	Turin	Fg Off H M Young – P – crew safe Sgt R G W Bristow Sgt W E Craven Sgt A P Clifford-Read – inj. Plt Off F G Malion – inj.	Ditched 20 miles south of Plymouth, 0445 hrs
	Whitley P5102	Turin	Sgt Pearce and crew uninj.	Force-landed near Brighton after ops
28 Nov 40	Whitley P5077 DY-B	Le Havre	Plt Off E R Osborn – P – M Sgt R Collier – 2P – M Sgt W Livesey – M Sgt G E West Sgt D Rowley – M	Shot down by flak over target and crashed in the Channel
15 Dec 40	Whitley P5012 DY-G	Berlin	Flt Lt K T Hannah – P – M Sgt K G Allardice – M Sgt J A Clemett – M Sgt W F Dennis – WOp – + Sgt A Sedgley – M	Shot down by *Fw* Hans Rasper, *4/NJG 1* off Egmond, Holland, 2323 hrs
16 Dec 40	Whitley T4289 DY-C	Berlin	Sqn Ldr O A Morris – P – crew safe Sgt A L Chapman Plt Off A G Eperon – O Sgt L E D Lindsay Sgt P S Pitt	Ditched off Bridlington, 0410 hrs
21 Dec 40	Whitley T4273 DY-O	Ops	Sgt D A Rix – P – crew uninj. Sgt R A A Doherty Sgt J Billington Sgt D R Mourton Sgt D A R Tallis	Suffered engine failure over North Sea. Returned to base and crash-landed, hitting Whitley P5005/DY-N, 2223 hrs

1941

Date	Ac & Serial	Mission	Crew	Details
2 Jan 41	Whitley T4227 DY-R	Bremen	Fg Off D C F Coutts – P – M Sgt T F Behan – P – M Sgt K H Smith – M Sgt N Stephenson – M Sgt J Kennedy – WOp – M	Shot down by *Ofw* Hans Hahn, *3/NJG 2* 50 km east of Withernsea, 1900 hrs
1 Mar 41	Whitley T4261 DY-S	Cologne	Sqn Ldr C E E Florigny – P – M Sgt A Bush – uninj. Sgt R F Martin – uninj. Sgt W E Hool – uninj. Plt Off R C Rivaz – uninj.	Ditched off Cromer, 2307 hrs
13 Mar 41	Whitley T4140 DY-H	Berlin	Plt Off E G Cubitt – P – + Plt Off F G Malin – P – inj. Sgt R D Davidson Sgt G E A Madgett – inj. Sgt N W Davies – AG – inj.	Returned on one engine and tried to land at Bircham Newton, overshot and crashed at Blackburn Wood, Docking/Courtyard Farm, Ringstead, Norfolk, 0100 hrs
	Whitley T4326 DY-K	Berlin	Sqn Ldr A M Watts-Reed – P – + Flt Lt F H Long DFC – P – + Sgt E H Goodall – WOp – + Sgt V Hallas – WOp – + Sgt W E Van Klaveren – POW	Shot down by flak and crashed Noord-Deuringen, 3 km N of Denekamp, Holland, 0005 hrs. Possibly claimed by *Oblt* Heinrich Wohlers, *St Kap 8/NJG 1*. Sgt Van Klaveren died of diphtheria, Berlin Weisald, 4 May 41
	Whitley T4273 DY-S	Hamburg	Sgt A L R Cook – P – + Sgt A C Elliott – P – + Sgt J M Oxley – O – + Sgt N R Skinner – WOp – + Sgt S H A Jess – WOp – +	Shot down by flak and crashed at Kampstrasse 80–84, Hamburg–Lokstedt
8 Apr 41	Whitley Z6468	Kiel	Wg Cdr F C Cole – P – M Sgt R C Smith – M Sgt A R Martin – M FS W E Craven – M FS J Derbyshire – M	Ditched in sea at 3 deg 48E 50 deg 05N on return, 0152 hrs
15 Apr 41	Whitley T4260 DY-S	Boulogne	Plt Off B A Childs – P – + Sgt J A Norris – P – + Plt Off R J W Williams – O –+ Sgt A P Clifford-Read – WOp – + Sgt R T Selley – WOp – +	Shot down by flak and crashed near Bourthes, Pas de Calais
18 Apr 41	Whitley T4334	Berlin	WO J I Charlton – P – POW Fg Off E G Libbey – P – POW Sgt L Barrows – POW Sgt G A Hartley – POW Sgt J J McCurdy – POW	Shot down by flak and crashed near Berlin, 0125 hrs
9 May 41	Whitley T4146	Ludwigs-hafen	Plt Off J F W Elliot – P – uninj. Sgt C T M Baldwin – uninj. Sgt Bershally – uninj. Sgt F A Braybrook – inj. Sgt H Timlin – inj.	Damaged in crash at North Farthing/Winfarthing, 5 miles N of Diss. Ac repaired

12 Jun 41	Whitley Z6565	Schwerte	Sgt N B Berndsson – P – crew uninj. Plt Off D N Sampson Sgt P S Thompson Sgt C Higson Sgt G W Griffin Sgt H Young	Damaged beyond repair
13 Jun 41	Whitley Z6746 DY-R	Schwerte	Sgt O W Rees – P – uninj. Sgt P Winter – P – wounded Plt Off S J Edwards – uninj. Sgt A E Hartle – uninj. Sgt N C Carter – uninj. FS R P Gowing – uninj.	Took off 2303 hrs. Attacked target from 10,000 ft, one stick, no bursts seen owing to searchlights. Sgt Winter wounded over Dortmund, landed Horsham St Faith 0515 hrs, returned to base 0753 hrs. Ac named 'Revenge'
	Whitley Z6489	Schwerte	Sgt J Chaplin – P – + Sgt J F James – 2P – + Sgt R W Dawson – O – + Sgt K R Winter – WOp – + Sgt J Hall – AG – + Sgt J M B Tunnah – AG – +	Shot down by *Lt* Reinhold Knacke, *2/NJG 1* at 0316 hrs and crashed at Gagelse Akkers, Waalre near Woensel, Holland, 0318 hrs
14 Jun 41	Whitley Z6510	Schwerte	Fg Off S V Alderton – P – + Sgt K Glassborow – P – + Sgt I P Hunter – P – + Sgt C T F Baldwin – O – + Sgt A C Fletcher – WOp – + Sgt J R Fraser – WOp – +	Shot down by flak and crashed in the early hours near Kirchellen, Germany.
27 Jun 41	Whitley T4297	Bremen	WO J M Culley – P – POW Sgt W M Featherstone – P – W, POW WO J N D Bailey – WOp – POW WO B R Wallace – N – POW Sgt B N Booth – AG – POW	Possibly shot down by *Oblt* Helmut Lent, *6/NJG 1* and crashed near Hipstedt, Germany
	Whitley Z6572	Bremen	Sgt D M Philip – P – + Sqn Ldr W C McArthur DFM – P – + FS S S Carlisle – AG – + Sgt W J Clarke – +	Crashed into the sea off the Wesser/Elbe Rivers
	Whitley Z6759	Bremen	Flt Lt R G Poulter – P – POW Sgt G D Jackson – P – M Sgt J Urquhart – WOp – POW WO N J Ranson – POW Sgt E W G Dickey – AG – POW	Crashed in the sea, Sgt Jackson washed off dinghy
28 Jun 41	Whitley T4269	Bremen	Plt Off M N F Jones – P – + Sgt A P Nicholl – P – M Plt Off A Bleakley – + Sgt R D Davidson – + Sgt E G Whitehead – O – + FS A Pratt – +	Crashed early hours near Brunsbüttelkoog, Germany
1 Jul 41	Whitley T4233	Duisburg	Fg Off A L Pullen – P – + Sgt J Bruckshaw – P – + Sgt J C Newlands – WOp – + Sgt F G Coulby – O – + Sgt D Sills – WOp – +	Shot down by *Hptm* Werner Streib, *Gr Kdr I/NJG 1* and crashed at Diergaarde-Echt, Holland, 0119 hrs

Date	Aircraft	Target	Crew	Notes
4 Jul 41	Whitley T4330	Essen	Sgt A Davis – P – crew uninj. Sgt R H Burr Sgt G R Davidson Sgt E M Cooke	Damaged in crash landing at Mill Common, Bacton, Norfolk, 0440 hrs
	Whitley P5014 DY-J	Essen	Sgt D F Gibson – P – + Sgt B A Cotton – P – POW Sgt A Lakin – O – POW Sgt W K H Bowden – WOp – POW Sgt N W Davies – AG – POW	Shot down by *Hptm* Werner Streib, *Gr Kdr I/NJG 1*. Crashed on the east bank of the River Maas at Arcen near Limburg, Holland, 0233 hrs
	Whitley Z6573	Essen	Sqn Ldr O R C Moseley – P – + Sgt H W Fish – P – + Plt Off H H Wells – + Sgt R M Milligan – + Sgt P J W Ennis – M	Shot down by *Oblt* Fritz Radusch, *1/NJG 1* and crashed near Stramproy, south of Weert, Holland, 0117 hrs
15 Jul 41	Whitley Z6748	Bremen	Plt Off B A Q Wynard-Wright – Sgt P C Eyre – uninj. Plt Off N L Shove – inj. Sgt J Garroway – WOp – inj. Sgt P J Jennings – uninj.	Crashed Anthorne near Kirkbright aerodrome, dawn
	Whitley Z6820	Bremen	Flt Lt G G Davies – P – uninj. Plt Off E G M Anderson – P – uninj. Sgt N Stockdale – AG – + Plt Off N J Bennett – N – uninj. Sgt W Swain – WOp – uninj.	Damaged by flak, 0217 hrs. Pilot awarded DSO.
23 Jul 41	Whitley Z6821	La Pallice	Plt Off D B Delaney – P – crew uninj. Sgt S E H Morgan Sgt K Harwood-Smith Sgt F A Braybrook Sgt A F Jaggers Sgt R K Craig	Crashed in forced-landing at base
26 Jul 41	Whitley Z6866	Hannover	Sgt H G Benfield – P – POW Plt Off I P B Denton – POW Sgt K S Carter – POW Sgt W R Gibson – WOp – POW Sgt R V Harnett – POW	Hit by flak and crashed at Maurik, Holland, 0235 hrs. Possibly claimed by *Ofw* Reinhard Kollak, *1/NJG 1*?
	Whitley Z6576	Hannover	Sqn Ldr E A Verdon-Roe – P – M Plt Off W L Rees – P – M Sgt A R Holmes – O – M Sgt W A McGinley – WOp – M Sgt L Nethercliff – AG – M	Shot down by *Oblt* Egmond Prinz zur Lippe Weissenfeld, *4/NJG 1* and crashed 10 km west of De Kooy, Holland, 0323 hrs
15 Aug 41	Whitley Z6746	Hannover	Sgt J Reid – P – crew uninj. Sgt G F Hoben – P Plt Off S R Whipple – O Sgt R C Perriam Sgt J Griffiths	Crashed on landing hrs at Topcliffe, 0510 hrs
	Whitley Z6829	Hannover	Sgt G K Powell – P – + Sgt F W Penn – P – POW Plt Off W W Bell-Towers – O – + Sgt L E D Lindsay – WOp – + Sgt R T Philp – WOp/AG – + Sgt T A Vermiglio – AG – POW	Shot down by *Ofw* Paul Gildner, *4/NJG 1* 8 km WSW of Terschelling and crashed into the Waddenzee, 0448 hrs

	Whitley Z6842	Hannover	Plt Off D N Sampson P – POW Sgt J D Hamilton – 2P – POW Sgt K G Lewis – AG – POW Sgt E Alderton – O – POW Sgt N W J Scott – WOp/AG – POW	Shot down by *Oblt* Ludwig Becker, *4/NJG 1* and crashed at Oudedijk, Terwispel, 10 km SSW of Drachten, Holland, 0106–0117 hrs
	Whitley Z6877 DY-O	Hannover	Sgt A W Hawkes – P – POW Plt Off G W Cole – 2P – POW Sgt K P Marlow – O – POW Sgt A Nicholas – WOp – POW Sgt D E J Hampson – AG – +	Possibly shot down by *Uffz* Benning, *I/NJG 3* who claimed a Wellington at 0136 hrs near Soegel, Germany, 0145 hrs
21 Aug 41	Whitley Z6862	Nonop	Sgt I C Hay – P – + Sgt N G Williams – P – + Plt Off P B Detlor – O – + Sgt D J M Bush – WOp – + Sgt C S Neveu – AG – inj.	Stalled on take off and crashed at Topcliffe, 1450 hrs
29 Aug 41	Whitley Z6863	Frankfurt	Sqn Ldr J O Lalor – P – + Sgt H J W Newnes – P – + Sgt M R Bowes – O – + Sgt F Potts – WOp – POW Sgt R C Watchorn – AG – POW	Shot down by flak SW of Koblenz; ac crashed near Macken, Germany
30 Aug 41	Whitley Z6951	Frankfurt	Sgt P E Carreau – P – + Sgt A E Masters – P – + Sgt W V Atkinson – O – + Sgt F G Kuebler – WOp – inj. Sgt C Higson – AG – inj.	Stalled and crashed at Docking, Norfolk, 0500 hrs
31 Aug 41	Whitley Z6868	Essen	Plt Off B B P Roy – P – crew safe Sgt L W Carr Sgt P L N Trehearn Sgt P A Taylor Sgt R Gayler	Ac blew up damaging Z6871 (Plt Off D B Delany), killing AC1 K M Ward
1 Sep 41	Whitley Z6837	Essen	Plt Off E G M Anderson – P – + Sgt T H Wood – P – + Sgt T C Boyle – O – + Sgt M Humphrey – WOp – + Sgt N C Carter – WOp – +	Shot down by nightfighter and crashed in early hours near Schaffen, Diest, Belgium
3 Sep 41	Whitley Z6946	Frankfurt	FS S T Modeland – P – + Sgt D M Bozer – P – + Plt Off J C Nixon – + Sgt A F Jaggers – WOp – + Sgt L M Bowen – +	Crashed at Kirton, Suffolk, 0335 hrs
7 Sep 41	Whitley Z6970 DY-R	Hüls	Sgt P C Eyre – P – + Sgt L H Stock – P – + Sgt K P Withyman – WOp – + Sgt T McGill – AG – +	Shot down by *Ofw* Willi Schmale, *III/NJG 1* and crashed at Sambeek, Holland, 0107 hrs. Claims by *Uffz* Gerhard Scheibe, *I/NJG 1* 0105 hrs and *Oblt* Helmut Lent, *4/NJG 1*, 0125 hrs

7 Sep 41	Whitley Z6574 DY-B	Hüls	Plt Off J R Croucher – P – M Sgt J R Tugman – P – M Sgt H L B Morphett – M Sgt A L Halsey – M FS J Glover – M	Ditched in North Sea 60 miles NE of Bircham Newton, 0137 hrs
9 Sep 41	Whitley Z6935	Kassel	Sgt E P Pike – P – uninj. Sgt J Glover – P – uninj. Plt Off S R Whipple – N – uninj. Sgt T Rodgers – WOp/AG – uninj. Sgt F Wrigley – WOp – +	Damaged in combat and landed at Waterbeach
11 Sep 41	Whitley Z6870	Night flying	Sqn Ldr J D Reardon DFC – P – + Sgt H E Moore – 2P – + Sgt J W R Griffiths – WOp – + Sgt A G Frampton – AG – uninj.	Stalled and crashed at Topcliffe 2250 hrs
30 Sep 41	Whitley Z6935	Stettin	Sgt E P Pike – P – crew uninj. Sgt W J Weller – P Sgt D L Boyd – N Sgt S H Jackson – WOp/AG Sgt I S Lloyd Sgt W M DeMille	Believed damaged beyond repair in combat and SOC
	Whitley Z6871 DY-A	Stettin	Plt Off D E Delany – P – uninj. Sgt D K Kibbe – P – + Sgt P L N Trehearn – uninj. Sgt C Miller – WOp – inj. Sgt R Gayler – inj. Sgt C Carr – uninj.	Crash-landed at Danby Beacon, 6 miles SW Leaholme
	Whitley Z6949	Stettin	Plt Off L B Reynolds – P – crew uninj. Sgt J R McMacklin – 2P Sgt J D Charrot – O Sgt G E Thompson – WOp Sgt S E Sumpton – WOp Sgt P J Hay – AG	Crashed and burned at Upper Heyford, 0515 hrs
13 Oct 41	Whitley Z6761	Nürnberg	Sgt J W Stell – P – crew uninj. Sgt J M Wilson Sgt D C Wilson Sgt C Miller Sgt D T McIlquham – AG	Ran out of fuel and crash-landed Market Deeping, Norfolk, 01513 hrs
1 Nov 41	Whitley Z6749	Hamburg	Plt Off V M Albrecht – P – M Sgt J Glover – P – M Sgt J C Brooks – O – M Sgt P A Champion – WOp – M Sgt D C Duguid – AG – M	Probably shot down by *Uffz* Heinz Grimm, *5/NJG 2* and crashed off Dutch coast
7 Nov 41	Whitley Z9219	Boulogne	Plt Off S J B Hamilton – P – crew uninj. Sgt H Malkin – P Sgt C E Sorsdahl Sgt D Cramp Sgt D T McIlquham	Crashed on take off from Topcliffe

8 Nov 41	Whitley Z9128	Berlin	Sgt T H Thorley – P – M Plt Off J C A Allchin – P – M Sgt V L Brown – O – M Sgt J A Steeves – WOp – M Sgt W C Clarke – AG – M	Ditched in North Sea on return leg, 0700 hrs
	Whitley Z6796	Berlin	Sgt R O Bryant – P – M Sgt R C Matthews – P – M Sgt E M Leftley – O – M Sgt R Brown – WOp – M Sgt W Miller – AG – M	Missing – last heard 0726 hrs
	Whitley Z6820 DY-A	Berlin	Sgt D R Pritchard – P – M Plt Off B B P Roy – P – M Sgt K Harwood-Smith – O – M Sgt S Thomson – WOp – M Sgt P H Stanton – AG – M	Missing; SOS heard 0743 hrs
	Whitley Z9212	Essen	Sgt G W McDonald – P – + Plt Off T H Taylor – P – POW Sgt A L Lord – O – POW Sgt T Rodgers – WOp – + Sgt I Stein – AG – +	Crashed near Cologne. Possibly shot down by *Lt* (Harro) Carstens, *III/NJG 1* at 2039 hrs near Wassenberg, Germany
30 Nov 41	Whitley Z6800 DY-L	Hamburg	Sqn Ldr J G Walker – P – + Sgt C T R Anderson – P – + Sgt J A Groom – O – + Sgt P A Taylor – WOp – + Sgt J Williamson – AG – POW	Hit by flak and crashed near Kiel
	Whitley Z9281	Hamburg	Sgt D Pike – P – crew uninj. Sgt J B Robinson – P Sgt G H Marks Sgt D C Grieve Sgt G Williams	Became lost and eventually ran out of fuel; crew baled out and ac crashed Springholm, 11 miles WSW of Dumfries
16 Dec 41	Whitley Z6973	Dunkirk	Sgt W G Caldwell – P – M Sgt D G Jack – P – M Sgt F E Baldock – O – M Sgt G E Thompson – WOp – M Sgt W A Evans – AG – M	Shot down by flak and crashed in the Channel

1942

Date	Ac & Serial	Mission	Crew	Details
6 Jan 42	Whitley Z9289	Cherbourg	Sgt A Hollingworth – P – + Sgt J T C Hazeldine – P – uninj. Sgt E A Brain – uninj. Sgt A G Buchanan – WOp – + Sgt L Jackson – AG – inj.	Suffered engine failure and when engine restarted, starboard engine caught fire. Crashed in quarry to the to the rear of Cresswell Street, Pogmoor, Barnsley, 1015 hrs
26 Jan 42	Whitley Z9283 DY-F	Emden	Sgt J D White – P – M Sgt J T C Hazeldine – P – M Sgt P May – O – M FS R K Craig – WOp – M Sgt J G Wilson – AG – M	Shot down either by *Oblt* Rudolf Schoenert, *St Kap* of 5/*NJG 2* or *Ofw* Heinz Struening, 7/*NJG 2* and crashed off Dutch coast

14 Apr 42	Halifax R9488	Non-op	Flt Lt H M Williams – P – + Flt Lt H N Ross – AG – + Sgt K H Sutton – AG – + Sgt N Grimoldby – E – + LAC J Livesey – + Sgt J K Morris – P – + Sgt K O'Connelley – WOp – + Sgt P L N Trehearn – O – +	Stalled and crashed at Baldersby, NE of Ripon, 1246 hrs
27 Apr 42	Halifax R9528	Dunkirk Docks	Sgt J W Barber – P – + Sgt F A Barker – P – E Sgt G W Butterworth – O – + Sgt W Nicoll – WOp – + Sgt G V Long – WOp – POW Sgt A R Evans – AG – E Sgt T E Johnson – E – E	Hit by flak and crashed at Dunkirk
28 Apr 42	Halifax W7653 DY-M	Cologne	FS L W Carr – P – E Sgt T W Ralston – P – POW Sgt R B Shoebridge – N –POW Sgt J Garroway – WOp – + Sgt I Edwards – WOp – + Sgt G H Lee – AG – POW Sgt T K Robinson – E – +	Shot down by *Oblt* Reinhold Eckardt, *St Kap, 7/NJG 7* near St Trond. Crashed at Hamois near Namur, Belgium, 0030 hrs
11 May 42	Halifax V9982	Conversion	Sqn Ldr P B Robinson – P – uninj. FS J F W Towse – P – inj. FS C C Harris – P – inj.	Crash-landed at Pick Hill, Northallerton, 1630 hrs
20 May 42	Halifax W7677 DY-O	Mannheim	Sgt H E Batchelder – P – crew uninj. Sgt J B Robinson – 2P Sgt G Hobsbawn – N Sgt F L Ringham – WOp Sgt T H May – B Sgt R H Rivers – AG Sgt F Bell – E FS F G Kuebler – 2WOp	Damaged by Bf 110 over Dutch coast, 0400 hrs; landed at Horsham St Faith, 0455 hrs. Pilot awarded DFM 16 Jun 42
	Halifax W1099 DY-A	Nickel-Vichy	FS C R Barr – P – crew uninj. FS D Conter – O Sgt R C Perriam – WOp Sgt E H Williams Sgt J G S Rocks – AG Sgt W Brown – E	Engine overheated and crash-landed at Cottesmore, 0025 hrs
2 Jun 42	Halifax R9532 DY-H?	Essen	Sgt E G Newell – P – + Plt Off T M Carter – P – + Sgt D C Grieve – WOp – + Sgt G M Selwyn – WOp – + Sgt J B Teesdale-Smith – AG – + Sgt C R Rowlinson – E – +	Crashed in early hours near Düsseldorf
	Halifax R9532 DY-D	Essen	FS B J Trelorar – P – crew uninj. Sgt D B Patterson – O Sgt L Williams – WOp Sgt J K Baker – AG Sgt A G Frampton – AG Sgt J Powell – E	Severely damaged by flak; control lost on final approach to Dalton and crashed, breaking its back

3 Jun 42	Halifax R9491 DY-N	Essen	FS F A Holmes – P – M FS G H H Marks – O – M FS F Booth – AG – M Sgt G F Jenkins – AG – M Sgt D Boddy – AG – + Sgt W L Crowther – E – M Sgt S Arnett – WOp – M	Ditched off Suffolk coast, 0257 hrs
5 Jun 42	Halifax R9408 DY-L	Essen	Sgt F Williamson – P – uninj. Sgt R Laughton – uninj. Sgt N W Haycock – AG – POW Plt Off D McRae – uninj. FS A W Saunders – uninj. Sgt D R Beale – uninj. Sgt E R Smith – uninj.	Ac hit by flak and control lost; pilot ordered crew to bale out but only AG succeeded before control was regained and order cancelled; ac landed 0340 hrs
17 Jun 42	Halifax W7652 DY-P	Essen	Sgt H E Batchelder DFM – P – POW Sgt R H Rivers – AG – W, POW Sgt G R D Hobsbawn – O – POW Sgt F Bell – E – POW Sgt F L Ringham – WOp – POW Sgt D M McCrae – N – POW	Shot down by flak over target, crashed at Hamminkeln, Germany, 0240 hrs
	Halifax W7651 DY-M	Essen	WO W R Davies – P – + Plt Off E F Lloyd – N – M Plt Off J E Sumpton – WOp – M FS F G Peebles – 2P – + Sgt I Duncan – B – M Sgt D Hanlon – E – + Sgt E Jackson – AG – + Sgt H Smith – AG – +	Shot down by *Oblt* Wilhelm Dormann, *3/.NJG 1*, 8 km SW of Hardenberg, crashed at Rosenburg (Radewijk), Holland, 0300 hrs
	Halifax R9530 DY-J	Essen	WO C R Barr – P – + FS D Conter – O – M Sgt J W Brown – E – + Sgt R C Perriam – WOp – M Sgt J G S Rocks – AG – M Sgt D McN Smith – AG – M	Shot down into the North Sea 60 km west of Walcheren by *Hptm* Herbert Boensch, *E/.NJG 2*, 0225 hrs
25 Jun 42	Halifax R9446 DY-F	Bremen	FS S E H Morgan – P – M Plt Off P J N Robinson – O – + Sgt J A Fraser – WOp – M Sgt R H Brett – AG – M Sgt D G Williamson – AG – M Sgt J J Southern – E – +	Crashed into sea
	Halifax V9987 DY-U	Bremen	FS F F Duff – P – + Sgt J R Shellard – O – POW Sgt A Hartley – WOp – POW Sgt G A Losh – E – POW Sgt W Weightman – AG – +	Crashed near Soltau. Sgt Losh killed in RAF air attack at Gresse/ Mecklenberg, 19 Apr 45
26 Jun 42	Halifax W7759 DY-L	Bremen	FS C C Harris – P – M Sgt V J F Bicat – O – M Sgt T H May – WOp – M Sgt J B Smith – AG – M Sgt J P Hankins – AG – M Sgt G C Pratt – E – M	Crashed into the North Sea in the early hours

	Halifax W7654 DY-Q	Bremen	Flt Lt K B Wright – P – M WO R F Bradbury – O – M Sgt L Starbuck – WOp – + Sgt P J Fernie – AG – M Sgt E R Taxiera de Mattos – AG – M FS I G I Lewis – E – M	Presumed crashed at sea in the early hours
27 Jun 42	Halifax W1153 DY-H	Bremen	Plt Off B V Hunter – P – crew uninj. FS C E Sorsdahl – N Sgt Jennings – WOp Sgt R W Kinsey – E Sgt D Hubbard – AG Sgt Stanton – AG Sgt Wood – B	Pilot was blinded by searchlight on return leg, starboard wing hit the sea, ripping off outer propeller and half of inner propeller
9 Jul 42	Halifax W1107 DY-D	Wihelms-haven	FS B J Treolar – P – POW FS D B Patterson – O – POW Sgt L Williams – WOp – POW Sgt A G Frampton – WOp – POW Sgt A G Parrott – AG – M Sgt J Powell – E – POW	Shot down by *Oblt* Rudolf Sigmund, *Gr Adj II/NJG 2* and crashed at Lauwerssea, NW of Westpolder, Holland, 0145 hrs
11 Jul 42	Halifax R9419	Dual instruction	Fg Off W Welsh – P – uninj. Sgt R Matthews – P – inj.	Attempted to force-land on a racecourse near Topcliffe, 1620 hrs
23 Jul 42	Halifax W7752 DY-R	Duisburg	Plt Off B G H Smith – P – crew uninj. Sgt R Moore – O Sgt S H Jackson – WOp Sgt G F Fargher – AG FS J B McCormack – AG Sgt D R W Schofield – AG Sgt K Marshall – E	Force-landed at Honington due to engine failure, 0430 hrs
26 Jul 42	Halifax W1153 DY-H	Hamburg	Plt Off B V Hunter – P – POW Sgt N A Penstone – O – + Sgt W H Golding – WOp – POW Sgt J Fryett – WOp – POW Sgt J K Baker – AG – + Sgt W E Mander – AG – + Sgt R W Kinsey – E – POW	Hit by flak and dirched 8 km off German coast
	Halifax W1142 DY-A	Hamburg	Sgt J M MacD Wilson – P – POW Plt Off W H Baber – O – + Sgt G M Jones – WOp – + Sgt J B Downes – AG – POW Sgt J W Vine – AG – POW Sgt W G Wilcox – AG – POW Sgt J S Higgin – E – POW	Shot down off German coast
30 Jul 42	Halifax R9442 DY-R	Saar-brücken	FS R F Stone – P – + FS Kirkwood – O – + Sgt E H Williams – WOp – + Sgt B Carroll – AG – + Sgt V H Twining – AG – + Sgt M A Barrett – E – +	Shot down by *Oblt* Reinhold Eckardt, *St Kap 7/NJG 3* and crashed at Corbais, 35 km SE Brussels, 0300 hrs

5 Aug 42	Halifax R9495 DY-L	Bochum	FS R S Tadman – P – + Sgt F A Frost – O – + Sgt A S C Ellis – AG – + Sgt N C Hain – WOp – + Sgt S R Lupton – AG – + Sgt J Colville – E – + Sgt W G McKinnen – AG – +	Crashed St Oedenrode, Holland. Possibly shot down by *Lt* August Geiger, *9/NJG 1*, 0135 hrs on 6 Aug 42
6 Aug 42	Halifax W7706 DY-O	Bochum	FS F H Schaw – crew uninj. Sgt S J E Lunn Sgt L C Fantini Sgt H Johnson Sgt L H Cailes Sgt R Levente Sgt A Huddlestone	Crash-landed West Raynham after nightfighter attack, 0430 hrs
9 Aug 42	Halifax BB211 DY-A	Osnabrück	Plt Off D B McLeod – P – POW Plt Off A D L Lamont – O – POW Sgt J F Long – WOp – POW Sgt D B Richards – AG – POW Plt Off M L McCarthy – AG – + Sgt R V Willshire – E – + Sgt H C Jones – AG – POW	Hit by flak and crashed at Emsbueren/Elbergen, 8 km south of Lingen, Germany
18 Aug 42	Halifax BB197	Training	FS J F W Towse – P – crew uninj.	Swung off runway at Pocklington and undercarriage collapsed, 0020 hrs
22 Aug 42	Halifax W1238 DY-H	Gee training	Sgt I L Berry – P – crew uninj. Plt Off J M Colquhoun – N WO C E Sorsdahl – N Sgt S Cooper – N Sgt D Hubbard – WOp Sgt W E Pattison – E Sgt R J Horton – AG Plt Off Lace – pax	Suffered engine failure and crash-landed at Gellyeadwgan, Llanfaredd, Radnor, 1805 hrs
29 Aug 42	Halifax W7712 DY-S	Saar-brücken	WO F A Schaw – P – uninj. Sgt W Storey – AG – fatally wounded Sgt R Levente – W Sgt T Metcalfe – O – uninj. FS J Reynolds – uninj. FS A W Summers – uninj. Sgt E R Smith – uninj.	Damaged by flak near Ostend, crash-landed Honington, 0111 hrs
2 Sep 42	Halifax W1248 DY-O	Saar-brücken	Plt Off H K Stinson – P – crew safe Sgt G G McIntyre Sgt C G Brazier Sgt A Hodson Sgt W A McMullan Sgt A W Bailey Sgt F Tooth	Crashed near Low Catton short of fuel, 0535 hrs

9 Sep 42	Halifax W7677 DY-Q	Frankfurt	Sgt F H J Farrell – P – + Sgt J G Phillips – N – + Sgt O K Barclay – WOp – + Sgt E T Heap – AG – E Sgt J L Griffiths – AG – E Sgt F Whitfield – E – POW Sgt K R Wright – B – POW	Hit by flak outbound 0036 hrs and crashed at Rambrouch, Luxembourg, 0100 hrs
	Halifax R9449 DY-T	Frankfurt	Sgt J B Robinson – P – crew uninj. Sgt L W Lofthouse Sgt R Laughton Sgt L C Fantini Sgt H Johnson FS C M Bowring Sgt E K Holmes Fg Off P Sniddy	Port engine failed to reduce revs, ac bounced over air traffic control and hit Halifax W1239/DY-G, Pocklington, 0347 hrs
10 Sep 42	Halifax W7752 DY-R	Düsseldorf	Plt Off B G H Smith – P – + Plt Off P A V England – P – + Sgt R Moore – O – + Sgt S H Jackson – WOp – + Sgt G F Fargher – AG – + FS J B McCormack – AG – M Sgt K Marshall – E – + Sgt D R W Schofield – AG – M	Hit by flak and crashed off Walcheren, 0250 hrs
14 Sep 42	Halifax W1271 DY-C	Bremen	Sgt T P Thirsk – P – uninj. Plt Off W R Plummer – O – W Sgt D Knight – E – W FS G H Rowe – WOp – W (+ 20 Sep 42) Sgt A M Long – uninj. Sgt A T Tuck – uninj. Sgt J F Ray – uninj.	Crash-landed Coltishall, 0410 hrs
	Halifax R9531 DY-R	Bremen	Sgt J L Hartshorn – P – crew safe FS J A T Simpson Sgt A M Conner – WOp Sgt R A Grimes Sgt J W Forland Sgt K White Sgt A Huddlestone	Crash-landed West Raynham
24 Sep 42	Halifax DT517 DY-G	Flensburg	Fg Off L G Mee – P – + Sgt D J Wood – 2P – + Sgt W Johnstone – O – + Sgt W H Davidson – WOp – + Sgt F A Youmans – AG – + Sgt L Jackson – AG – + Sgt J C Coulthard – E – + Sgt J T Spirit – AG – +	Crashed in North Sea in early hours
	Halifax W1055 DY-F	Flensburg	Sgt R C E Bassom – P – + Sgt S Cooper – O – M FS W D Reynolds – WOp – + Sgt A G Sherrard-Smith – AG – + Sgt C Stainton – AG – + Sgt J Bennett – E – M Sgt R J Gould – WOp – M	Crashed in North Sea

1 Oct 42	Halifax W7858	Flensburg	Sgt R Mathews – P – + Sgt S G E Dunn – N – M Sgt R J Peters – WOp – M Sgt G H Sadler – AG – M Sgt T H Parker – AG – M Sgt D H Tarver – E – M Sgt D S Benner – 2P – M	Crashed in North Sea
	Halifax W1066 DY-H	Flensburg	Sgt P C Cato – P – + Sgt C A McIntyre – O – + Sgt F J Robinson – WOp – + Sgt R L Millbank – AG – + Plt Off A I McGillivray – AG – + Sgt A I James – E – + Sgt F Tooth – O – +	Crashed near Kiel
5 Oct 42	Halifax W7746	Aachen	Plt Off R E Williams – P – + Sgt J Thorpe – N – + Plt Off L F McRae – WOp – + Sgt R Morgan – AG – + Sgt T E O'Connell – AG – + Sgt J N Bourne – E – + Sgt F R Scott – WOp – +	Crashed near Brussels
	Halifax W7824	Aachen	WO F A Schaw – P – + Sgt G McGowan – 2P – POW Sgt T Metcalfe – O – POW Sgt D K Meagher – AG – POW Plt Off G R Harsh – O – POW Sgt L H Cailes – AG – POW Sgt R Levente – POW Sgt P T Regester – O – POW	Crashed near Cologne
13 Oct 42	Halifax W1167 DY-J	Kiel	FS J L Hartshorn – P – crew uninj. FS J A T Simpson Sgt A M Conner – WOp Sgt L Neill FS C W Forland Sgt K White FS J B Bell	Caught fire and crash-landed at Pocklington, 1945 hrs
18 Oct 42	Halifax L9510	Training	Sgt P A J Grant – uninj.	Crash-landed Pocklington 1100 hrs after top escape hatch blew out on approach, ac then swung off runway and undercarriage collapsed
24 Oct 42	Halifax DT512 DY-Q	Genoa	Wg Cdr S B Bintley – P – + Fg Off A J Graham – WOp – + Gp Capt E J Corbally – uninj. FS J A T Simpson – uninj. Sgt R R Long – uninj. Fg Off V B Davies – uninj. Sgt K White – uninj. FS G Richmond – uninj.	Hit by W1181/DY-D (FS I L Berry) at Holme on Spalding Moor, 0345 hrs
30 Oct 42	Halifax DT518	Training	Sgt C J Ketchell – P – crew uninj.	Swung on take off and undercarriage collapsed

2 Nov 42	Halifax L9565	Training	Sgt S W Templar – P – crew uninj.	Undercarriage collapsed on landing, 2120 hrs
3 Nov 42	Halifax L9584	Training	Sgt P A J Grant – P – crew uninj.	Undercarriage collapsed on landing, 1905 hrs
9 Nov 42	Halifax DT539 DY-A	Hamburg	Sgt D T Marler – P – + Sgt J H Zealand – N – + Sgt M K Callan – WOp – + Sgt S Broome – AG – + Sgt W A Moir – AG – + Sgt P Richardson – E – + Sgt E H Kingsland – O – + FS F W Read – 2P – +	Hit by flak and crashed on the seadike at Oosterend, Holland
	Halifax W7864 DY-F	Hamburg	Sgt G A Neville – P – M Sgt T E Dunlop – O – M Sgt N Sidorchuck – WOp – M Sgt M V Riddle – AG – M Sgt C C Brook – AG – M Sgt F W Hope – E – M Sgt J K Player – O – M FS T R N Featherstone – 2P – M	Possibly shot down by *Hptm* Helmut Lent, *Gruppen Kommandeur IV/NJG 1*, 40 km west of Wijk Aan Zee, 2242 hrs
22 Nov 42	Halifax W7194 DY-A	Stuttgart	Plt Off G B H King – P – + Plt Off T H Follett – N – + Sgt H Clarkson – WOp – + Sgt F R Thompson – AG – + Sgt D P Johnson – AG – + Sgt H T Cheetham – E – + Sgt J Nicholson – B – +	Crashed Hangest Sur Somme
3 Dec 42	Halifax W7916 DY-L	Frankfurt	Sqn Ldr J G G Walkington – P – + Plt Off A R Haines – N – E FS L C Fantini – WOp – POW Sgt H Johnson – AG – POW Sgt L C Molloy – AG – + Sgt J Law – E – + Sgt R C A Douglas – B – POW Wg Cdr J R A Embling – 2P – E	Shot down by nightfighter and crashed near Couvron et Aumer, Aisne, France, 0615 hrs. Wg Cdr Embling was OC 77 Sqn (designate) and awarded DFC
	Halifax W7913 DY-C	Frankfurt	Sgt H Morrisy DFM – P – + Sgt R F H Kenyon – P – + Plt Off D E Pike – P – + Sgt G A Robson – WOp – + Sgt J W Taylor – AG – + Sgt T McCallum – AG – + Sgt J M B Albrecht – E – + Sgt E L R Brown – O – +	Crashed in the early hours between Resteigne and Grupont, south of Rochefort, Belgium
	Halifax W7884 DY-H	Frankfurt	Sgt H A E Charman – P – POW Plt Off D W McKim – N – POW Sgt G E Nutter – WOp – W, POW Sgt C J Pope – AG – + Sgt T I M Edwards – AG – + Sgt E N Neilson – E – W, POW Sgt F S May – B – POW	Shot down by *Lt* Heinz Martin Hadeball, *8/NJG 4* at 0425 hrs and crashed at Laumersheim, Germany, 0430 hrs

6 Dec 42	Halifax W7911 DY-B	Mannheim	Sgt P A J Grant – P	Crashed near Abbeville, France
			Sgt S Brownhill – N – +	
			Sgt J McCartney – WOp – +	
			Sgt F J Eden – AG – +	
			Sgt W Jackson – AG – +	
			Sgt D C Langford – E – +	
			Sgt J G Clements – B – +	
	Halifax W7924 DY-E	Mannheim	Sgt F D Buchwalter – P – M	Crashed near Friedrichshafen, Germany
			Sgt H Jones – N – M	
			Sgt C R Pendelpho – WOp – M	
			Sgt W E Hawke – AG – M	
			Sgt J T Pinkney – AG – M	
			Sgt D M Sannholm – E – +	
			FS C Carr – B – M	
	Halifax W7919 DY-N	Mannheim	Flt Lt B K Lindsay and crew uninj.	Damaged in combat with a Ju88
8 Dec 42	Halifax W7925 DY-S	Gardening	Sgt C J Ketchell – P – M	Believed crashed in North Sea
			Sgt G C Haig – N – M	
			Sgt W C Parry – WOp – M	
			Sgt W N Hopwood – AG – +	
			Sgt F E A Box – AG – +	
			Sgt C G Adnams – E – M	
			Sgt C A Massey – B – M	
11 Dec 42	Halifax W7915 DY-J	Turin	Fg Off N S Milnes – P – crew uninj.	Crash-landed at Bradwell Bay and hit nissen hut. Pilot awarded DFC, nav DFM
			FS A M McDonald – N	
			Sgt W R Laws	
			Sgt J L S Cowings	
			Sgt L Lazenby	
			Sgt G C McMillan – E – inj.	
			Sgt P R Dunsford	
	Halifax W7668	Turin	Plt Off P Beesley – crew uninj.	Landed at Scampton with undercarriage unlocked, 0106 hrs
12 Dec 42	Halifax W7933 DY-D	Ops	Sgt G J Morgan – P – +	Crashed at Lowthwaite Farm, Helmsley, 0225 hrs
			Sgt C R Wooley – N – +	
			Sgt W H Casson – WOp – +	
			Sgt F Allen – AG – +	
			Sgt J A McPhee – AG – +	
			Sgt R L Lines – E – +	
			Sgt B Norris – B – +	

1943

Date	Ac & Serial	Mission	Crew	Details
4 Jan 43	Halifax W7910	Training	WO J F W Towse – P – crew uninj.	Force-landed Aclear Farm, Huby 1410 hrs
28 Jan 43	Halifax W7918 DY-T	Düsseldorf	Flt Lt B K Lindsay – P – M	Hit by flak and crashed in Waddenzee, Holland, 0030 hrs
			Fg Off J M Colquhoun – N – POW	
			Sgt A F Turner – WOp – POW (reported missing 5 Mar 45)	
			Sgt R Thompson – AG – POW	
			Sgt W A Bennett – E – +	
			Flt Lt G T O'Hanley – O – +	

Date	Aircraft	Target	Crew	Remarks
2 Feb 43	Halifax W7882 DY-P	Cologne	FS N A Ross-Thompson – P – + Sgt R W Goffin – O – + Sgt D H Watt – B – + Sgt H J Naylor – WOp – + Sgt R F Lilleywhite DFM – AG – + Sgt D V Gwillam – AG – + Sgt G Guerrier – E – +	Hit by flak and crahsed at Luyksgestel, Holland, 2100 hrs
3 Feb 43	Halifax W7921 DY-M	Hamburg	FS M W Lofthouse – P – + Sgt W B Haxby – N – POW Sgt R L Alexander – N – + Sgt W S Thompson – WOp – + Sgt A Short – AG – + Sgt J W Crouch – AG – POW Sgt D H Wynard – E – POW	Believed crashed near Badbergen, Germany. Possibly shot down by *Lt* Werner Rapp, *III/NJG 1*, 2048 hrs near Brokstreet
11 Feb 43	Halifax W7879 DY-O	Wilhelms-haven	Sgt H E R Saunders – P – + Sgt Hill – inj. Fg Off H Farquharson-Ley – N – + Sgt A W Flansburgh-Washbourne – WOp – + Sgt M N Reilly – AG – + Sgt F Cooper – AG – + Sgt T C Coles – E – + Sgt H E Amos – B – +	Suffered engine failure on take off and crashed at North Dalton 1839 hrs
14 Feb 43	Halifax W7880 DY-J	Cologne	FS J L Hartshorn – P – + Sgt H A Cheasman – B – + FS A M Conner – WOp – + Sgt A O Gilbert – AG – + FS H G Farah – AG – + Sgt J W Kilyon – E – + Sgt F W Cox – O – +	Believed to have been shot down by *Oblt* Manfred Meurer of *3/NJG 1*. Crashed 2030 hrs at Venray/Veulen, Holland
	Halifax W7922 DY-L	Cologne	Flt Lt H K Stinson – P – inj. Sgt N A Griffiths – inj. Fg Off R J Wiggs – uninj. Sgt J H Nightingale – uninj. Sgt A Hodson – uninj. FS I O Newton – uninj. Sgt A W Bailey – uninj. FS G Richmond – uninj.	Caught fire at Pocklington, 1740 hrs
25 Feb 43	Halifax DT800 DY-P	Nürnburg	Sgt C H Bray – P – + Sgt L V W Herbert – N – + Sgt C J D Smith – WOp – + Sgt J Dudley – AG – + Sgt I L Sanitsky – AG – + Sgt E L Widgery – E – + Sgt T B Barfoot – B – +	Lost control on outward leg and crashed at Badliss Hall Farm, Ardley, Colchester, 2024 hrs
26 Feb 43	Halifax HR669 DY-E	Cologne	Sgt M G Gibbons – P – + Sgt L J Langham – N – + Plt Off L J Dowdall – WOp – + Sgt D S Richings – AG – + Sgt J W Hunt – AG – + Sgt T E Russell – E – + Sgt J L Wilson – B – M Sgt H E Bradshaw – P – +	Initially buried Cologne, now buried Rheinberg

	Halifax W7919 DY-N	Koeln	Sgt E J Frith – P – + Plt Off R S Burgher – N – + Sgt T J Cox – WOp – + Sgt A R James – AG – + Sgt J Wilby – AG – M Sgt J Peak – E – + Sgt J Steward – N – +	Crashed near Cologne, 2120 hrs
	Halifax DT779	Gardening	WO J L Lee – P – crew uninj. Sgt G A Jones Sgt J N Underwood Sgt F M Traynor Sgt R A M Mather Sgt J K Campbell Sgt B C White	Undercarriage collapsed on take off from Pocklington, 1829 hrs
8 Mar 43	Halifax JB840	Nürnburg	FS R C F Hibden – P – POW Sgt F R Slocombe – N – POW Sgt H M Simpson – WOp – POW Sgt R Atkinson – AG – POW Sgt E G Sawkins – AG – POW Sgt W Hughes – E – E Sgt A R Mansford – B – E	Shot down by nightfighter and crashed near Brizeaux, France, 2245 hrs
12 Mar 43	Halifax JB836	Essen	Fg Off A D A Barnes – P – M Sgt A L Thurlow – O – M Plt Off E H Beeton – WOp – M Sgt V N Elkins – AG – M Sgt W P Quinleven – AG – M Sgt J S Lowdell – E – M Sgt G C Felsenstein – B – M	Missing
	Halifax DT799	Essen	Sgt H C A Newland – P – + Sgt R W Floyd – O – + Sgt D J Druett – WOp – + Sgt M H C Crow – AG – + Sgt A E Beaven – AG – + Sgt C S Jones – E – POW Sgt J D Haigh – B – +	Crashed near Bochum, Germany
	Halifax DT739 DY-P	Essen	Sgt E W L Charlebois – P – + Sgt D A P Horne – N – POW Sgt W S Hedges – WOp – POW Sgt H F Powers – AG – POW Sgt E A Hughes – AG – + Sgt H R Kemp – E – POW Sgt A D Williams – B – POW	Believed hit by flak near target and crashed 3 km east of Ahaus-Wessum, Germany, 2110 hrs. Possibly claimed by *Hptm* Herbert Lutje, *St Kap 8/NJG 1*, 2118 hrs
29 Mar 43	Halifax JB848 DY-G	Berlin	FS W P Comrie – P – + Plt Off D W F Harper – N – + Sgt F W Dorrington – WOp – + Sgt J King – AG – + Sgt M C C Squiers – AG – + Sgt W J McGrath – E – + Plt Off E H Jenkins – N – +	Crashed at West Green near Pocklington after being caught in the slipstream of another ac, 2159 hrs

3 Apr 43	Halifax JB867 DY-V	Essen	Sqn Ldr J E H Marshall – P – uninj. Fg Off T McLoughlin – AG – + Plt Off McDonald – N – uninj. Sgt C B Mitchell – uninj. FS Jones – uninj. Sgt A W Johnson – uninj. Sgt Dunsford – uninj.	Ac landed safely at Pocklington
16 Apr 43	Halifax HR663 DY-T	Pilsen	Sqn Ldr W I Lashbrook – P – E Fg Off K G Bolton – N – E Sgt W R Laws – WOp – E Sgt L Neill – AG – wounded POW Plt Off G G Williams GM – AG – + FS D C Knight – E – POW Fg Off A Martin – B – E	Shot down by *Oblt* Rudolf Altendorf, *St Kap 2/NJG 4*. Crashed at Mez near Givry, Belgium (11 km SSE of Mons), 0400 hrs
20 Apr 43	Halifax DT747 DY-	Stettin	Sgt W A Griffiths – P – + Sgt T S E Bennett – P – + Sgt W L Marsh – N – + Sgt A Jenkinson – WOp – + Sgt A C Weir – AG – + Sgt B C J White – AG – + Sgt D V Smith – E – + Sgt J K Campbell – B – +	Crashed near Saedden, 5 km NW Esbjerg, Denmark
21 Apr 43	Halifax HR712 DY-M	Stettin	Sgt P R Oliver – P – POW Sgt G L Doidge – N – + FS G H Bartman – WOp – + Sgt F W Day – AG – + Sgt J B M Irving – AG – + Sgt G S Meldrum – E – POW Sgt A F Warner – B – +	Crashed in Slipshaven Harbour, 2 km SEA of Nyborg, Denmark, 0226 hrs
26 Apr 43	Halifax JB918 DY-T	Duisburg	Sgt J G Grainger – P – + Sgt K Oatridge – N – + Sgt W A Willis – WOp – + Sgt H Beck – AG – + Sgt U R Wells – AG – + Sgt F G Harris – E – M Sgt W Foley – B – +	Crashed in North Sea off Texel
5 May 43	Halifax JB869 DY-H	Dortmund	Sgt W B J Happold – P – + Sgt J H Barratt – N – POW Sgt J Brownlie – WOp – POW Sgt T H Jones – AG – POW Sgt D R McGregor – AG – + Sgt G S Bowles – E – + Plt Off J Baxter – B – +	Crashed near Münchengladbach, Germany
	Halifax HR667 DY-U	Dortmund	Sqn Ldr J B Flowerdew – P – M Plt Off D E Grant – N – M Sgt J G S Dutton – WOp – M FS K H Buck – AG – + Sgt G Rose – AG – + Sgt P E Tiller – E – M Plt Off H G R Chiverton – B – M	Shot down by *Lt* Robert Denzel, *12/NJG 1* and crashed at Voorweg, Westergeest, Holland, 0036 hrs

	Halifax JB867 DY-V	Dortmund	FS J Bowman – crew rescued Sgt D Galbraith Sgt G C Parry Sgt J J Prinsloo Sgt S J Tregunko Sgt H R H Mock Sgt J H Lovelest	Ditched 75 miles off Flamborough Head, 0314 hrs
13 May 43	Halifax JB799 DY-E	Duisburg	FS M Q Moffatt – P – + Fg Off J D Erzinger – N – M Sgt C H Hurle – WOp – + Plt Off G Davies – AG – M Sgt W J Holman – AG – M Sgt C G Gowen – E – + Sgt D F Moon – B – M	Crashed in the North Sea in the early hours
14 May 43	Halifax JB964 DY-G	Bochum	Sgt V H Hatchard – P – + Fg Off F A James – N – POW Sgt J Leedham – WOp – + Sgt J A Coughlin – AG – POW Sgt J S W Fowles – AG – + Sgt W T Lee – E – + Sgt S Brown – B – +	Shot down by nightfighter on return leg in early hours and crashed in between Cologne and Münchengladbach, Germany
	Halifax W7935 DY-Y	Bochum	FS A M Sargent – crew safe Sgt A Campbell Sgt M Galloway Sgt A G Newberry Sgt J C Smith Sgt C R Webb Fg Off J R Bullock	Damaged by flak and ditched 23 miles east of Yarmouth
24 May 43	Halifax JD112 DY-H	Dortmund	FS A McA Sargent – P – POW Sgt A Campbell – N – + Sgt M Galloway – WOp – POW Sgt H D Newberry – AG – + Sgt J C Smith – AG – + Sgt C R Webb – E – POW Fg Off J R Bullock – B – +	Shot down by *Maj* Rolf Leuchs, *II/NJG 1* (flying with *IV Gruppe*) and crashed into t'Grootslag polder, Oude Gouw, west of Enkhuizen, Holland, 0055 hrs
28 May 43	Halifax JD149 DY-H	Essen	Plt Off J D Jeffrey – P – + Fg Off H Entwistle – N – + Sgt S Zareikin – WOp – + Sgt J L S Lowings – AG – + Sgt T Heslop – AG – + Sgt K J Smith – E – + Plt Off R N Fewtrell – B – +	Shot down by *Lt* Heinz Grimm, *Stab IV/NJG 1* and crashed in the Waddenzee, 3 km west of Oosterland, 0144 hrs
30 May 43	Halifax W7934 DY-J	Wuppertal	Sgt R A Ward – P – + Fg Off R E C Allen – N – + Sgt J Martland – WOp – + Sgt P Smith – AG – + Sgt J A Stewart – AG – + Sgt R L Hoddle – E – + Sgt P H Sheerman – B – +	Crashed at Guesten, 6 km NE of Juelich, Germany

12 Jun 43	Halifax JB868 DY-T	Bochum	Sgt R R Hale – P – M Sgt A C Woodley – P – M Sgt A E Muir – N – M Sgt W A Hobbis – WOp – M Sgt W Hallows – AG – M Sgt R Quevillon – AG – M Sgt A E J Gibbs – E – + Fg Off E D Wilcock – B – M	Crashed near Borkum, Germany
21 Jun 43	Halifax JD206 DY-T	Krefeld	Sgt G S Honey – crew safe Sgt R A Ward Sgt J Brennan Sgt F R Hayward Sgt D A Wagner Sgt A J Dick Sgt R O Tudberry	Hit by flak at Overflakee and ditched in North Sea; picked up by 277 Sqn and landed at Felixstowe
24 Jun 43	Halifax JB834 DY-C	Wuppertal	Sgt J A Marsden – P – M Fg Off J E Lewis – N – M Sgt R H Barnes – AG – M Sgt T A Hicks – AG – M Sgt P A G Warwick – AG – + Sgt J S R Ablett – E – M Plt Off J A Perkins – B – M	Missing
	Halifax JD144 DY-Q	Wuppertal	Sgt K R W Sheppard – P – + Sgt A G Tovey – N – + Sgt F A Gettings – WOp – + Sgt J J McDonald – AG – + Sgt M H Clack – AG – + Sgt C Rushton – E – POW Sgt W R Cole – B – POW	Sgt Sheppard buried Fosse, SW Namur, Belgium; Sgt Tovey buried Antwerp, remainder buried Florennes
26 Jun 43	Halifax JB843 DY-F	Gelsen-kirchen	Sgt K Gore – P – + Sgt J H Wright – N – + Sgt F H Mitchell – WOp – + Sgt D A H Gough – AG – + Sgt J B Foskett – AG – + Sgt T M Sugden – E – + Sgt T E Judd – B – +	Crashed at Breezand/Koedijk, Holland, 0240 hrs
3 Jul 43	Halifax BB428 DY-Q	Cologne	FS R C Jenkins – P – M Plt Off R Hodgson – N – M Sgt J Peck – WOp – M Sgt W McConnell – AG – M Sgt L C Watson – AG – POW Sgt J Galloway – E – POW Sgt A E Garlick – B – M	Crashed at Ruppichteroth/Winterscheid, Germany
10 Jul 43	Halifax BB249 DY-Z	Gelsen-kirchen	FS A T Fraser – P – + Sgt T J E Stockton – N – POW FS J G H Mansell – WOp – + Sgt R F Glass – AG – + Sgt H Edwards – AG – POW Sgt W Morse – E – + Sgt R N Brand – B – POW	Shot down by *Hptm* August Geiger, *St Kap 7/NJG 1* and crashed at Eprave, 6 km SE of Rochefort, Belgium, 0240 hrs

13 Jul 43	Halifax JD297 DY-Q	Aachen	Wg Cdr H R Coventry – P + Flt Lt F E King – N – + Sgt W Brown – WOp – + Sgt W Hardy – AG – + Flt Lt G F Hogg – AG – + Sgt G T Pine-Coffin – E – Fg Off C S Read – B – +	Crashed near Maubeuge, France. Possibly shot down by *Hptm* August Geiger, *St Kap 7/NJG 1* who claimed a Halifax at 0210 hrs, 14 Aug 43 near St Faysles-Veneur
	Halifax JB894 DY-X	Aachen	Sgt R G Amos – P – + Sgt B P Dowthwaite – N – + Sgt J R Fradley – WOp – + Sgt D H Brown – AG – POW Sgt J Raw – AG – + Sgt J R Smith – E – + Sgt W H J Smith – B – +	Shot down by *Flak Abt I/514* and possibly a nightfighter; crashed between Brunssum and Scherpenseel, Holland, 0204 hrs
25 Jul 43	Halifax JD316 DY-K	Hamburg	Flt Lt T Bakewell – P – + FS T L Colvin – P – + Plt Off F G Smith – N – POW FS J H Page – WOp – + Sgt F J Edwards – AG – + Sgt A L Wood – AG – + Sgt J Swinton – E – + Plt Off D Hill – B – +	Believed hit by another ac's bombs and then shot down by nightfighter, 0119 hrs. Crashed near Soltau, Germany
26 Jul 43	Halifax JD169 DY-J	Essen	Sgt J N Whitehouse – P – M Plt Off G S Smith – N – M Sgt F C Brown – WOp – M Sgt A W Evans – WOp – + FS F Turner – AG – M Sgt M Spencer – E – M Flt Lt D C Moon – B – +	Ditched off English coast: possibly shot down in error by RAF nightfighter
27 Jul 43	Halifax JD150 DY-A	Hamburg	Sgt G H Brown – P – + Fg Off W J J Hitchcock – N – + Sgt J W Rooke – WOp – + Sgt E G Gough – AG – + Sgt W A R Sinclair – AG – + Sgt J A Tyler – E – + Plt Off R F W Allison – B – +	Shot down by *Fw* Hans Meissner, *II/NJG 3* and crashed near Rendsburg, Schleswig Holstein, Germany
28 Jul 43	Halifax JB864 DY-B	Hamburg	Fg Off G M Clarke – P – + Sgt P S C Thorne – N – POW Sgt C A Bailey – E – + Sgt D Harrison – AG – + Plt Off W J Slater – WOp – POW Sgt H G Bartle – E – + Fg Off E W Slipp – B – POW	Shot down by flak and crashed in early hours at Keekkamp, Hamburg-Sasel. Sgt Thorne was killed escaping 2 Feb 45
30 Jul 43	Halifax HR711 DY-C	Hamburg	Sgt J J Gaston – P – + Sgt F Ball – N – M Sgt J R S Williams – WOp – M Sgt L Brown – AG – M Sgt A Verras – AG – M Sgt T S Yarwood – E – M Sgt L Cocking – B – M	Crashed in early hours

	Halifax W7883 DY-R	Hamburg	FS T A MacQuarie – P – + Sgt C G Whiteley – N – + Sgt E E Wright – WOp – + Sgt J F A Trehearn – AG – + Sgt R H Morgan – AG – M Sgt G P Woodroffe – E – + Fg Off A F Williams – B – +	Shot down by *Lt* Sachsenberg, *II/NJG 3* and crashed near Neumünster, Germany in the early hours
6 Aug 43	Halifax JD412 DY-X	Training	Sgt T G McAlpine – P – crew uninj.	Overshot and hit obstruction, 2335 hrs
9 Aug 43	Halifax JD408 DY-R	Mannheim	Sqn Ldr L J Pestridge – P – POW Plt Off A R Hunter – N – POW FS K P Walker – WOp – POW Sgt L G Dunn – AG – POW FS F A Sherrington – AG – + Plt Off J Burdon – E – + Fg Off L Bays – B – +	Attacked by nightfighter over Trier, crew baled out and landed near Idar-Oberstein, Germany
	Halifax JB782 DY-W	Mannheim	Sgt V H Thomas – P – POW Sgt N Wilbraham – N – + Sgt W H Buffery – WOp – + Sgt P Perry – AG – POW Sgt J A Walls – AG – + Sgt C Lafford – E – + Sgt A C Marsh – B – +	Nothing known
10 Aug 43	Halifax JD369 DY-A	Nürnburg	Sgt G W Ward – P – + Sgt J A McLearnon – N – POW Sgt P Bostle – WOp – POW Sgt W H Davey – AG – + FS R G Shaw – AG – + Sgt J A Irving – E – + Sgt R E Chapman – B – + Fg Off S R Vivian – 2P – +	Crashed near Ramsen/Bollanden, Germany
	Halifax JB794 DY-G	Nürnburg	FS E Storey – P – + FS W C A Poulter – N – inj. Sgt F R Newman – WOp – + Sgt J H T McEwan – AG – inj. Sgt T Lawman – AG – inj. Sgt R H Bowers – E – + Sgt W M McArthur – inj.	Struck obstruction on landing at Pocklington and crashed 300 yds east of airfield, 2335 hrs
17 Aug 43	Halifax JD296 DY-B	Peene- munde	FS W B Lambert – P – crew uninj. Fg Off W L Cook Sgt W A Rice Sgt H E Bentley Sgt J Hope Sgt E J Dyke Sgt C H Thomas	Crash-landed at Ashbourne, Derbyshire
23 Aug 43	Halifax JD378 DY-C	Leverkusen	Sqn Ldr D J G Jackson – P – POW Fg Off F R Booth – N – POW Sgt C E Kaye – WOp – POW Sgt W T Dolan – AG – POW Sgt J B Haynes – AG – POW Sgt C Williams – E – + Sgt W J Vernon – B – POW	Crashed in early hours near Kreuzau near Dueren, Germany

23 Aug 43	Halifax JD407 DY-R	Berlin	Sgt G S Roadley – P + Sgt W G Jennings – N – M Sgt J Chalkley – WOp – M Sgt N G Webb – AG – M Sgt R A Kirk – AG – M Sgt E B Woodrow – E – M Sgt R F Roberts – B – M	Crashed in early hours in sea
	Halifax JD127 DY-U	Berlin	Wg Cdr S J Marchbank – uninj. Fg Off W G Corbett – uninj. Sgt E G Clarke – uninj. Sgt J H Conrey – uninj. Sgt J J Duncan – uninj. Sgt E R Crane – uninj. Plt Off H F Pullen – inj.	Swung on take off, pilot retracted undercarriage to avoid hitting the air traffic control tower; ac exploded 2043 hrs
28 Aug 43	Halifax JB835 DY-X	Nürnburg	FS G Sproat – P – + FS F H Gould – N – + Sgt D W Firth – WOp – + Sgt R W Horton – AG – POW Sgt N R Gauntlett – AG – + Sgt L Rees – E – + Sgt C F Painter – B – +	Crashed early hours near Genappe- Sur-Sambre, Belgium
	Halifax BB365 DY-E	Nürnburg	FS K A Heaton – P – uninj. Sgt M D E Scott – B – uninj. Sgt Davenport – uninj. Sgt N G Davidson – AG – uninj. Sgt C Rodgers – E – uninj. FS D D Rae – AG – uninj. FS Howard – uninj. Sgt J P Hague – N – +	Landed at Tangmere, 0430 hrs
29 Aug 43	Halifax DT702 DY-K	Nürnburg	Flt Lt A Gibson – P – crew uninj. Fg Off D L Mayes – N Sgt F W Powell – WOp FS J Conley – AG WO A C Evans – AG Sgt D J Varney – E Sgt D B Atkins – B	Swerved off runway and undercarriage collapsed at Pocklington, 1608 hrs
31 Aug 43	Halifax JD128 DY-M	München- gladbach	FS J A Chappell – P – + Sgt G Lees – N – + Fg Off E I Smallfield – WOp – + Sgt L D Zander – AG – + Sgt L G Smart – AG – + Sgt A S J Harris – E – + Sgt J J Jones – B – +	Crashed in early hours
	Halifax JN909 DY-B	Berlin	Sgt E T S Rowbottom – P – + Sgt J K Keele – N – + Sgt A R Pearce – WOp – + FS R L Collins – AG – POW Sgt M L McClay – AG – + Sgt R H Day – E – + Sgt R V Wallace – B – POW	Crashed near Sauerbeck, near Münster, Germany

7 Sep 43	Halifax JB921 DY-B	Munich	Fg Off R Atkinson – P – POW Plt Off G A Butcher – N – POW Sgt J S Kirkby – WOp – POW Sgt A Ridley – AG – +. Plt Off W G Brown – AG – + Sgt B H Cockroft – E – + Sgt H F Moore – B – POW	Hit by flak and crashed near Penzberg, Germany, 0100 hrs
17 Sep 43	Halifax HR919 DY-O	Modane	WO E M Cartwright – P – uninj. Sgt D J Nicholson – N – inj. Sgt G R Fletcher – WOp – inj. Sgt H Brown – AG – inj. Sgt A W Snowden – AG – inj. Sgt R W Barber – E – inj. Sgt E F Jones – B – +	Crashed at Garrowby Hill on return, 0446 hrs
22 Sep 43	Halifax HX154 DY-K	Hannover	FS J Hanby – P – POW Plt Off F J Williams – N – POW Sgt A Taylor – WOp – POW Sgt R Maund – AG – + (buried Hannover) FS F Windmill – AG – POW Sgt H Edlin – E – POW Sgt C Anderton – B – POW	Thought to have been shot down by nighfighter near target
1 Oct 43	Halifax HX180 DY-E	Cross Country	Sgt W Hennys – P – crew uninj.	Stalled and crashed at Elvington, 2115 hrs
3 Oct 43	Halifax JD467 DY-V	Kassel	FS McPhail – P – crew uninj. Sgt J J Young – N Sgt I V Morgan – WOp FS V F M Carr – AG FS G C Robertson – AG Sgt R C Chatterton – E Sgt L P Seabury – B	Port inner engine fell off 3½ miles SE Pocklington; ac landed safely and pilot awarded DFM
	Halifax JD276 DY-Z	Training	Sgt C T Lockwood – P – + FS W A Miller – P – + Fg Off V L Hyatt – B – + Sgt J J McShane – E – + WO D W G Randall – WOp – + Sgt T Smith – AG – + Sgt C R Garrick – AG – +	Overshot with full flaps and crashed ½ mile SE of Pocklington, 0030 hrs
9 Oct 43	Halifax HX173	Hannover	FS R Ellis – P – + Sgt H F Rowlatt – N – POW Sgt J Woollerton – WOp – POW Sgt J Mason – B – POW Sgt S Williams – AG – + Sgt T G Palgrave – E – + Sgt J M N Buchanan – AG – POW	Crashed Steimbke/Lichtenhorst, Germany, 0120 hrs
18 Oct 43	Halifax HR804 DY-T	Training	Sgt W Hennys – P – crew uninj.	Swung on take off from Pocklington and undercarriage collapsed, 1935 hrs

20 Oct 43	Halifax BB370	Cross Country	FS K Whittington – crew uninj.	Overshot and undercarriage collapsed in a ditch at Picklington, 2315 hrs
22 Oct 43	Halifax JN908 DY-Z	Kassel	Flt Lt E S Kelly DFC – P – POW FS D Crump – 2P – POW Plt Off J C Fell – N – POW Fg Off J D Wroughton – WOp – W, POW FS D E Cosford – AG – POW FS T H McCarthy – AG – POW Sgt E W Jerrum – E – POW Sgt R Fowler – B – +	Probably shot down by *Fw* Hans Kurz, *3/NJG 2*, 2111 hrs and crashed at Willebadessen/Niesen, Germany
	Halifax HR911 DY-L	Kassel	Plt Off D W Brookes – P – + Plt Off J H Walton – N – POW Sqn Ldr A Abels DFC – B – POW Sgt R Sykes – E – + Sgt S Fautley – WOp – POW FS W A Spencer – AG – + Sgt K G Sewell – AG – +	Shot down by *Hptm* Rudolf Altendorf, *St Kap 12/NJG 5*, 2114 hrs and crashed 2121 hrs at Silixen, Germany
11 Nov 43	Halifax HX158 DY-O	Gardening	FS R H Campbell – P – M Fg Off L D Dingley – N – M Sgt C Healey – WOp – M FS A G Dyson – AG – M Sgt F Thrall – AG – M Sgt L G Yorke – E – M Sgt J C Arrowsmith – B – M	Shot down by flak ship and ditched off Dutch coast
22 Nov 43	Halifax LW333 DY-K	Berlin	Plt Off W Hughes – P – + Sgt W W Cottle – N – + Sgt R A Dabnor – WOp – + Sgt R B Bainbridge – AG – + FS D Willington – AG – + Sgt J Boxall – E – + Sgt F T Dunn – B – +	Collided with Halifax JD146 of 77 Sqn and crashed at Barmby Moor, 2345 hrs
25 Nov 43	Halifax HR811 DY-C	Frankfurt	Flt Lt H R Phillips – P – POW Fg Off C J McPherson – 2P – + Fg Off A Bolton – B – POW Sgt G G Lyall – N – POW Sgt J J Duncan – AG – POW Sgt A D Raine – WOp – POW FS A Lee – E – POW Sgt R F C Bryant – AG – POW	Shot down by flak over target, crashed near Burgstadt/Mitenberg, Germany
	Halifax JD366 DY-Y	Frankfurt	Sgt D M Pearson – P – + Sgt N W Durrant – N – + Sgt L James – WOp – + Sgt J A Adams – AG – + Sgt H A S Addison – AG – + Sgt W R Shore-Marston – E – + Sgt J Haddow – B – +	Crashed near Oestrich-Winkel, Germany

26 Nov 43	Halifax HR804 DY-T	Frankfurt	Sgt J W Symons – P – + Sgt R W Chandler – N – uninj. Sgt G E Bennett – WOp – uninj. Sgt N Medd – AG – uninj. Sgt T Jones – AG – + Sgt R W Buckle – E – + Sgt R D Walker – B – uninj.	Crashed on return at Warter Priory near Pocklington, 0355 hrs
	Halifax HX188 DY-F	Stuttgart	Fg Off W H A Dick – uninj. Sgt K J Petersen – AG – + Fg Off C S Pattrick – uninj. Sgt J Holben – uninj. Plt Off G A Henderson – uninj. FS M Bernbaum – uninj. Sgt G Holmes – uninj.	Badly damaged by nightfighter
3 Dec 43	Halifax JD303 DY-S	Leipzig	Fg Off E L J Key – P – + Fg Off T H Jackson – N – + Sgt G W Guy – WOp – POW FS R J Ardent – AG – + Sgt C W Phillips – AG – + Sgt W R Cox – E – + Fg Off J A Tippins – B – POW	Crashed at Luederitz, Germany
20 Dec 43	Halifax JD467 DY-R	Frankfurt	FS R Fiddes – P – + Sgt R B Hoynes – N – + Sgt D Williams – WOp – + Sgt H R Kitchener – E – + Sgt K J Dunger – B – + Sgt A Curry – AG – POW FS A E Adams – AG – POW	Crashed Kuispenich, Holland?
22 Dec 43	Halifax JN949 DY-D	Training	Flt Lt A Hilton – P – uninj. Fg Off E Whittington – P – uninj. Rest of crew uninj.	Overshot runway on take off for engine run, Pocklington, 1124 hrs
29 Dec 43	Halifax HR867 DY-A	Berlin	Plt Off A C Fraser – P – POW Fg Off H H Hesketh – N – POW Sgt R Day – WOp – POW FS N L Pearce – AG – POW FS T P O'Hare – AG – + Sgt R Mundy – E – POW Sgt R R McWhinnie – B – POW Fg Off E L Carlson – 2P – W, POW	Hit by flak and crashed near Berlin
	Halifax JD412 DY-X	Berlin	Sgt E A Stokes – P – M Sgt H W Parr – N – POW Sgt C E Habberley – WOp – POW Sgt E H Ricketts – AG – POW Sgt J Thompson – AG – POW Sgt T G Hatton – E – POW FS H Bretheron – AG – POW	Nothing Known

1944

Date	Ac & Serial	Mission	Crew	Details
20 Jan 44	Halifax LW337 DY-F	Berlin	Fg Off G A Griffiths – P – POW Sgt K F Stanbridge – 2P – + FS R C Wilson – N – POW FS E A Church – WOp – + FS C G Dupies – AG – M Sgt H J Bushell – AG – POW Sgt J Bremner – E – M Fg Off L A Underwood – B – POW	Hit by flak and nightfighter and crashed near Berlin
	Halifax HX187 DY-H	Berlin	Fg Off A W Dean – P – POW Sgt A Whittle – 2P – POW Sgt S R Stone – N – POW Sgt D S Veale – WOp – POW Sgt J H L Towler – AG – POW Sgt A Watson – AG – + Sgt A Landen – E – + Fg Off J Nelson – B – +	Hit by flak and nightfighter and crashed near Ahrensfelde, Germany
	Halifax JN951 DY-N	Berlin	FS E Render – P – POW FS F A Dobson – N – M Sgt F Mowbray – WOp – M Sgt J E Lyons – AG – M Sgt R Frankish – AG – M Sgt G H F Gover – E – M Fg Off E A Richardson – B – M	Crashed near Wensickendorf, Germany
	Halifax JD302 DY-O	Berlin	FS R W Proctor – P – inj. Sgt G A Wood – N – uninj. Sgt J C A Holcroft – WOp – uninj. Sgt C A Watson – AG – uninj. Sgt G B McRitchie – AG – uninj. Sgt T A Dearden – E – uninj. Fg Off J A W Turnbull – B – +	Crash-landed near Norwich on on return
	Halifax LW227 DY-X	Berlin	WO R G Wilding – P – POW Sgt R W Chandler – N – POW Sgt T K Buxton – WOp – POW WO F F Yeager – WOp – POW Sgt H Sheppard – AG – POW Sgt J L Corrigan – E – POW Sgt J C Heap – B – POW	Shot down by nightfighter and crashed at Neuruppin, Germany
	Halifax JD461 DY-Y	Berlin	FS R Compston – P –POW Sgt E W B Evans – N – POW Sgt W J M Eastwood – WOp – POW Sgt E R S Smith – AG – + Sgt D V Metcalfe – AG – POW Sgt D Courtney – E – POW FS F Moss – B – +	Crashed near Neu-Zittau, Germany
	Halifax HX153 DY-U	Berlin	Flt Lt D H Phillips – crew uninj. Plt Off T W Maddock Sgt W Lemon Sgt Diblick Sgt G F Cairns Sgt I Davies FS K M C Barton Sgt J M Smith	Starboard engine set on fire by nighfighter

21 Jan 44	Halifax HR716 DY-P	Berlin	Fg Off A H Hall – P – crew uninj. Fg Off A J Painter – N Sgt C G Woplin – WOp Sgt R D Loke – AG Sgt R J Clarke – AG Sgt N Pearce – E FS I A Weir – B	Crew baled out and pilot crash-landed ac at Clitheroe Farm, 5 miles north of Driffield, 0010 hrs
	Halifax HX149 DY-J	Magdeburg	FS J W Gregory – P – POW Fg Off D C E Bradshaw – N – POW Sgt J T A Mitchell – WOp – + Sgt D Bellamy – AG – POW Sgt K S Chrisfield – AG – + Sgt I Davies – E – + FS R J Irvine – B – POW	Shot down by nightfighter
	Halifax JN952 DY-L	Magdeburg	WO M F Headley – P – M WO E T Watt – N – POW Sgt J A White – WOp – POW FS J F Blair – AG – M Sgt R H Stately – AG – POW Sgt J Boland – E – M Fg Off O K Nelson – B – M	Nothing known
	Halifax HX150 DY-M	Magdeburg	FS H T Ellis – P – M Fg Off F J Payne – N – POW Sgt S E Adams – WOp – POW Sgt J S Fraser – AG – M Sgt L J Wilson – AG – + Sgt R Symcox – E – M FS W Millar – B – POW	Shot down by nightfighter 40 miles SE of Flensburg and possibly crashed near Bergen–Becklingen, Germany
	Halifax LW274 DY-R	Magdeburg	Sgt J M Smith – P – M Fg Off A L Clogg – N – M Sgt D C Forster – WOp – M Sgt R W Chadwick – AG – M Sgt N Taylor – AG – M Sgt R C Betts – E – M Fg Off L W O'Neill – B – M	Missing
28 Jan 44	Halifax JN950 DY-G	Berlin	Flt Lt A E Kilsby – P FS W J Wood – 2P Fg Off S Whittington – N FS G F C Marsh – WOp FS W C Vear – AG Fg Off W J C Seely – AG – W Sgt W M J Savell – E FS D Copeland – B	Damaged by nightfighter
	Halifax LW277 DY-Y	Berlin	Plt Off E W Linsell – P – POW Plt Off M J Connolly – N – POW Sgt C Cullis – WOp – POW Sgt L D Hammond – AG – + FS W H Coderre – AG – POW Sgt J R Coward – E – POW WO W T Scott – B – POW Sgt D E Ward – 2P – POW	Hit by flak over Berlin and crashed at Elsgrund, Germany?

29 Jan 44	Halifax JD165 DY-J	Berlin	FS D M S Pugh – P – inj. Fg Off J C Graham – N – + Sgt A Cohen – WOp – inj. Sgt C Williams – AG – inj. Sgt A A Burgess – AG – M Sgt R F Purkiss – E – M Sgt E Campbell – B – M	Ditched off Montrose on return leg, 0900 hrs
15 Feb 44	Halifax HX155 DY-Q	Berlin	Plt Off A Kularatne – P – M Sgt R Whittaker – 2P – M FS W F Johnson – N – M Plt Off J A Downs – WOp – M Plt Off A Stapleton – AG – + Fg Off J M W Filmer – AG – M Sgt K W Sherlock – E – M Plt Off W M M Manser – B – M	Shot down near Berlin
	Halifax LW339 DY-F	Berlin	Flt Lt A Hilton – P – + FS R J Paige – N – + Sgt L F Carr – WOp – + Sgt F A Paskell – AG – + Sgt A Dean – AG – + Sgt E A Gosling – E – POW WO R F Sykes – B – +	Hit by flak and crashed at Bartelshagen, Germany
16 Feb 44	Halifax HR978 DY-Y	Berlin	FS K O Harris – P – crew uninj. Sgt G Smith Sgt G W Parrett Sgt W B Grant Sgt K G Thomas Sgt E E Fisher Sgt J C Richardson	Hit trees in circuit at Leconfield damaging starboard engines, 0043 hrs
20 Feb 44	Halifax HX185 DY-B	Leipzig	Fg Off W B Dean – P – POW Sgt R C Trett – N – POW Sgt A J Milner – WOp – POW Plt Off W W Stenning – AG – POW Sgt W C Loosemore – AG – POW Sgt M A Clarke – E – POW Plt Off I M Dryden – B – POW	Shot down by Bf 110 over target and crashed Brandenburg/Stendal area, Germany 0230 hrs
	Halifax JN972 DY-H	Leipzig	FS K G Cummings – P – + Fg Off P J McInerney – N – POW Sgt N F Lingley – WOp – + Sgt R P Rees – AG – + Sgt J Torrance – AG – + Sgt L G K Giddings – E – POW FS G C Clarke – N – +	Crashed in early hours near Sulingen, Germany
26 Feb 44	Halifax LW331 DY-D	Gardening	FS S J Rodgers – P – M WO J A R W Lalonde – N – M Flt Lt T Leithead – WOp – M Sgt E R Burns – AG – M Sgt J W Brown – AG – M Sgt D G Llama – E – M FS J Metka – B – M	Ditched off Bridlington in the early hours

Date	Aircraft	Operation	Crew	Remarks
24 Mar 44	Halifax HR978 DY-V	Laon	FS J Garside – P – M Sgt J C Owens – N – M Sgt L D Maynard – WOp – M Sgt T A Smith – AG – M Sgt G Walker – AG – M Sgt R Callow – E – M Fg Off R J Roach – B – M	Missing in early hours
17 Apr 44	Halifax LW322 DY-A	Gardening	Flt Lt P B Jackson – P – crew uninj. FS L P Wiseley – FS T H Bolitho – Sgt J White – Sgt R D Moore – Sgt D M Hamilton – Fg Off K Wakeham –	Swung on take off, uncarriage collapsed, port outer caught fire, 2035 hrs
23 Apr 44	Halifax HX151 DY-M	Gardening	Fg Off A H Hall – P – + Fg Off A J Painter – N – M Sgt C G Woplin – WOp – + Sgt R D Loke – AG – M Sgt R J Clarke – AG – M Sgt N Pearce – E – + FS I A Weir – B – +	Shot down by *Lt* Walter Brieglieb, *10/NJG 3* and crashed in the sea at Smalandsfarvandet east of Omo, Denmark, 2342 hrs
28 Apr 44	Halifax JN948 DY-N	Aulnoye	Flt Lt A L Silverman – P – + Plt Off R J Blake – N – + Sgt L F Webb – WOp – + Sgt D B Robertson – AG – + Sgt R B Russell – AG – + Sgt R F Collier – E – + FS J R McClelland – B – +	Crashed in the early hours 800 metres south of Dourlers (Nord), 6 km north of Avesnes, France
2 May 44	Halifax JD304 DY-Y	Ferry	Fg Off J Dodds – crew uninj.	Tyre burst on landing at Marston Moor and undercarriage collapsed, 1714 hrs
6 May 44	Halifax JN919 DY-R	Cross Country	Sgt H Davies – P – crew uninj.	Caught fire and crew baled out; crashed at Lonesome Hill Farm, 2250 hrs
7 May 44	Halifax LW138	Instruction	Fg Off J H Rank – P – crew uninj. Sqn Ldr A E Kilsby – P	Crash-landed due to engine failure, 1215 hrs
28 May 44	Halifax MZ649 DY-Y	Bourg Leopold	Fg Off A H S Huycke – P – POW Fg Off G H Godsell – N – POW Fg Off G H Scott – WOp – POW FS L Collins – POW Sgt T A Eburne – AG – + Sgt R Lethbridge – AG – + Sgt J Welsh – POW	Shot down by nighfighter off Overflakkee in early hours possibly claimed by *Hpt* G-H Greiner, *St Kap 11/NJG2*

9 Jun 44	Halifax MZ659 DY-T	Gardening	Plt Off S W Sambell – P – crew uninj. Sgt A L Curphey – FS J M Beecroft – Sgt C H Kidds – Sgt A A Aylmer – Sgt S M Magill – Sgt J M Craig –	Ran out of fuel and crashed at Carnaby, 0512 hrs
	Halifax LW140 DY-M	Gardening	WO G D Jekyll – P – + Fg Off D Lillington – N – + Fg Off V P Hillrich – N – + Sgt R C Downs – WOp – + Sgt T W Rodger – AG – + Sgt J T G Catterwell – AG – + Sgt V B Florent – +	Crashed at Wassand near Catfoss on return leg 0355 hrs
12 Jun 44	Halifax MZ651 DY-Z	Massy Palaisseau	FS R P Singleton – P – + Sgt S J Thomas – N – + FS M F J McNamara – WOp – + FS P A Robson – B – + Sgt N Lishman – AG – + Sgt J D Francis – AG – + Sgt H R Smith – E – +	Crashed in early hours near Autheuil, 9 miles north of Evreux, France
16 Jun 44	Halifax MZ652 DY-Z	Sterkrade (Fischer Tropsch Werke)	Fg Off A V Maxwell – P – + Fg Off W A Rushforth – N – + Sgt R W Peel – B – + Sgt P Stamper – WOp – + Sgt N W Amstein – AG – + Sgt L McKenna – AG – + Sgt E Walker – E – +	Crashed in Germany
	Halifax MZ292 DY-C	Sterkrade	FS J G Kelso – P – + Sgt J C Gibson – N – M Sgt T E Hill – B – M Sgt R Bartram – WOp – + Sgt D W Jennings – AG – + Sgt N Howarth – AG – + Sgt A Smith – E – M	Shot down by nightfighter off Dutch coast
17 Jun 44	Halifax LW192 DY-H	Sterkrade	FS E F Braddock – P – + Sgt W A C Reid – N – + Sgt R L Putt – B – + Sgt J O Booker – WOp – + Sgt E A Finch – AG – + Sgt G Hadfield – AG – + Sgt E W Zaccheo – E – +	Attacked by nighfighter and exploded in mid-air, wreckage fell at Buren, 20 km north of S'Hertogenbosch, Holland, 0203 hrs
	Halifax MZ301 DY-M	Sterkrade	Sqn Ldr D R Fisher DFC DFM – P – M Fg Off A G Striowski – N – M Plt Off G C Burglass – B – M Fg Off L A Watts – WOp – M Flt Lt R E Cooke – AG – M Sgt P J Parker – AG – M Sgt K Clough – E – M	Crashed in North Sea in early hours

	Halifax MZ642 DY-U	Sterkrade	Sgt A J M Barr – P – + Sgt J F Tweed – N – POW FS A M Duggleby – WOp – + Sgt H J Wakeford – WOp – + Sgt W Chapman – AG – + Sgt F Bowman – AG – + Sgt J Bender – E – +	Shot down by nightfighter and crashed at Luur, Steenderen, Holland, 0200 hrs
24 Jun 44	Halifax MZ648 DY-X	Noyelles	Fg Off P Bailey – P – W Sgt D R Cunningham – AG – uninj. Sgt R Jackson – E – W Fg Off R Bruton – B – uninj. Fg Off A Newham – WOp – uninj. Sgt V Taggart – AG – uninj. Fg Off D King – N – uninj.	Badly damaged by flak during daylight operation, landed at Ford
25 Jun 44	Halifax MZ753 DY-M	Montorgueil (Day)	Sqn Ldr G B Treasure – P – + Fg Off S J Bailey – N – + Fg Off G Fraser – B – + Sgt R W Collins – WOp – + Sgt L T Archer – AG – + Sgt B D Bland – AG – + Sgt D Sykes – E – +	Collided with Halifax LL549/KN-L of 77 Sqn captained by FS D M Stevens and crashed near Fontaine L'Etalon, France
	Halifax MZ752 DY-K	Montorgueil	Sqn Ldr J O C Kercher – P – crew uninj. Fg Off J V Sampan – N Fg Off N McGregor – B FS J C Jarvis – WOp Sgt D A Blythe – AG FS D W Hartley – AG Sgt L D Cooledge – E	Overshot runway at Pocklington, 1125 hrs
29 Jun 44	Halifax LW143 DY-O	Blainville Sur L'Eau	FS N D Campbell – P – + FS A D Eagle – POW FS S J Wilson – POW FS N A Pardon – WOp – + Sgt R L Leverington – AG – POW Sgt R W Joyce – AG – POW Sgt D E Leslie – E – POW	Crashed in early hours near Marissel, France
	Halifax LW159 DY-Q	Blainville Sur L'Eau	Plt Off H Rogers – P – + FS L Williams – E – N – E WO R J Wilson – B – + Plt Off R J Messer – WOp – + FS J A Ligertwood – AG – + Plt Off L C Potter – N – + Sgt G E Frost – E – +	Shot down by nightfighter in the early hours and crashed near Coeuvres et Valsery (Aisne), 10 km NNE of Villers-Cotterets, France
	Halifax NA502 DY-S	Blainville Sur L'Eau	Plt Off G J Mulvaney – P – E Sgt J A Miller – N – E FS J B Duell – B – + FS L K Whellum – WOp – POW Fg Off G S Heath – AG – E FS S E Bastick – AG – E Sgt D G B Smith – E – +	Crashed in early hours 2 km NE of Ons-en-Bray (Oise), France

	Halifax MZ644 DY-V	Blainville Sur L'Eau	Sgt B R Jardine – P – + Sgt E J D Merrill – N – E Sgt M R Reid – WOp – E Sgt B Crayden – AG – E Sgt W S Whyte – AG – + Sgt J A Waught – B – E Sgt D F Dales – E – +	Crashed in early hours at Foret de Wassy (Haute Marne), 9 km south of St Dizier, France
	Halifax MZ646 DY-W	Blainville Sur L'Eau	Sgt K Robinson – P – + Sgt J C Watkins – N – POW Sgt J E G Woodward – B – + Sgt R W Lucas – WOp – + Sgt W N Partridge – AG – + Sgt F J Higman – AG – POW Sgt J Fingleton – E – +	Crashed 0030 hrs after nightfighter attack, dead buried Gresnay La Riviere, 37 miles ESE Beauvais, France
4 Jul 44	Halifax MZ771 DY-M	Domleger	Plt Off A J Crabb – P – uninj. Sgt P C Kansas – AG – W WO R H Dixon – uninj. FS T D Wise – uninj. Sgt N H E Guttridge – uninj. Sgt G Taylor – uninj. Sgt R S Robinson – uninj.	Damaged by flak in fuselage, wings and starboard inner engine
24 Jul 44	Halifax MZ298 DY-F	Les Hauts Boissons	Plt Off H W E Donald – P – M FS N Brand – N – M FS R T Lathlean – B – + Sgt R W Skeates – WOp – M FS D A Rogers – AG – + FS R B Seth – AG – safe Sgt W J Cook – E – M	Ditched
25 Jul 44	Halifax LL552 DY-X	Stuttgart	FS A J Page – P – + Sgt R M Simpson – N – + Sgt F Court – B – + Sgt R Leyland – WOp – + Sgt E Ord – AG – + Sgt R H Brewer – E – POW Sgt J Watkinson – N – +	Crashed in early hours near Pienbcourt (Eure), France
	Halifax MZ745 DY-Z	Stuttgart	Flt Lt J Weaver – P – crew uninj. Plt Off M Granda – N Sgt W Humphreys – B Sgt B G Chute – WOp Sgt S Sheeran – AG Sgt W P Barber – AG Sgt W Roberts – E	Damaged in combat with Ju 88, 0220 hrs. Port outer engine, aileron, port rudder and elevator damaged
28 Jul 44	Halifax LW142 DY-N	Foret de Nieppe	Flt Lt W F Rabitt – P – uninj. FS B G Spiller – N – W FS B G McLean – uninj. FS H W Brabin – uninj. Sgt C Hood – uninj. FS A J Concannon – uninj. Sgt A J Allen – uninj.	Damaged, landed Ashfield

30 Jul 44	Halifax NA503 DY-U	Battle Area	FS J E M Hulme – P – + FS H R Riddle – N – + FS L P Jarratt – B – Sgt C H Matthews – WOp – + FS M W Nielsen – AG – + Sgt F L Booker – AG – + Sgt G A Herbert – E – +	Hit trees and crashed at Blockley, Gloucs, 0940 hrs
3 Aug 44	Halifax LW134 DY-L	Foret de Nieppe	FS R R Mitchell – P – crew uninj. Sgt W McCorkindale Sgt J F Latimer FS R W Scott FS T L Maguire FS A F Thornton Sgt A Kellard	Overshot on landing, 2203 hrs
11 Aug 44	Halifax MZ371 DY-G	Ops	Fg Off A H Munroe – P – crew uninj.	Port inner failed on take off, 1340 hrs
13 Aug 44	Halifax LW195 DY-H	Braun-schweig	Fg Off S W Sambell – P – POW Sgt A L Curphey – N – + FS J M Beecroft – POW Sgt G H Kidds – POW Sgt S M Magill – POW Sgt A A Aylmer – POW Sgt J M Craig – E – +	Crashed in early hours near Rinteln, Germany
	Halifax MZ647 DY-R	Ruessel-heim	Flt Lt P E Young – P – M Fg Off K L Walker – 2P – + FS R H Osbourne – N – M FS J York – B – M Sgt J V Finney – WOp – + Sgt J G Gordon – AG – M FS A H Harvey – AG – M Sgt J C Doughty – E – +	Crashed in early hours
16 Aug 44	Halifax NA504 DY-Y	Kiel	FS L W Coughland – P – M Fg Off W Peldow – N – M Sgt F S G Heal – B – M Sgt C H Townsend – WOp – M Sgt G W Todd – AG – M Sgt L O'Toole – AG – M Sgt H Brown – E – M	Missing
3 Sep 44	Halifax MZ694	Venlo	Fg Off O C Cronshaw – P – uninj. Fg Off H Norminton – B – W Sgt A Hollingsworth – N – uninj. Sgt A H Macaulay – WOp – uninj. FS J M Fraser – AG – uninj. Sgt P D D Horne – AG – uninj. Fg Off J P Oliver – E – uninj.	Damaged by flak during daylight raid, landed Attlebridge

12 Sep 44	Halifax MZ699 DY-T	Münster	Plt Off P H Groves – P – +	Crashed 1840 hrs 2 km to the right
			Sgt C L Munroe – N – POW	of Kinderhaus railway station,
			Sgt A B Davies – B – POW	Coerde, 4 km north of Münster,
			WO R A Paquette – WOp – POW	Germany
			Sgt F Hooker – AG – POW	
			Sgt L Duncan – AG – +	
			Sgt C E Waterman – E – POW	
	Halifax LL555 DY-W	Münster	FS V G Fitt – P – uninj.	Ac damaged
			Sgt N N Brown – B – uninj.	
			FS M Lavadie – N – uninj.	
			Sgt A Miller – WOp – uninj.	
			Sgt P Dodd – AG – uninj.	
			Sgt C K Prime – AG – uninj.	
			Sgt P G Green – E – uninj.	
17 Sep 44	Halifax MZ289 DY-J	Bomb disposal over North Sea	Capt R C Thompson – P – M	Crashed 40 metres from Aaldonk–
			FS G S Reader – N – +	Reichswald road, Ottersum, Holland
			Sgt R I White – B – M	
			WO H L Locke – WOp – M	
			Sgt G V Greening – AG – M	
			Sgt G B Gibson – AG – M	
			Sgt R Aitchison – E – M	
31 Oct 44	Halifax NA599 DY-Y	Cologne	Sqn Ldr A H Jarand – P – uninj.	Hit by another ac's bombs but
			WO J D Galbraith – N – uninj.	returned to Pocklington
			Plt Off L M Carter – WOp – uninj.	
			Sgt J Wilson – AG – uninj.	
			FS J Symes – AG – uninj.	
			FS C Telfer – AG – inj.	
			Flt Lt J Kirkpatrick – E – uninj.	
			Fg Off J C Holmes – B – inj.	
2 Nov 44	Halifax MZ798 DY-M	Düsseldorf	Lt J E Begbie – P – +	Damaged by friendly bomber and
			Fg Off H Worden – B – +	then shot down by Ju 88 and crashed
			Sgt C J Jauncey – E – +	south of Louvain, Belgium, 1945 hrs
			Sgt Robertson – safe	
			Sgt Griffiths – safe	
			Sgt Matthews – safe	
			Sgt Scott – safe	
	Halifax LW141 DY-U	Düsseldorf	Fg Off J Redmond – P – M	Possibly crashed Inden/Lammersdorf,
			Fg Off R H Lemmon – N – POW	Germany
			Plt Off J A Picken – B – +	
			FS W Wilson – WOp – M	
			Plt Off J Binstead – AG – M	
			Plt Off N J Pearmain – AG – M	
			Sgt F W Lightfowler – E – M	
5 Nov 44	Halifax MZ772 DY-Q	Bochum	Fg Off A C Cameron – P – M	Crashed on border between Aachen
			Fg Off R F Hudson – N – +	and Laurensberg, Germany
			Fg Off M P Frobisher – B – +	
			Fg Off E Bolton – WOp – +	
			Sgt J M Wilby – AG – +	
			Sgt E C M Swart – AG – +	
			Sgt T Jones – E – +	
9 Nov 44	Halifax LW191	Ferry	Fg Off J Marvin – P – crew uninj.	Swung off runway at Woodbridge and
				undercarriage collapsed, 1245 hrs

16 Nov 44	Halifax NA165 DY-Q	Juelich	Fg Off E J Francis – P – uninj. Sgt J K Finney – AG – W Plt Off O J E Shirley – uninj. WO G A Loveday – uninj. FS A Sheppard – uninj. Sgt R F Alderton – uninj. Sgt E S Horsham – uninj.	Landed at Woodbridge, 1700 hrs
21 Nov 44	Halifax NR187 DY-S	Sterkrade	WO E W Fogg – P – crew uninj. WO R Williams – N FS W Mathews – B FS F Seymour – WOp Sgt R A Allen – AG Sgt J F Hewitson – AG Sgt S P Armstrong – E	Landed with port inner fluctuating, overshot runway at Pocklington and undercarriage collapsed, 2006 hrs
9 Dec 44	Halifax MZ800	Dual instruction	Sqn Ldr L J Ward – P – crew uninj. WO T D Lamb – P	Tail wheel torn off and undercarriage collapsed after striking boundary hedge at Pocklington, 1530 hrs
24 Dec 44	Halifax MZ871 DY-G	Mülheim	Fg Off E Roberts – P – + Plt Off J B Lea – N – POW Plt Off J D P Ball – N – POW FS J F Murphy – WOp – POW Sgt J G Williams – AG – M Sgt J L Simpson – AG – + Sgt J C A Steggell – E – POW	Crashed near Neuss, Germany
	Halifax LW168 DY-O	Mülheim	Plt Off E Hislop – P – + Plt Off G R Hawthorne – N – POW FS K P Lindenboom – B – M FS R G Clements – WOp – POW Sgt D Worthing – AG – POW Sgt J Temple – AG – POW Sgt A Coope – E – POW	Hit by flak and crashed near Krefeld, 1430 hrs
29 Dec 44	Halifax MZ426 DY-D	Koblenz	Flt Lt W H Russell – P – uninj. Plt Off C J Forrester – W Fg Off J D Sharpe – uninj. FS V Smith – uninj. Sgt R S Mopalee – uninj. Sgt F Magee – uninj. Sgt D F Murphy – uninj.	Damaged in combat

1945

Date	Ac & Serial	Mission	Crew	Details
1 Jan 45	Halifax LW158 DY-P	Dortmund	Plt Off M O Laugham – P – inj. FS Knight – inj. FS J H Sherridan – B – + Sgt S Westwood – inj. Sgt J Bettney – inj. Sgt E Davies – inj.	Undershot on landing and hit house, 2225 hrs
2 Jan 45	Halifax NR186	Training	Flt Lt J Marvin – P – crew uninj.	Overshot and crashed, 2210 hrs

5 Jan 45	Halifax MZ796 DY-M	Hannover	Fg Off J A Bergman – P – POW Fg Off C C Smith – N – + Fg Off D W Dale – B – POW FS E L Stevens – WOp – + FS H A Dunphy – AG – + Sgt C N Aune – AG – + Plt Off J F Shirley – E – +	Hit by flak and crashed at Neustadt/Mariensee, Germany
	Halifax LL597 DY-X	Hannover	Flt Lt J T Jones – P – POW Sgt J H D Bay – N – POW FS G A Wilson – B – POW Sgt W Shaw – WOp – + Sgt J Harding – AG – + FS R English – AG – + WO R Jones – AG – + Sgt S J Franklin – E – +	Nothing known
	Halifax NA602 DY-Y	Hannover	Capt R W F Heiden – P – + FS W Quill – N – + Plt Off E M Boorman – B – POW FS J F Valery – WOp – + Sgt G I Johns – AG – + Sgt R D Jones – AG – + FS M J E Tyler – AG – + Sgt P Morgan – E – +	Crashed on Heilingen–Otterhagen road, 200 metres north of Hannover–Neustadt road, Germany
16 Jan 45	Halifax LW179 DY-Y	Magdeburg	Sqn Ldr A H Jarand – P – + WO J D Galbraith – N – + Plt Off E L Davies – B – + Plt Off L M Carter – WOp – + FS C Telfer – AG – + Sgt J Wilson – AG – + Sgt E E Pope – E – +	Crashed near Langelsheim/Wolfshagen, Germany
7 Feb 45	Halifax LW142 DY-N	Goch	Plt Off R W Smallwood – P – + Fg Off W W Russell – N – + Fg Off B R James – B – + Sgt P D Hewitt – WOp – + Sgt J M Lennon – AG – + Sgt W B Scott – AG – + Sgt J Gallacher – E – +	Crashed Hamme Mille, Belgium in the early hours
	Halifax NA175 DY-Q	Goch	WO W R Smith – P – + FS W A McPherson – N – uninj. FS A G Kingdom – B – inj. Fg Off J Crisp – WOp – uninj. Sgt W Ollerton – AG – uninj. Sgt B Peckham – AG – inj. Sgt J G Grist – E – uninj.	Shot down by nightfighter 14 miles from target on return leg, crew baled out and ac crashed near Leopoldsburg
21 Feb 45	Halifax NP950 DY-U	?	Flt Lt W R McEvoy – P – crew uninj.	Overshot and crashed, 0431 hrs
5 Mar 45	Halifax RG502 DY-Q	Chemnitz	Fg Off J A Hurley – P – + FS H H Briggs – N – + Fg Off A V Valentine – B – POW Sgt J T Smith – WOp – + Sgt T Cooney – AG – + Sgt K E White – AG – POW Sgt A J E Morton – E – POW	Crashed near Volyne, Czechoslovakia

18 Mar 45	Halifax PP179 DY-A	Witten	Fg Off R D Jeff – P – + Sgt J Sutherland – N – + FS W N Birkett – B – + Sgt G R Grimsdell – WOp – + Sgt G E Emerson – AG – + Sgt E G Hick – AG – + FS J G Fraser – E – +	Crashed near Dortmund/Brechten, Germany
10 May 45	Halifax RG503 DY-O	Bomb Disposal	Flt Lt L Fenny – P – crew safe	Ditched 54 deg 28N, 0045E, 1548 hrs
23 May 45	Halifax PP209 DY-D	Transit base – St Athan	Flt Lt J Withington – P – crew uninj.	Landing accident, 1507 hrs
30 Jul 45	Halifax RG482 DY-D	Non-op	Flt Lt S B Dalmais – P – + Sgt R D Frost – N – + Sgt J Milne – B – + Sgt W H Bradshaw – WOp – + Sgt R L Williams – E – +	Swung on take off and crashed, 1535 hrs
8 Nov 45	Liberator KN742	Training	Flt Lt E A Robinson – P – + Fg Off W Marquis – 2P – + Fg Off S Brown – N – + FS A Miller – WOp – + FS R K Lewis – E – +	Second pilot raised take-off flaps too early, ac sunk, hit trees and burst into flames at Abington Pigot, Bassingbourne, 2327 hrs
13 Nov 45	Oxford NM596	Delivery flight	Flt Lt J Dodds DFC – P – inj. Fg Off T E Wallis – Co-P – inj.	Swung off runway on landing and hit a contractor's lorry, Bassingbourne, 1357 hrs

Post War

Date	Ac & Serial	Mission	Crew	Details
19 Nov 54	Canberra WJ638	Sqn Cdrs Check	Sqn Ldr W E Martin – P – crew uninj. Plt Off K G Speer – P	Belly landed at RAF Gütersloh, 1745 hrs after undercarriage failed to lower; ac suffered minor damage
28 Oct 55	Canberra WT480	Continuation training	Flt Lt B Sherwin – P – inj. crew uninj.	Ac drifted to port on take off from RAF Gütersloh; pilot retracted undercarriage and ac belly landed at 1417 hrs

No 102 (Ceylon) Squadron Gallantry Awards

First World War*

Name	Award	Date Gazetted
Lt A J E Broomfield	DFC	Not known
Lt E H Canning	DFC	,,
2/Lt E J Clarke	DFC	,,
Lt A F Corker	DFC	,,
Lt J Day	MC	,,
Capt H Fall	DFC	,,
Lt H Hammond	MC	,,
Lt W J Harvey	MC	,,
Lt E F Howard	MC	,,
Lt H Howard	MC	,,
Capt R T Jones	DFC	,,
Capt T J C Martyn	MC	,,
Lt G B Nicholas	DFC	,,
Lt W O'Reilly-Patey	DFC	,,
Capt H C Senior	DFC	,,
Lt A B Whiteside	MC	,,

Total: 9 DFCs; 7 MCs.

* It is assumed that these awards were gazetted for service with No 102 Sqn.

Second World War†

Date	Award	Date Gazetted
Plt Off K N Gray	DFC	2 Jan 40
Plt Off F H Long	DFC	,,
Sgt A Stokes	DFM	17 Jan 40
Sgt W C McArthur	DFM	17 May 40
Sqn Ldr P R Beare	DFC	9 Jul 40
Wg Cdr J C MacDonald	DFC	,,
Sgt R W P McFarland	DFM	30 Jul 40
Sqn Ldr R G Harman	DFC	13 Sep 40

† These awards were made for service with 102 Squadron and the lists are believed to be as complete as humanly possible –
Author.

FS R T Langton	DFM	13 Sep 40
Sgt R Bailey	DFM	22 Oct 40
Sgt E Binks	DFM	,,
Sgt D Parr	DFM	,,
Sgt F G E Tizard	DFM	,,
Flt Lt J D Warne	DFC	,,
Plt Off J F Painter	DFC	,,
Sgt G H Miller	DFM	,,
Flt Lt J W Stephens DFC	Bar to DFC	21 Nov 40
LAC C J McCutcheon	DFM	22 Nov 40
Plt Off G L Cheshire	DSO	6 Dec 40
Sgt H Davidson	DFM	,,
Sgt J J Gale	DFM	17 Jan 41
Sgt A Stokes	DFM	,,
Sgt G O Maughan	DFM	11 Feb 41
Flt Lt J J McKay	DFC	,,
Fg Off G L Cheshire DSO	DFC	7 Mar 41
Plt Off R N Pearce	DFC	,,
Sgt E Shaw	DFM	,,
Flt Lt H M Young	DFC	9 May 41
Fg Off D N Lowson	DFC	,,
Sgt D A R Tallis	DFM	9 May 41
Fg Off A D Frampton	DFC	,,
Plt Off J V Verran	DFC	6 Jun 41
Plt Off P Dobson	DFC	18 Jul 41
Flt Lt G C Davies	DSO	8 Aug 41
Wg Cdr C V Howes	DFC	22 Aug 41
Fg Off R James	DFC	,,
Sgt J C Banks	DFM	,,
Sgt W Swain	DFM	24 Oct 41
Plt Off S J Edwards	DFC	,,
Sgt D P D Archer	DFM	21 Nov 41
Sgt M B Berndsson	DFM	,,
Plt Off N J Bennett	DFC	23 Dec 41
Sgt F A Braybrook	DFM	,,
Sgt P G Brett	DFM	,,
Plt Off K D Whisken	DFC	14 Mar 42
Sgt H E Batchelder	DFM	15 Jun 42
FS T O McIlquham	DFM	4 Jul 41
Sgt D Sills	DFM	28 Jul 42
Sqn Ldr E D Griffiths	DFC	22 Sep 42
Sgt C Miller	DFM	,,
Sgt F A Barker	DFM	20 Oct 42
Sgt H Morrissy	DFM	18 Dec 42
Wg Cdr S B Bintley AFC	DSO	28 Dec 42
FS A W Summer	DFM	,,
Sgt E R Smith	DFM	,,
Sgt C A L Walton	DFM	,,
FS C M Bowring	DFM	,,
Sgt A Huddleston	DFM	,,
Sgt T J McLean	DFM	5 Jan 43
Sgt R F Lilleywhite	DFM	,,

Flt Lt P R Gaskell	DFC	11 Jan 43
Flt Lt W B Vaughan Davies	DFC	,,
Plt Off R Gayler	DFC	,,
Flt Lt N S Milnes	DFC	15 Jan 43
FS A M McDonald	DFM	,,
Sgt J L Griffiths	DFM	5 Feb 43
Sgt E T Heap	DFM	,,
Flt Lt S J B Hamilton	DFC	10 Feb 43
Wg Cdr G W Holden DFC	Bar to DFC	9 Feb 43
Flt Lt E M Lewis	DFC	10 Mar 43
Plt Off B C Sandall	DFC	,,
FS R J Horton	DFM	,,
Sgt E K Holmes	DFM	,,
Fg Off A R Haines	DFC	13 Apr 43
Flt Lt N L Shove	DFC	19 Apr 43
Fg Off J W Weller	DFC	,,
Flt Lt H K Stinson	DFC	15 May 43
WO A S Younger	DFC	,,
Flt Lt S T Whipple	DFC	18 May 43
Wg Cdr G W Holden DFC & bar	DSO	11 Jun 43
WO J F W Towse	DFC	15 Jun 43
Flt Lt K J Bolton	DFC	6 Jul 43
Sgt W R Laws	DFM	,,
Sgt A D Garlick	DFM	8 Jul 43
Plt Off J R McCormack	DFC	13 Jul 43
Sgt W S Lambert	DFM	,,
Fg Off A Martin	DFC	22 Jul 43
Sqn Ldr W I Lashbrook DFM	DFC	,,
Sqn Ldr J E H Marshall DFC	Bar to DFC	13 Aug 43
Wg Cdr H R Coventry	DFC	,,
Flt Lt E W Cranwell	DFC	,,
Flt Lt G F H Ingram	DFC	,,
Flt Lt F E King	DFC	,,
Flt Lt D C Moon	DFC	,,
FS A Sharpe	DFM	,,
Plt Off F A Sutherland	DFM	,,
Plt Off A E Fenton	DFC	18 Aug 43
Plt Off T McKinley	DFC	,,
Plt Off G W Rushbrook	DFC	,,
Sgt S C Richards	DFM	,,
FS N A Beale	DFM	10 Sep 43
Plt Off D Hutchison	DFC	14 Sep 43
Sgt L Lazenby	DFM	,,
Sgt W Hughes	DFM	29 Sep 43
Flt Lt A R Middleton	DFC	12 Oct 43
Fg Off D H Jones	DFC	,,
Fg Off A M McDonald	DFC	,,
Plt Off J Bell	DFC	15 Oct 43
Plt Off F J Steen	DFC	,,
Sgt J Clack	DFM	,,
Flt Lt H S Hartley	DFC	22 Oct 43
Flt Lt T H Dargavel	DFC	,,

Plt Off J Bowman	DFC	22 Oct 43
Fg Off H P Jeffreys	DFC	31 Oct 43
FS A G Harris	DFM	,,
FS N McPhail	DFM	,,
FS V R Moss	DFM	,,
FS J R S Power	DFM	,,
FS E E de Joux DFM	CGM	11 Nov 43
Sqn Ldr G R Hay DFC	Bar to DFC	,,
Plt Off J Hughill	DFC	13 Nov 43
Plt Off S W Templar	DFC	,,
FS P B Jackson	DFM	23 Nov 43
Sgt W R Doherty	DFM	1 Dec 43
Flt Lt J L Causton	DFC	6 Dec 43
Flt Lt A Gibson	DFC	,,
FS J Muldoon	DFM	,,
Fg Off W T Carroll	DFC	,,
Flt Lt A C Walter	DFC	,,
Fg Off D L Mayes	DFC	,,
FS W H Hughes	DFM	,,
WO A C Evans	DFC	9 Dec 43
FS T Sayer	DFM	,,
Fg Off G Russell	DFC	,,
Plt Off R A H Dube	DFC	,,
Sqn Ldr A E Millson DFC	Bar to DFC	27 Dec 43
Sqn Ldr P G A Harvey	DFC	,,
Flt Lt I T Hartley	DFC	,,
Fg Off F A B Hoskins	DFC	,,
Fg Off T Topham	DFC	,,
Plt Off H L Mackay	DFC	,,
Flt Lt A Carey	DFC	17 Jan 44
Wg Cdr F R C Fowle	DFC	11 Feb 44
Flt Lt E S Kelly	DFC	,,
Fg Off J Ashbrook	DFC	,,
Fg Off D J Hewlett	DFC	,,
Plt Off K Mountney	DFC	15 Feb 44
Flt Lt A E Kilsby	DFC	20 Feb 44
Sgt W M J Savell	DFM	26 Feb 44
FS G Marsh	DFM	,,
Fg Off S Whittingham	DFC	1 Mar 44
Sqn Ldr J Finch	DFC	15 Apr 44
Plt Off W B Lambert	DFC	21 Apr 44
Sqn Ldr A E Millson DFC & bar	DSO	18 May 44
Flt Lt N McPhail DFM	DFC	19 May 44
Plt Off V F M Carr	DFC	,,
Plt Off C G Robertson	DFC	,,
Sqn Ldr B G Glover	DFC	23 May 44
Fg Off W L Cook	DFC	,,
FS E H Bentley	DFM	,,
Flt Lt V W Armitage	DFC	2 Jun 44
Flt Lt J W Ward	DFC	6 Jun 44
Wg Cdr S J Marchbank	DFC	,,
Plt Off J Burns	DFC	,,

Fg Off H J Plank	DFC	6 Jun 44
Flt Lt K H Whittington	DFC	27 Jun 44
Sqn Ldr C G Lomax	DFC	30 Jun 44
Fg Off K Wakeham	DFC	,,
Flt Lt P B Jackson DFM	DFC	,,
Fg Off W R McKinnon	DFC	,,
Flt Lt D H Phillips	DFC	3 Jul 44
Plt Off G J Cairns	DFC	1 Aug 44
Fg Off E R Crane	DFC	15 Aug 44
Flt Lt R B Walmsley	DFC	,,
Plt Off H W Lawes	DFC	17 Aug 44
FS L O Lynch	DFM	4 Sep 44
Flt Lt J Kirkpatrick	DFC	14 Sep 44
Fg Off H S Horsfall	DFC	,,
Fg Off J J Hanrahan	DFC	,,
Fg Off W H A Dick	DFC	15 Sep 44
Sqn Ldr A E Kilsby DFC	Bar to DFC	,,
Fg Off W Wigham	DFC	18 Sep 44
Plt Off R T Champion	DFC	,,
Plt Off W J Graham	DFC	,,
Plt Off W J Wood	DFC	19 Sep 44
Flt Lt K J B Askins	DFC	12 Oct 44
Flt Lt A R S Smith	DFC	,,
Fg Off G P Clark	DFC	,,
FS B Davies	DFM	,,
Fg Off W G Corbett	DFC	,,
Fg Off D W Moore	DFC	13 Oct 44
Plt Off D Cooper	DFC	16 Oct 44
Plt Off P Geraghty	DFC	,,
Plt Off B A Read	DFC	,,
Sgt H C Wenborn	DFM	23 Oct 44
Flt Lt R A V Hazlehurst	DFC	12 Nov 44
Plt Off J E Dickinson	DFC	16 Nov 44
Plt Off G E Davies	DFC	12 Dec 44
Fg Off H H Lawrence	DFC	21 Dec 44
Flt Lt H R Dodd	DFC	15 Jan 45
Fg Off C J Lywood	DFC	19 Jan 45
WO E G Canelle	DFC	,,
Sqn Ldr L J Ward	DFC	15 Feb 45
Flt Lt H F Pullen	DFC	,,
Flt Lt H Taylor	DFC	,,
Flt Lt E C Creaney	DFC	,,
Plt Off J F Coldicott	DFM	,,
Plt Off P R Dunsford	DFC	,,
Fg Off R E C Hogg	DFC	,,
Fg Off P McNee	DFC	20 Feb 45
Plt Off A A Edwards	DFC	,,
Plt Off S J Ellis	DFC	,,
Plt Off R G Pitts	DFC	,,
Plt Off G W Thomas	DFC	,,
Plt Off S A Thomson	DFC	,,
Capt G A Gillett	DFC	15 Mar 45

Flt Lt J V Sampson	DFC	22 Mar 45
FS J C Jarvis	DFM	,,
Flt Lt A J Crabb	DFC	,,
Flt Lt N S Rabbitt	DFC	,,
Fg Off A H Granda	DFC	,,
Wg Cdr L D Wilson DFC AFC	DSO	23 Mar 45
Flt Lt J F Weaver	DFC	,,
Plt Off W W S Bond	DFC	26 Mar 45
Sgt L J Barnett	DFM	,,
Plt Off B G Spiller	DFC	,,
Plt Off W P Barker	DFC	,,
Fg Off N McGregor	DFC	27 Mar 45
Plt Off W Humphreys	DFC	,,
Plt Off A J Concannon	DFC	,,
Plt Off R H Dixon	DFC	,,
Plt Off D B McLean	DFC	,,
Plt Off P C Kanas	DFC	,,
Flt Lt J S Ross	DFC	12 Apr 45
Fg Off P Bailey	DFC	,,
Fg Off D G King	DFC	,,
Fg Off R W Bruton	DFC	16 Apr 45
Fg Off A Newham	DFC	,,
Plt Off J D Allen	DFC	,,
Plt Off S A Craigie	DFC	,,
Plt Off J D Wise	DFC	,,
Plt Off H J Hammond	DFC	,,
Fg Off A Arthurson	DFC	21 May 45
Fg Off J Cocks	DFC	,,
Fg Off O C Cronshaw	DFC	,,
FS A F Anderson	DFM	,,
FS A J Bolton	DFM	,,
FS G Lewis	DFM	,,
Fg Off W A Johnson	DFC	,,
Flt Lt F A Budden	DFC	22 May 45
Flt Lt D A White	DFC	,,
FS P H Pexton	DFM	25 May 45
FS R Stead	DFM	25 Sep 45
FS J H Wilson	DFM	7 Dec 45

Total: 1 CGM, 74 DFMs, 167 DFCs, 5 Bars to DFC, 5 DSOs.